Private School of HARD KNOCKS

by Anita Hayes

RoseDog Books
PITTSBURGH, PENNSYLVANIA 15222

ISBN: 978-1-4349-9875-0

Printed in the United States of America

First Printing

For more information or to order additional books, please contact:
RoseDog Books
701 Smithfield Street
Pittsburgh, Pennsylvania 15222
U.S.A.
1-800-834-1803
www.rosedogbookstore.com

This book is dedicated to my longtime friend, Helen Ridley Scarff, and all dog lovers.

CHAPTER ONE

Everyone has had a youthful life, and two important people would have guided you to your adult life in the best way they could. My mother was born in Paltamo, Finland, on July 15, 1920, although her Canadian citizenship states that she was born in Paltamo, Kivesjarvi, Kainuu, Finland. She was the youngest of five siblings. She had two brothers and two sisters. She was named Elsa Amanda Oikarinen. Paltamo is very far north of Finland, just south of Lapland. To its right is the Russian border. The northern Finns are slightly different than the southern Finns in dialectic and native costume. Their family was considered well to do, with nannies and farm helpers. The Oikarinen family owned most of the land around the lake, and still does to this day. Considering she was the youngest, my mother learned to read, write, and colour before she officially went to school. The schoolhouse was within walking distance from their home, and it schooled the local farmers' children. In winters, everyone skied to school. The winters in Finland are very long, dark, and cold. Cross-country skiing is part of their transportation. In the summers, the Finns take great pride in their farms and grow vegetables, fruits, and flowers. They milk their cows and look after their farming stock. Because the summers are so short, the growing period is important for their food supply for the upcoming winter; they basically work the land all day long. Once the vegetables and fruits are ready for picking, everyone works together then freeze all the food. The Finns have great pride in strawberries. Potatoes and fish are an everyday meal, and form part of breakfast, lunch, and dinner, along with various breads, especially *pulla*, a Finnish bread.

When World War II commenced in 1939, my mom fought with the Lotta Svärd (Women's Finnish Army) against the Russians and got five miles into Russia with German and Finnish soldiers. However, the Russians drove them back. She was in Oulu, Finland when it was bombed by the Russians. She was evacuated to Narvik, Norway, and was taken to Hamburg, Germany, which was already in ruins. Mom had been in Berlin, Germany; Wien, Austria; and Salzburg, Austria. To get around, she also learned to speak Dutch. The times then were very bleak. She would look after the soldiers who came in from the frontlines, all frostbitten. She sewed clothes for the soldiers and taught kindergarten. My mother learned to speak many languages. Throughout those years, she did what most did during those times—try to survive.

Her departure from Europe October 1948.

October 5, 1948. I have just had dinner at home. My work in the children's home isn't easy; it gets into my nerves. Today, we have studied prayers a little in German. At 2:00 P.M., I must go again. We are waiting for some peaceful guests from Tailfing camp. It is ten minutes to seven o'clock in the day time.

On November 15, 1948, Mom received her medical report from the German military so she can escape from Europe in general. I don't think she had any idea of where she was going to end up in or start up from, but she wanted to be out of Germany so badly. Her document, *fiche individuelle*, had her name, citizenship, and date and place of birth: Oikarinen, Elsa Amanda OIKARINEN, Finlandaise, July 15, 1920, Balingen. They had her picture on it, stapled on the right hand corner. Her medical report was in German:

Arztliche Bescheinigung. Hiermit bescheinige ich, das ich heute Fraulein Oikarinen Else, geboren am 15.7.1920, wohnhalf in "Westward Ho!" Transit Camp Kapfenberg/Steiermark, Osterreich, arztlich untersucht habe und fuglemen Befund erhoben habe: Faulein Oikarinen ist mittlerer Grobe, proportional and gut entwickelt; Knochen und Muskulatur gut entwickelt. Die Haut ist zart rosa und ohne Ausschlage. Dir Drusen sind nicht schmerzhaft und vergroBert. Mund und Rachen sind ohne krankhafte Veranderungen. Der Brustkorb ist gut gewolbt mit simmetrischen Exkursionen beim Atmen. Lunge und Herz sind perkutorisch und auskulttorisch ohne krankhaften Befund; in einer Minute 18 Atemziige und 72 Pulsschlage. Die Bauchorgane sind nicht empfindlich; Die Geschlechtsorgane ohne Besonderheiten. Die Augen und Ohren pathologist Befund, das Behen und Horen ist normal. Die Glieder sind gut entwickelt und gesund. Das Nervensystem zeigh keine abnorme Reaktioinen; de Geisteszustand zeight keine krankhaften Veranderungen. Diagnose und article Meinung: Faulein Oikarinen Else ist geistig und korperlich vollkommen gesund und ist voll rbeit s kraftig und arbeitsfahig. Signed Lagerarzt —Dr. Josa Rapp

With these documents she can leave.

HER MEDICAL REPORT IN ENGLISH

This is to certify that this person, Frans Oikarinen, Else, who was born July 15, 1920, a resident of "Westward Ho" Transit Camp Kapfenberg, Steinach, Austria, Ostfriesische, (Aizlich) to investigate to have medical check-up, property and so on in the following define to have temperature or what do you have to gain from it Frans Oikarinen sein average generous propotional and trusting to approve developer; bone structure and so on muscular trusting development. Die skin specialist sein tender rose and so on loan granted with no problem. To tip the balance. Die Gland sein compliance pain reliver and so on and to increase. Theft of food for personal consumption and so on. Throat sein loan was granted without problem morbid his meanless is almost pathological change of job. Give to woman to boast sein to put correct forced artifical he has treated he badly (partner) to foreign illness trip to move on breathe suffering from a lung disease and so on heart attack - heart beat sein periodic and so on to cure loan granted without second thought.

Stretching in single skull unit Minute 18 at lot of staying power and so on 72 pulse sein failure abnormal muscle, pancreas sein exhausted sore, touchy, sensitive, die sexually transmitted disease loan granted special. Die.

To have a closer look and so on. Ear specialists loan granted without problem. Pathological diagnosis that is, and so on. I'll be in touch and so on keep in touch normal. Die equal balance sein make good to develop to show and so on healthy. And such bundle of nerves to point at nobody abnormal reaction with absent minded slow motion not a bad idea to get on my nerves do access diagnose and so on medical in my opinion Rot Oikarinen Elsa is rails and so on body language full board healthy and so on sein she can leave.—*Dr. Josa Rapp*

During her time, Mom was trying to get back to Finland, but that never became a reality. She ventured to England, boarding the *Cunard White Star S.S. Scythia* as an immigrant to Halifax. Pier 21 was the gateway into Canada and is now a museum. It is back to its original state. Visiting there had been emotional for Mom. Mom learned English while working at the St. Stephen Hospital in New Brunswick, the Queen Elizabeth Hospital in Toronto and, finally, in the Vancouver General Hospital.

Mom met Dad in a rooming house at 1111 Dunsmuir (long since gone). They were neighbours. When they got married, neither one had any money. Mom's wedding ring came from a pawnshop on Hastings Street. A Finnish friend of my mother, Mr. Alho, who worked as a gardener on Marine Drive, filled their place with flowers. However, later, my grandfather said to my father, "She is not the right girl for my son." Possibly, he was right.

Mom was born a Cancer—the day of material inducer. July 15 people are able to realize their worldly goals by inducing others and manipulating materials to do their will. Those born on this day display an impressive control over their environment. With people, their first step is usually to arouse or activate them, and they exert positive pressure to get them to move in the right direction.

The wise, talented use of material is a recurrent theme in the lives of July 15 people. They may be bound to this world in a variety of ways: as a rich man to money, a real estate agent to property, a father/mother to a home, a painter to paints and canvasses, or a musician to an instrument. In the case of an artist, although the mode of expression is earthy and grounded, the content often moves toward more nonmaterial and spiritual directions as the artist progresses through life.

Although their motives proceed from desire and attraction, potentially healthy forces, July 15 people will be prone to be attached to objects once they have attained them. They must learn the lesson of nonattachment at some point in their lives, or run the risk of complacency, jealousy, or even all sorts of fixed sexual obsessions.

July 15 people can be highly useful members of society when directing their energies toward the betterment of its institutions. A willingness to share wealth, good fortune, or material possessions with others is an important component of an evolved July 15 personality; less evolved types are likely to simply hoard these things for themselves, or perhaps, with their immediate family

Because of their unique connection to the material world, July 15 people face an important decision whether to be slaves to it or masters over it. The word mastery here should not imply an exploitative domination, but an ever-changing relationship with their environment where nonaction plays as significant a role as action in maintaining harmony.

Those born on this day, indeed have a great responsibility to their fellow human beings, particularly as their magnetic influence over them can be so considerable. Consequently, as early in life as possible, July 15 people must form their ethics and live according to a set of principles in which they truly believe in, because their influential talents do not at all imply a corresponding depth in the moral sphere. Although highly responsible in discharging their duties, they must beware of using others for their own selfish ends and of teaching, either by word or example, empty values to their children, employees, or associates.

Those born on the fifteenth day of July are ruled by the planet Venus. They have great impact and control over others. The challenge to those born on this day is not to get stuck in the material world and its passions, but first to understand, second to matter, and third to harness desire toward positive ends.

The tarot card "The Devil" indicates a fear–desire dynamic working where sexual attraction, irrationality, and passion are concerned. The Devil holds us slave through our need for security and money, he represents our base nature grasping for security; he controls us through our irreconcilable differences, which exist in our male/female nature. But the card reminds us that although we are bound to our bodies, our spirits are free to soar. July 15 people must also understand their desire, their source, and motivation and learn to be honest about them.

Those born on July 15 must beware of overindulgence and excess of all sorts, which generally result in both physical and mental harm to themselves. Excess drinking, causing cirrhosis of the liver and stomach ulcers, and the deleterious effects of smoking put them at risk. By gaining control over their emotional drives, July 15 people can insure better personal health. Overeating can also be a problem for July 15 people, which can be managed by adopting vegetarian or low-fat diets with an emphasis on grains, fruits, and fresh-grown garden vegetables. Those born on this day can focus their obsessional nature on competitive and low-contact sports, as well as physical self-improvement (jogging, swimming, aerobics), usually with healthy results.

The advice is to harness your material talents; use them toward positive ends. Beware of addictions and obsessions, which will ultimately slow you down, or set you back. Growth is a continual process of change. Your strengths are influential, dynamic, and inspirational, while your weaknesses are being materialistic and controlling.

The element of Cancer is water. Its use, as a solvent, is vital for bringing ions of salts into solution. Although it is the only element capable of appearing in the liquid, gas, or solid state, it is, like fire, very consistent from one situation to another. Water is not only an ubiquitous element but also one of the most ubiquitous words. Water is a paradox. Though resistant to pressure, it can change its state dramatically, forming steam or ice. Though yielding, water can wear down a stone, or find a way in where tools could not.

Water mixes well with two of the other elements, earth and air, making good growing soil with the former and clouds or humidity with the latter, all of which are essential for life. Water is anathematic to the fourth element—fire.

The cardinal water sign, Cancer, represents the water-sign nature in its purest and most basic form. Concerned with feelings, Cancer is protective of itself and others. Like the Crab, it seeks privacy in its own home and is extremely sensitive to intrusion. In addition, it is capable of extremely aggressive action and can change to attack mode in an instant. Its ruler, the Moon, governs not only the tides, but also has profound effects on human emotions as well. Both the Moon and the Crab symbolize the life of the Unconscious. Water-sign people apprehend the world primarily through the feeling mode. Emotional considerations often take an overriding propriety in their daily lives. Many water-sign people are highly empathic or sympathetic, and so, they are hurt when others do not reciprocate. Their sensitivity to criticism and rejection is very high. Consequently, they can usually tell when someone approves or disapproves of them even before a word is said.

Water-sign people have a natural feeling for what people need. Consequently, they can be very good persuaders and can play on the emotions of others to get their way. Because their feelings run deep, they are often serious and profound individuals. Humor has a special meaning to water-sign people not only because it can lighten their mood but also because of its ability to dissolve barriers between people. In fact, bringing people together in intimate settings is a special joy for water signs because they usually have only a few close friends.

Water-sign people can be highly sensual—as much as earth signs. However, their brand of sensuality is more of an easy, flowing (albeit clinging) type and is at its best when it does not get too demanding or heavy. Generally, water-sign people become very deeply involved with their love relationships, so much so that they often have difficulty detaching themselves. These signs describe both my mother and father.

—Taken from *Horoscopes: Your Daily Fate and Fortune*. Maryland: Ottenheimer Publishers, 1983.

ANITA ELIZABETH HILLIS

I was born in the Salvation Army Grace Hospital in Vancouver, BC on December 7, 1953, at 8:53 A.M. I weighed three pounds and eleven ounces at birth, and I was named Anita Elizabeth. Anita is a common name in Finland, which means little Ann, while Elizabeth is for the coronation of Elizabeth II in 1953. I have a rare mixture of Finnish, Irish, and Canadian thrown in with gusto. I was two months premature and spent two months in an incubator, but not necessarily expected to live; babies under four pounds usually don't survive, especially in the 50s. While pregnant Mom was working at the Vancouver General Hospital, in the infectious disease ward. While there she contacted Polio. Mom was the first to get compensation from getting a disease while on the job. I was brought on early. Apparently, I was quite a fighter. I was always kicking, moving, and crying all the time. In order to be allowed to come home, I needed to be five pounds. Mom received some nice baby gifts: Grandma Hillis sent two nightgowns; Aunt Eleanor bought a sweater, bonnet, and booties; Fred and Anne Bonnett, a baby blanket; Mrs. Alho, a baby blanket; and the other gifts were a pink bonnet, two pairs of blue booties, and bathing dishes. Mr. and Mrs. Alho were my mother's very good Finnish friends; they were close until the couple died. Aunt Eleanor is my dad's sister.

Of course, in those days, Dads weren't allowed in the delivery room. Dad was working and came to visit later. Mom said, "Have you seen the baby?"

"Nope," he answered.

So Dad went to see me. I was red faced and screaming blue murder, and the nurse said to him, "That's what you got." I would only assume why I was kicking and crying all the time was just to show how strong I was, though I was so small. I would think that if I were rather limp, some serious medical problems would occur, or I might have even faced death. Mom was released from the hospital, but I stayed. Mom would apparently visit frequently. Dad would deliver mother's milk every morning before work, and when Mom ran out of it, he delivered *lactic acid*. Considering they didn't have a car, Dad would take the bus from the house to the hospital, and he'd have to transfer twice. Then, he would pay another fare to get to work.

One day, the nurse was patting me on the back very rapidly. Apparently, the nurse fed me the wrong formula, and I was choking on it. I had reached four and a half pounds. After getting the wrong formula, I had to start all over again. Mom walked into the room right at that minute, and she was livid. Mom, who worked as a nurse's aid for many years all over Europe and Canada, knew immediately what was wrong. I would have hated to have been the nurse looking after me right then. It was just a delicate situation, especially back in the 50s, when medical research on premature babies was not as advanced as it is today. Daddy-O said, "I showed my disposition early." Mom and Dad had bought a house on Ontario Street, right across the General Wolfe Elementary School. They paid $5,000.00 for the house, and Dad paid cash. It was a double lot, right next to the corner Chinese grocer. It was a small, white house with a closed-in front porch. Inside was made of old, solid mahogany and oak. The kitchen had huge old wood stove, with the black iron top. I remember it well. There's no doubt why Mom had no problem with that old stove. She probably felt at home with it, because in Finland, they still have the wooden stoves. Mom and Dad worked. I was a healthy youngster, but tiny. I was received in Holy Baptism into the Christian faith at the Augustana Ev. Lutheran Church on October 31, 1954. The priest was Leonard H. Maigaard.

The church is situated at the corner of King Edward Blvd and Ontario Streets.

The grocery store, school, and church were all within walking distance from our house. On January 22, 1954, Mom became a Canadian citizen. She received her official form in January 25. So, life is complete. There was a new baby, a paid-off house, and jobs. This new life had to have been a dream of the new world and peace.

Those born on December 7 are one of a kind. It is the Day of Idiosyncrasy as said in the book *The Secret Languages of Birthdays.* During most of their lives, they find it difficult to fit in with those around them, whether at school, at work, or at home. Those born on this day often grow up thinking of themselves as abnormal, peculiar, or just plain weird. Whether they really are or not, they believe they are, and often live up to their own expectations.

December 7 people are usually drawn to those who are also a tad peculiar. In any case, they have respect for people who have the courage to go their own way, no matter what it is they do. Secretly, of course, many born on this day would like to be accepted on conventional terms and enjoy just blending into the crowd from time to time. They may succeed in forcing themselves to fit in, but the struggle usually takes its toll on their nervous system.

In their adolescence and early adulthood, December 7 people are often undecided as to what profession or line of work they wish to pursue. Not uncommonly, they try a number of different occupations, very different in nature, before they finally hit on one that suits them best. Usually, they then stick to this one for life, but are not necessarily happy at it. Part of the reason why it is so difficult for them to adopt a satisfactory social role is that they are ambivalent about society itself. Also, what they like to do best, what really comes naturally to them, is not always what they can make money at. Consequently, they can suffer many anxieties and frustrations, and perhaps, wind up, believing they have failed.

December 7 people really need to take a lot of time off, and not put too many demands upon themselves. As children, their prodigious talents may raise high expectations that are difficult to meet; they may become rebellious, neurotic, and isolated, forced to form a shell around themselves to guard their sensitive natures from disappointment or rejection. Those born on this day, who are fortunate enough to have both caring and sensitive parents, stand a much better chance of finding themselves in this life. If they are still more fortunate in meeting individuals who see their potential and bring their talents along, their uniqueness becomes a great asset—they don't have to make an unnatural effort to stand out or be recognized.

However, December 7 people must be careful not to become too peculiar or insulated against the world, particularly as they grow older. As dreamers and fantasizers, they run the risk of winding up living a strange mental state that has little to do with the daily lives of most people. They should at the very least keep busy with certain minimal social and family activities, maintain close contact with their friends, write letters and, in general, continue to communicate, no matter how difficult it may be. In personal relationships, making an effort to bring attention to themselves may not be a bad idea at times. Indeed, they should keep in mind that it is the squeaky wheel that gets the oil and that self-pity, in all its insidious forms, is poison.

The numbers and the planets of those born on the seventh day of the month are ruled by the number seven and by the planet Neptune. Neptune is the watery planet ruling visions, dreams, and psychic phenomena, and December 7 people may be prone to these unstable influences. The combination of Neptune with Jupiter (Jupiter rules Sagittarius) grants idealism and expansiveness to those born on this day, but also presents dangers of naïveté and malleability. Those ruled by the number seven typically enjoy change and travel. The seventh tarot card of the Major Arcana is "The Chariot," which shows a triumphant figure moving through the world, manifesting his physical presence in the correct path, in which he must continue on. The good side of this card posts success, talent, and efficiency; the bad side suggests a dictatorial attitude and a poor sense of direction.

On the health of December 7 people, the nervous system is extremely sensitive, so stresses should be kept to a minimum in order to avoid anxieties taking hold. All escape-oriented and addictive drugs should be absolutely shunned. Making frequent trips to bucolic areas of restful, natural beauty can do a world of good. There, fresh air may inspire December 7 people to exercise, whereas in the city, they may not find the time. Being around small children (not necessarily their own) can also be a great job and highly beneficial to their health. As far as their diet is concerned, December 7 people should seek a wide range of tastes and textures, with an emphasis on enjoyment. Few dietary restrictions need be observed, except in the case of allergies. Allergic conditions (whether to dust, cat hair, soaps, or foods) may have a strong psychological component. Under no circumstances should December 7 people allow themselves secret worries about real or imagined diseases. The advice for Sagittarius is to bring yourself regularly into social contact with others. Don't expect too much from yourself and learn to take it easy without feeling caged. Their strengths are: imaginative, sensitive, and highly individual; the weaknesses are: peculiar, nervous, and withdrawn. Alas, Sagittarius is the fire sign, the combustive element. Fire can refer to intense feelings as fire can mean "to ignite flammable materials, or to incite people's emotions, but also to **shoot a gun** or dismiss someone from a job." A fiery person is someone who is emotionally volatile, or even someone with red hair. The mutable fire sign, Sagittarius, is often depicted drawing the arrow on its prey, but indeed, the Archer speeds its shaft toward the highest philosophical targets also. A gentle love of animals characterizes this sign. Sagittarius is capable of change but also of erratic behavior. Being highly idealistic, Sagittarius values honor above all else. This fiery sign must be put in the service of expansive and high-minded endeavours. Fire-sign people apprehend the world primarily through the intuition mode; hunches, gambles, and flying the world primarily through the intuition mode. Hunches, gambles, and flying by the seat of their pants rather than by a map all characterize this exciting and, at times, unstable personality. Fire-sign people do not need to be told when to act, or to read about it in a book, they know. More often than not, they are guided by a sixth sense, which rarely proves wrong unless they themselves doubt it. Thus, they often do better when they follow their first impulses than when they think things over too much. Worry can be particularly destructive to their positive outlook and undermines their usually high self-confidence. Fire-sign people have a strong sense of themselves. Often criticized as egotistical, they are self-centred, but not particularly self-indulgent. Usually, they are moving too fast to pamper themselves, and may dislike it when others display possessiveness or intimacy openly. Their orientation is more sexual than sensuous, and, like many air-sign people, more passionate than sensual. Fire-sign people generally enjoy the excitement of competitive sorts and challenging physical endeavours. You couldn't have a better description of me than this.

CHAPTER TWO

From kindergarten, Mom always had me dressed so cutely. I wore designer clothes—hers. She sewed all my dresses until the time she could teach me to sew. She always had my hair curled and in pigtails. She had colourful ribbons in my hair always ironed. Never would she put wrinkled clothes on me or in my hair. I was a walking doll. But, with a mind of my own, as an only child, I certainly would say my peace. I was always personable and never scared to approach anyone and speak with them. I was always selling myself. For some reason, I had this fascination for money and an unbelievably natural affinity with dogs and cats. I simply loved money, dogs, and cats at five years of age. Apparently, one Christmas, which my mother told me years later, I loaded up my wagon with all my toys and took them down to Main Street and sold them all. I came home with a few pennies and was very proud of my selling ability. I believe that only happened once. Other instances would include me playing in the dirt with the neighbour's kid; I had a mouth full of dirt. When Dad opened my mouth, he found a penny. I was independent. One morning, Dad was about to take me to Sunday school, I demanded to go by myself and will cross the street—a busy street—by myself. From where we lived, my Dad could watch me. I made it. Dad did his part around the house, and Mom was working as he told me, I was just able to sit a little wobbly. When I was a baby, I was in the tub with Dad; he was washing me when the phone rang. Dad went to answer it. When he came back, I was face down in the bathwater. Dad grabbed both my little legs and shook me upside down. I was breathing. (Apparently, Dad got Mom angry over this). I guess Mom decided she would bathe me in the kitchen sink. I didn't like it; the neighbours could see me. According to Mom, I was so embarrassed, so she didn't bathe me in the sink anymore. I was a very small girl, small for my age, and was always the smallest in the classroom. I hated to be called "little." One day, Mother and I were shopping at Woodward's, Vancouver's premier department store on Hastings Street, and I wanted to go on the escalator by myself.

Apparently, a nice looking man in a business suit said, "What a cute 'little' girl," picked me up, and put me on the escalator. I got mad because I heard the word little. I turned around and spat at him, an act which stuck with me into adulthood. Needless to say, Mom was embarrassed. Evidently, I did this again to a woman walking down the street, passing our house. She said that magical word, "What a cute 'little' girl." I spat at her. I asked Mom if I got her, and she said that my spit didn't go that far. I guess I am simply not shy about approaching people, a trait that still is with me today. I was on the bus, and a lady sat next to me. She was wearing a red fox fur, and I said, "Nice kitty. Nice kitty." The wind in the trees, for me, is called "Windflowers." I'm a nature lover!

On my adventurous days, I was searching out my dresser drawer when I pulled the dresser over on myself. But I was saved when the drawer slid out and left the unit in a shape like that of a teepee. Of course, being raised on the waterfront town of Vancouver, my family would always walk along the Stanley Park's seawall, Kitsilano Beach, and so forth. I was fascinated when the water went gurgling down our bathtub drain, so I wanted Dad to pull the plug at Kitsilano pool to see where it went.

Just down the street from Woodward's was a landmark restaurant called the White Lunch. We frequented this place before. One afternoon, while entering the swinging doors of the restaurant, it knocked me out for a loop, and a whole tray of meals flew all over the floor. We resolved that matter and continued on with lunch. I've always admired the art on the wall of this restaurant, and I loved the mash potatoes and gravy. The White Lunch is no longer there. In fact, the thriving business of Hastings Street is gone today and is now considered in Vancouver East as a drug area. My understanding is that the politicians are cleaning up this area for the underprivileged. In my youth, it was the place to shop. Army & Navy was another department store that I thought was rather dingy as a kid. There were tables of loose bras, panties, and such. People were thriving through this stuff. I never thought it was classy. Early on, I had the designer fever. I would say that Army & Navy was the Wal-Mart of its day. I remember you'd have to go through the lane to get to the other building. It was the norm. On Hastings Street were pawnshops, beer parlours, and hotels that were the centre of the town during their day.

One day, I brought home this big collie and begged my mom to keep it. I was a true "Lassie" lover. Mom put the dog in the covered porch. When I think back, this poor dog was trying to go home. I wasn't just content with cats. Dogs are my thing. This poor dog scratched at the floor and wanted to go home. Mom let the dog out in the morning. During Halloween, Dad would take me out to trick or treat. He took me out for many more years. He would also entertain me with firecrackers; they were legal then. I always had a sort of costume on, like a little "Heidi," and I wore that same thing every year. One Christmas, the neighbours brought over a dollhouse for me. I was jumping up and down at the door. This dollhouse was made of metal and came with tiny furniture. It was my favorite for sometime. When it came to kindergarten, I only had to cross the street. Mom would have me impeccably dressed and with polished saddle shoes. One of my favorite games in kindergarten was banging on different levels of wood with a hammer. I like boy's toys. When it came to a nap, we all had our own blanket. I had a small, pink blanket. I can remember so clearly that one little boy peed on the floor and some other kid put his blanket on top of the pee. I guess there was some confusion in the corner that day. The janitor arrived with sawdust. At the school, they had large cement stairs. A boy knocked me over, and I had to get stitches on my forehead.

I remember the teacher carrying me through the hall. Apparently, I ended up at the children's hospital for observation. All was okay. I was a very independent little girl, and Mom gave me lots of freedom. I used to walk to Queen Elizabeth Park on my own, which was some walking distance from my home.

I loved the flowers and the little stream that went through the park. I told some people that I was waiting there because a whale will be coming through under the bridge soon. I had all kinds of stories and imagination at that park. Queen Elizabeth Park is a Vancouver sightseeing park. If you visit Vancouver, you can't miss the park. Many wedding photos are taken there. Since my youth, they have added a conservatory with birds and, of course, food concessions. There was an odd kid on a bicycle selling ice cream—young entrepreneurs. The family spent five years on Ontario Street.

There was a house that caught Mom's eye. It was a real quaint house at 1577 West 64th Avenue at Granville. The house next door was also for sale. Although brand new, the floor plan was odd and more expensive then. It also had a garage, which was of no use to our family. Dad was the kind of guy who wouldn't move, but Mom was the one who pushed Dad. They bought the house, which actually put us in a much better area, not too far from millionaire homes on SW Marine Drive, Maple Grove Park area, and Shaughnessy, with Shaughnessy being Vancouver's old money. Although schools and churches were not nearby, the bus route and stores were close. It was a great move. The house was originally grey in colour outside, made of wood, with a living room with a fireplace, two bedrooms, eat-in kitchen, and bath. There was no dining room. The house had a fenced yard with a garden and a plum tree. There was an outside picnic area with a table, which dad later dismantled. Dad later had the house stuccoed white and black with turquoise trims. It really improved its curbed appeal.

My first priority was to find some friends. First, I stopped by this house where a black man was outside, cleaning the windows. His name was Mr. Beckwith. I told him I was new in the neighbourhood, and that I was out looking for friends. (Needless to say, the Beckwiths would become more special to me later). As I continued down 64th street, I met Evelyn, and I brought Evelyn over to my place. As time went on, I met the rest of the kids in the neighbourhood. There was Helen, who lived one house away from me; Doug, from across the street; and, down the road, were Bruce, Philip, Rene, and Jill. Helen, Evelyn, and I became best of friends for years to come.

I went into grade one at David Lloyd George Annex at 62nd and Granville. I wasn't a smart kid; it took me time to catch onto whatever the teacher was teaching, but, once I got it, I got it. Grade one was difficult for me, although I was passed onto grade two on trial. I actually missed the whole grade one. I needed glasses and couldn't see a thing all year. Nothing registered. I asked to go back to grade one. Needless to say, I was the only one in class who wore glasses. And boy, were they ugly glasses. But, with them, I did much better in my studies because I could see.

The first Barbie doll was launched, and, of course, every little girl had to have one. Mom bought me a Barbie. She would sew cloths for my doll, and, now and then, I'd get store-bought Barbie clothes. I also really liked my ThumbleLenia doll. It was like a real baby. (I remember Evelyn was not allowed to take her dolls outside). It was a great neighbourhood with lots of kids the same age as me.

One weekend, Buzzie (David) and I went to the school grounds. I had a small shovel with me. Buzzie and I were in the same grade. He only lived down the street. I started digging a hole in the dirt near the sidewalk and filled it up with orange berries I found on the ground. We thought it looked rather pretty. Well, on Monday, I was in BIG trouble. The teacher dug it out of us kids who dug a hole in the school grounds. The teacher phoned my parents about this, and all hell broke loose. The hole had to be refilled. Thinking about that hole, I didn't think it was that bad, considering a classmate had a poo on the front steps of the school and considering kids bringing knives and guns to school today.

I remember when it was student time. I always had my work taken back with him or her (teacher in training) to university as my drawings, stories, and printing was always attractive and neat. In other words, the teacher in training had something to show for his or her teaching abilities. Miss Edgecombe was my grade two teacher. She was elderly and a good teacher who took an interest with the kids. Her sister, Mrs. Wagner, taught grade three in the same school. One incident that I remember is when one of the other teachers came to the school to show off her new baby. She brought small bags of popcorn for everyone. I always sat in the front row. Her instructions were "Give everyone behind you one bag, and the last one was for you." I was the only one in the classroom that didn't get a bag of popcorn. I didn't think that was very nice. The rejection stayed with me throughout my life. When similar incidents occurred, I'd always remember the popcorn day.

Mom was sick from time to time, and she'd have to go into the hospital for days or weeks. I seemed to have always been staying with the neighbours. Evelyn's mom took me in for a few days while mom was away, and Dad was at sea working. I remember complaining to Mom one sunny day that Evelyn's mom made me wear leotards to school because I, apparently, peed on my pants. The complaining became a big deal. I supposed Mom approached Evelyn's mom, and, for some reason, I was never allowed to play with Evelyn or go over her place ever again. I didn't understand why, neither did Evelyn. It was odd.

Dad's job was seasonal, and, during the winter, he collected Unemployment Insurance. There were lots of boozing and fighting when he was home, although Dad, today, says his boozing was strictly social. There were many times when Mom would run to the neighbor's only to be turned away, so from then on, she and I went to a hotel. One time, I ended up at Mrs. Beckwith's house. We walked to the children's shoe store, and she bought me a pair of shoes that day. I picked out a fancy, black velvet pair with a little glass star in the front. I really liked those shoes, but I never saw them again.

I never saw any physical abuse toward Mom. Mom and Dad's arguments were strictly verbal. Mom would normally lock Dad out of the house. He'd break a window in the basement and sleep in his out-of-bounds room, only to repair the window the next day. At that time, I doubt that I had any knowledge of their arguments; I was content in my room with my toys.

Then, it was time for a dog. I badly wanted a dog, so Mom, Dad, and I went to see a place where there were a bunch of puppies. We were going to get a German shepherd puppy, but when I saw this little white thing come out of the house, I wanted it. It was a white Pekingese pup. I named him Puff. I have a natural rapport with dogs and cats, especially dogs. When I was not doing homework, I would be playing with my friends and my puppy. The puppy taught me responsibility early.

Us kids—and there were many on the block—would play games such as Snap, Solitaire, Taxi (a British Game), Sorry, Monopoly, Memory, pick-up sticks, and marbles.

Barbie was included with the girls, cars with the boys. Although, I liked to play cars with Philip on a mound of dirt, I always wanted a train set but never got one. Toys were rather simple back then; there weren't any electronic games then like today. We made our own fun the old-fashioned, creative way—through imagination. Helen was just a house away, and she would put on carnivals in her backyard and donate the funds to charity at our school. We had these carnivals regularly. One day, I decided to put on a paper hunt at Helen's backyard. I came over there with loads of paper such as cutouts and pictures and hid them all amongst the bushes, trees, and flowers, but nobody wanted to go hunting for them, so Helen's yard was full of paper. I certainly wasn't going to go and pick it all up by myself. Helen's dad ended up cleaning it all up. Helen's mom doesn't remember that carnival though.

We kids also thought up our own roller-coaster. I had a wooden wagon with a brake on the back. Philip and Helen would put their wagons ahead of mine, and we'd tie them together. We'd go on the boulevard and around the trees and roots, as if we were on a roller coaster. Of course, during summer, we sold lemonade in front of our homes. It was a test of whose mother made the best lemonade. Our entrepreneurial endeavors were short lived when it was tougher to sell lemonade, or when we simply got bored. Rene's parents were both schoolteachers. They had a nice house and a finished basement. I don't know what happened exactly, but Philip, of whom was an accomplice with another chap, had taken the hose that was connected to Rene's house, put it through the mailbox in the door, and turned it on full blast the whole length; the family was out on holiday when Phillip and his accomplice did that. When Rene and his family got back home, their finished basement was totally flooded. Forty-two years later, Philip, who we still speak with, said to me that he did not do it, but that he was very near by.

We all created our fun. I had a certain amount of freedom, much more than the other kids. One luxury I never had as a kid, though, was that neither my mother nor father drove, so when I had a ride with other kids' parents, I really loved the car. And, whenever I could get a ride in a car, I was gung ho. Life was good; going to school, Mom was home with me, and Dad worked on ships. I rarely saw my dad during summer months. During the winter months, Dad was around a lot. Dad would teach me penmanship and coloring. Today,

I have good handwriting, and I became very good at colouring. I was always told to stay with the lines. Dad and I also played ball and catch, which would later give me the opportunity to be good in baseball and running.

My reading and arithmetic was poor. Mom used to send me to the neighbours to read twice a week, and it proved worthy. My best subjects in school, wherein I excelled and got As, were art, music, and sports. I loved social studies; I was good at it. I liked science, but I was not good at it. English wasn't my best subject either at that time. At the annex, we had a good principal, Mr. Buckley. He ran the annex and the big school, David Lloyd George. (It was the annex which will be closed some forty years later). Once we graduated to grade four, off to the big school we would go. And to us, it was a *big* school.

During the months Dad wasn't working, we'd all go to the United States, mostly Seattle, since mom had a nurse friend there with whom we stayed for nothing in return. I got to know Seattle just as well as my own hometown of Vancouver. We always travelled by Greyhound and always got the front seat. When Disneyland opened in Anaheim, California, off we went there by Greyhound. I remember chatting up a storm with a good-looking man in uniform. I told him that when I grow up, I am going to marry him. The travellers on the bus had a good laugh. When I woke up in the morning, he was gone. I was disappointed. While on the Greyhound bus, I'd count how many swimming pools in California I could see; it gave me a great thrill. When it came to hotels, Dad was cheap; we never stayed in anything fancy, just your average Motel 6 type of place, or less. Dinners were always at ordinary cafeterias—your basic mom-and-pop diners. We never stayed at an expensive hotel and never ate at our present hotel after my mom's friend from Seattle died.

While at Disneyland, Dad bought me a white balloon. I lost hold of my balloon and told Dad to quickly climb the tree to get my balloon. But, of course, he couldn't. My balloon wasn't replaced. We spent several days at Disneyland. Other sightseeing places we went to was Hollywood's Grauman's Chinese Theatre where stars leave their foot and handprints on the cement. We also went sightseeing around Beverly Hills, Los Angeles, and Long Beach. We spent many hours at the beach. At one time, while around the ocean, the tide was in.

I said to Dad, "The ocean is full; why don't they pull the plug?" I saw this as water was running down in the bathtub and felt the ocean worked the same way. Always fascinated with water, I never could master the art of swimming. I remember finding a sand dollar on Long Beach. Mom and Dad neither had a driver's license, and it was too expensive to take a tour, so we always went by local bus. We rode with the locals. That's how you really get the feel of the people living there. Los Angeles was another city we frequented, and I got to know it just as well as home. I loved Los Angeles. On the way back up the coast of California, we stopped in San Francisco and once again, not necessarily, staying at the best hotel. I guess it was beer time for Mom and Dad. Once off the Greyhound, they sat me on the suitcase outside the beer parlour and told me not to move. People would ask me where my Mom and Dad were, and I said, "In there," and motioned my hand toward the beer parlour. One lady was fit to be tied for doing such a thing. I remember that well. One time, Mom was buying a leather Mexican purse in one of the stores and Dad took off to the bar. I went after him and got lost. I was amongst the adults on a very crowded sidewalk. A woman took my hand, and I was able to find the store my mom was in. My direction and memory helped me find my way back to Mom. To this day, I have a good sense of direction in a strange town or just when plain travelling to where I want to go. I don't need to be shown how to get somewhere twice. I don't think Mom even knew I was missing until the lady brought me back to the store, as Mom was at the cash register. One thing Mom told me was to never to cry. I was a strong-minded girl.

Back on the Greyhound heading north, we stopped in Seattle for one night and stayed at the Vance Hotel. The Vance Hotel is familiar to me to this day. Mom, Dad, and I would always go to the Pike Place Public Market for farmers by the waterfront. It is, to this day, the neatest market and far excels Vancouver's newer Granville Island. From fish to handicrafts, it's always on the agenda when in Seattle—my first stop. Then, we would continue onto Bellingham, a small town, and our last stop before the border. Bellingham had a small station with a cafeteria, souvenir shop, candy shop, and stinky bathrooms. The stop in Bellingham Greyhound Depot was always a major stopover, about a forty-five-minute break, then onto the border. While travelling by Greyhound, you always had to get off the bus, retrieve your suitcase, and open it at the border. As I became older and frequented the United States, I got very good in breezing through customs. It takes a good hour to get through, sometimes more, especially if someone suspicious was on board, or the Customs officials found something. Sometimes, the bus was short of passenger when entering Canada.

When Dad was working in the summer, Mom and I went to the beach, usually Kitsilano Beach and Second Beach in Stanley Park. Although I couldn't swim, I'd do the dog paddle around the pool and ocean. Can you imagine: I lived by the ocean and mountains, and I don't swim or ski? Come to think of it, I hated swimming in salt water, I find the ocean unclean. I always swallowed salt water. I didn't like walking through the seaweeds growing on the sea floor, the rocks, sticks, and, in later years, the garbage. I'd get sand stuck in my private parts and had to pick it out. I did not like showering in a public place either. Nonetheless, our trips to the beach lasted for years; there was no way out of going to the beach. When summer was over, the reality of school sets in.

Passing onto grade four meant going to the big school; David Lloyd George was further away, and I would walk by myself or with friends, depending on who I bumped into along the route. My homeroom teacher was Mrs. Boyce. I could not stand Mrs. Boyce. She was a tall, buxom blonde whose handwriting even bothered me. I don't think she liked me either as she placed me behind Nikki; Nikki had severe farting problems all day long. Mrs. Boyce must have gotten a thrill in placing me there. Teachers can be cruel, and she was way up there. Mrs. Boyce was always flirting with Mr. Armstrong, which made us kids sick of them both. However, kids favoured Mr. Armstrong. When needed, I would complain to Mom about Mrs. Boyce but nothing happened. Of course, I met new friends: Brenda, Linda, and Leanne. We would become friends for many, many years to come. Mr. Hugh was my science teacher. He was a short, fat man, but he was okay; he was not a mean teacher. Mr. Timmins was a fair, good teacher. He liked kids, and they liked him, too. Mrs. Cotton was my favourite teacher. She paid special attention to the less bright learners. My marks raised in her classroom. I had an excellent music teacher and art teacher. Those were my most difficult studying years. Physical Education (P.E.) was okay; except Mrs. Boyce taught me P.E. I was very athletic and always came in first at Sports Day events. Jill and I would come in first at the three-legged run. We would tie a nylon stocking around our legs to come up with the three legs, and, boy, could we run. She was much taller than I, so it looked odd. I played baseball, and Mrs. Boyce was the boss. Although a very good player, I was always the spare and did not get to play much. I'd complain to my mother but, still, nothing happened. When we girls came to puberty, Mrs. Boyce would always be looking at us girls going through shower. I hated this and would complain to Mom. Finally, I got a doctor's note saying I did not have to take a shower after P.E. I'd sit in the gym alone. I didn't mind. (To this day, I'll rather bathe at home after a workout). The winter Olympics were on, and our school had a makeshift one of its own. I decided to enter the speed skating event. We had to be at Kerrisdale Arena at around 5:00 or 6:00 A.M. The ice was cleared of debris and was crystal clear. The younger kids went on first. By the time it was our turn, the ice was all chopped up almost to a snowy texture. I was first on all the laps. But, when I was getting close to the finish line, I fell. I got up quickly and continued on. Nonetheless, rather than getting the gold, I got a bronze. Deep down, I wasn't pleased. Had the arena been cleared of the excess ice, I would have been first. School was a social place. I wasn't all that academic as I think I should have been. Besides us close trio, Arlene invited me over to her mom and dad's place. En route there, she was telling me that her dad was building this place. I was thinking there is going to be this glorious mansion. But, when we got there, it was an old-looking shack built with different materials that her father would find as scrap at the dump, garage sales, and just about anywhere. Once inside, I saw that there were no walls dividing the rooms. In fact, there weren't any rooms. To get to the master's bedroom, you must climb a ladder, though it was more like a ledge.. It also had no walls. I assumed that if you had a bad night and rolled over the wrong way, you'd fall to your death. I asked if I could have a glass of water, so I opened the cupboard, and I could see outside. The back of the cupboard was finished with chicken wire. I went home and told Mom and laughed and laughed. Even to this day, I still think it's funny.

My great love, dogs. I have such a natural affinity with dogs. Dogs would just pick me out in a crowd. And one did. I named him Boy. He was a

Norwegian Elk Hound and was very well trained. For some reason, this dog jumped over his fence every day and came looking for me. He and I walked to school together, and, at 3:00 P.M., he waited for me, just on the sidewalk, before entering the school grounds, just like "Lassie, Come Home." We spent the weekends together, and he went home in the evenings. We played at the school grounds and the park. Boy lounged around in my backyard and became rather protective of the surroundings by barking at the neighbours. It was a great love between kid and dog. He had an owner somewhere, but I didn't know where this dog actually lived. Our relationship lasted for a good six months. One day, I was walking out of the corner grocery store when a couple was walking across the street with Boy. Boy left their side despite their commands and came running over to me. Now, it was solved in their mind as to where their dog took off to almost daily. We walked down 64th Street, and I said they should give me this dog. He really liked me. Apparently, they were moving out of Province and were taking the dog with them so long, Boy.

I looked after the other dogs on the block, walking them and playing with them. One day, Mrs. Simms's dog got out of the yard and was running on Granville street—a very busy street. I went over to that busy street and rescued the dog. I was a hero on the block. I simply focused my energy on animals. At this time, I no longer had Puff. I had to sell Puff in order to get a bicycle.

School was the same, year after year, in the elementary grades. We kids pretty well did the same things during the summer months. This one time, there was this odd house on the way home from school. But the house wasn't as odd as the person who lived in it. Everyday, at 3:00, the occupant of the house would always be naked in his foyer, on the telephone that was right there. We kids were always on the other side of the street, rather puzzled. We looked anyway and then took peeks. It was the shortest way home, maybe not necessarily the best way, but we went that way anyway. I told Mom while, of course, was giggling. In those days, people did not phone the police like they do today. Another incident was when we kids told Mr. Buckley, our principal, of the day when a man had pulled over in his car and called us over. He had a sock over his wee wee; it was sticking straight up. We giggled when we were telling Mr. Buckley. Thinking back, he didn't take it lightly. Another naked incident that happened frequently was when a couple would visit their grandmother across the street from my house. The two small boys who visited with them never failed to always strip off their clothes and run naked around the block, with their mom tailing behind. I didn't know what their fascination about nakedness was, but I thought it was funny. I was sure the parents felt very embarrassed. Around once a week, a chap, his collie trailing behind him, walked to the corner store. I just loved that dog. It lived right across the park from where I played. In those days, leashes weren't a big thing; this dog would just walk behind his master and, at home, relaxed on their front porch.

Back to school, one time, for homework, I was supposed to make a treasure map out of brown paper. Considering we had a fireplace, I decided to burn the edges of my treasure map to make it look real. I'd play by the fire and slowly put my map in the flame, slowly moving it around as to just fringe the edges. My first two maps caught fire and were toasted. For my third map, I decided not to have the real look and handed my map in on a plain brown paper bag.

One time, Mom was cleaning my closet. She put my red rubber boots in the fireplace. Well, little did we know, the neighbourhood was being filled with thick, black smoke coming out of our chimney. There was a loud knock at the door; it was a firemen. Someone had called the fire department. They asked if we have a chimney fire. I didn't believe so, but Dad was just walking home at that very same time, and, when he got in the house, there was an argument about the burning of the boots. Dad would always come home with a glazed donut that I really liked. I remember, one time, the Chinaman at the grocer didn't give Dad a bag, so he had to put the donut in his pocket. It just seemed like a big deal!

Mom took sick leave again. Apparently, she had this huge lump full of pus just to the right of her tailbone. The doctor had cut into it like a hot cross bun. Pus was just oozing out of this thing. Mom had me help her pick this, and, every time I went to pick it, she was in pain. The pus slowly came out, but reformed again, never to be cleaned fully, and boy, did it stink. It got to the point where neither I nor the neighbours wanted to come over to pick it. It was so thick you'd want to take a spoon and scoop the pus out. Mom became very, very ill. It was my understanding today that she had cancer. Apparently, I was once again to stay at a neighbour's house. But, I got to pick out from which of two families I would stay for Mom's durations at the hospital: Mr. and Mrs. Beckwith, or Mr. and Mrs. Krivel. I chose Mr. and Mrs. Beckwith because they have a dog. I assumed Mr. and Mrs. Krivel weren't amused. Shortly after, they bought their kids a dog. Mr. and Mrs. Beckwith were wealthy people, although their house was modest. Mrs. Beckwith had moved from a mansion in Shaughnessy with her new husband, Carl. My bed was the couch, which was in gold silk with matching elegant pillows. Her dining room was no longer set up. She had one room filled with her fine silver, china, and art. You could see richness, elegance, and once-upon fine dining. Cindy, their Shetland sheepdog, a tri colour (black and white), was my favourite. Mrs. Beckwith bought Cindy at Sunnyslope Kennels, which was, at that time, one of Vancouver's best dog kennels, owned by the Arpels. There was a great atmosphere there, and I'd go off to school daily. Mrs. Beckwith had me washed and clothed, and off I'd go. My stay with them was long, and I don't think I remember why. I did remember Dad telling me, in the basement, that I might have to go to an orphanage—my biggest fear. I ran up the stairs and told Mom that I am going to an orphanage. Mom and Dad had a fight over this. Apparently, Mom was very sick and chances of death were high. I thought that, if this happened, I would be able to stay with Mrs. Beckwith. Mom did return home, and family life, for me, resumed. However, it was not perfect. I do remember one weekend when Mom had to return to the hospital. Dad was home, so there was no need for me to go anywhere. I guess Dad stole a huge bag of popcorn from a vendor in Stanley Park and brought it home. Being as cheap as he is, he wanted to go out to the bar, but he would never think of getting a babysitter. Daddy-O sat me down on the couch, turned on the TV, placed the popcorn beside me, and told me NOT to open the door. I was fine; I babysat myself. Helen was over one Saturday, and Dad was out. We decided to jump up and down on the bed. I really made a mess of my room. When Dad came home, he caught us screaming and jumping up and down. He wasn't amused. We even included the laundry that was in the wicker basket. Anyway, Helen had to go home.

All of our parents had some oddity. Mrs. Novikoff, Philip's mom, was the most different of the bunch. She was very meticulous about her home; it was always spotless. One day, Helen had to use the bathroom and she said no because she had just washed the floor. Helen ran all the way home and peed on her kitchen floor while trying to make it to the bathroom. We thought Philip's mom was mean. That was the talk of the block for a while. Philip N. was a bugger. One day, Evelyn, Philip N., myself, and the other Phillip were walking home from school. Phillip pooed his pants, and it ran down his pant leg; Philip N. picked up the poo with a stick and chased Evelyn with it all the way home. (They lived next to each other). I was laughing all the way home and told Mom about it. I don't know what possessed us one day, but Helen, Evelyn, and I (before I couldn't play with Evelyn) decided we were going to find out who had the strongest chair. All three of us had our little chairs and started to throw them against the fence one by one to see whose chair will hold out—mine did; it was the strongest.

One day, I was pouring milk in a glass for Helen at her house. I told her to tell me when to stop. She didn't so I kept pouring. Her mother and sister weren't amused. *You've got to stop pouring; you've got to tell me*. I never did that again.

Mom made friends with Sharon's and Mark's mom. They were very poor in money and class. Their father wasn't with them, and they all lived with their mom's father—Sharon's and Mark's grandfather—in a small rented shack; he worked as a garbage collector. He drove a truck with a canopy on top. You could only enter from the door at the back of the truck. We three kids would ride in the back. Mom and Sharon's mom were in front of us while her dad drove. We went to Cultus Lake a lot with them. It was fun, as I always enjoyed riding in vehicles. Cultus Lake has an Indian reservation not too far away, and I can remember very clearly how many natives were on the beach. One time, there was definitely a big party. I had never seen so many drunken natives having sex on the beach and leaving their beer bottles there as well. I wasn't amused; it left a social stigma of natives being drunk all the time.

Carol's mom and dad had a cabin in Penticton. I used to go with them for the weekends in the summer very often. I loved the drive and the travels. Their cabin was right on the waterfront with a rowboat. Carol and I would go out in the boat a lot. We'd take the fishing rods and go fishing. I caught a rainbow trout one time, and I was proud. We had that for supper that night.

One morning, I was very, very ill. My head was so sore. Carol's dad and brother were also very ill. Carol and her mom were okay. Apparently, there was a propane leak that affected the three of us, and it was wicked. I thought I was going to die. As soon as her dad could, he fixed the leakage. But still, I was in bed the whole day, and her dad was equally sick. Other than that, our trips were fun. I soon learned that Mom paid Carol's family to take me there on weekends.

CHAPTER THREE

Mom and Dad's marriage was going down the drain. Although, I truly didn't understand what was going on, Dad said that Mom and her friends were planning a divorce while he was at sea. There was tension in the house. I noticed that Dad slept on the couch, and Mom would cook fish oil above the stove every night. This was so stinky, and it filled the house. I couldn't stand it. Mom used the oil over her legs at night to keep Dad out of the bedroom. Dad slept out on the couch for many nights. The story went, but not confirmed, that Dad had picked up a hooker when the ship docked and contacted venereal disease. If this was true, Mom was devastated. I believe Mom and Dad had a great love, but now, it was toasted. She would seek companionship elsewhere. In the background was a Finnish man named Martti Kankanen whom I hadn't seen yet. Mom was all of a sudden draped in furs and jewellery, and an unlimited amount of money was at my disposal. Dad wasn't ever a spender, and Mom loved the gifts. To conclude Mom and Dad's relationship, Mom, Dad, and I were to meet at the theatre. I remember Mom walking ahead of us while I held Dad's hand, looking up at him with great concern. I have a picture of this taken by a street photographer. From then on, Dad wasn't around. Mom said he had gotten a job on the deep-sea freighters and was going around the world. That, he did.

Martti was in; Dad was out. Martti stuck around five to many more years. Because of the unlimited amount of money, Mom had braces put on my teeth. I also participated in winter and summer activities that cost money. One of my favourite summer vacations was a camp called Holiday Acres. It was a camp based in Aldergrove, BC. I went there for three summer's in a row, until I was too old. The first year, I stayed for two weeks. Mom put me on the Greyhound bus for the trip to Aldergrove. I would be picked up by the owner's son by the road side. I was a great traveller and had no problem ever travelling alone. The owner's son was there, and off we went down a gravel road to Holiday Acres. It had your average house where the owners lived, a riding ring in the front, and, behind the riding ring, was the cottage. All the girls were on one side, and the boys were on the other side of the wall. Of course, there was a sink and shower in each area. There were those fold-up beds all over, and you could pick where you would like to sleep. The earlier you got there, the better the chance of you getting the best bed. On the other side of the cottage were outhouses that led to the barn. There were hitching posts enough to accommodate thirty horses. Along the left of the barn was a creek and road that ventured out onto the 100 acres where we rode and where the horses would prefer to take off after they had been ridden. The kids would leave to go home on Saturdays, and new kids would arrive on Sundays; it's a week by week thing. Once, we were all in house on Sunday; it was orientation time. Near the house was another building equipped with a kitchen and eating area. Behind that was the open pit for roasting wieners and marshmallows. We all joined in the dining area at first, then by the fire pit later in the evening. We got to know each other as time went on. Most of us kids were from Vancouver. In fact, we were all from the same area of town and from schools that were rather close. As the years went by, us kids who grouped together would meet every year at Holiday Acres. The weather in Aldergrove was always sunny; it rained rarely. Monday morning was time to pick out a horse. One of the counsellors would go out to the back 40 to retrieve the horses. We were taught to saddle and bridle the horses. At this point, no one was assigned to any one horse. We were just learning how to start up. We brushed the horses first. They were always very dusty. Then we'd put on their blanket, saddle, and bridle. Us kids would walk a horse to the riding ring and try out different horses that were in the centre of the ring. One counsellor put me on Peanuts. He was the most vicious pony. He hated everything and everybody. He was always attacking other horses, and us. He was also very picky on who could ride him, so, as I am going around the ring, Peanuts decided to get down on his front legs and back legs. I heard the counsellor scream, "GET OFF!" I did, just as Peanuts decided to roll over with his saddle on and everything. That was the last time I rode Peanuts. It was two kids to a horse. You were lucky if you had one of your own. We took turns in the morning riding session or the afternoon riding session. The system worked well. Peanuts naturally had only one rider. That person could ride the morning and afternoon sessions. I wanted a big horse. The way it was picked was this: Ron, the counselor, would call a horse's name and you would stand up. He'd pick which kid would get what horse. I stood up for almost all the larger horses. Soda, the best horse, always went to the most experienced rider. I got a palomino named Comet. Comet was assigned to me for a week. Considering I was staying for two weeks, I had to go over the same procedure of standing up when the horse you wanted was called. I got Comet for the full two weeks. Once you were assigned a horse, you could go and get your horse and stay in the centre ring. If you had a partner, which I did, you two would decide who would go out first. Everyone wanted to be the first out as the horses were fresh and full of pee and vee. The system did work fine, and everyone had their turn. The first set of kids would set out. Basically, you would have the morning to bum around, read comic books, and get to know the other kids. When the horses returned around noon, it was lunchtime and a break for the horses. We'd meet our partner and horse, remove the saddle and blanket, and let them rest. After lunch, we'd start up brushing and saddling again, and off we'd go. I loved riding; Comet and I were a team. He listened, and I wasn't hard on him. There were many trails to go through on the 100 acres. We all had fun. There was a pond out back, and Comet decided to go into the pond. I jumped off.

Ron, the counselor, got mad. "Stay on your horse," he screamed. Now, this way, he had to go into the pond and retrieve Comet. However, Comet wouldn't budge, and he stayed in the centre of the pond. Once our ride was through, the horses would gallop back to the barn, as they knew it was "take-the-saddle-off" and "let-me-loose" time. The horses all ran out to the back 40. It was suppertime by then, and all of us kids piled into the dining area. The meals were always good, and we were hungry after a full day of country-fresh air. We'd had to peel potatoes and carrots. Once we all had washed and cleaned, the dining room was hayride time. There were two huge Clydesdales, rather old, that pulled the hay wagon. The wagon was a huge old thing that accommodated all of us kids. We'd travel down the gravel road and sang songs. After the hayride, we'd all hung around the fire pit and roasted wieners and marshmallows. Then, it was bedtime, only to repeat the same things the next day. Of course, during the time us kids were there, we grabbed ourselves a boyfriend or a girlfriend. My friend was named Neil. He went to the Prince of Wales School in Vancouver. It was all pure, clean fun. One afternoon, we went swimming. We all walked to the watering hole. There was a big tree by the watering hole where a rope hung. With it, you could climb the tree and swing into the water like Tarzan. One day, I was just about to go into the water when this HUGE green water snake was joyously swimming around. One boy picked up the snake and started chasing me with it. Considering I was a first class runner, I was well ahead of him and made it back to the cottage. That was the last time I decided to go near that watering hole.(Years later, an out-door pool was put near the cottages). There weren't any disasters or fighting that happened while I was there. It really was a happy camp. Evelyn, who was not allowed near me, or me near her, would go to Holiday Acres the week I wasn't there. It was prestigious for the mothers to see which kids could stay the longest. With Mom's new wealth, for the next two more years, I went for the whole month, leaving a limited time for Evelyn to go to Holiday Acres. (I believe it was a Mom thing). The odd kid would stay all summer. To me, a month was enough. Once, upon my return home, Mom couldn't get over how dirty I was, plus my clothes. "But that was camp, Mom.".

One more last treat before school was the P.N.E., the Pacific National Exhibition. Mom and I went there every year. We'd start off at the first building on the first day with exhibits of crafts, then onto the food building where we always ate as the food there was cheaper than at some of the food carts around the grounds. I usually had pizza and always with scones. From there, we'd go through the "buy-some-junk" building where merchants would set up their wares. Mom and I usually bought the latest in vegetable-shredding machines where the salesman had a microphone wrapped around his head, enticing everyone to buy one. Every year, we also bought the nonfog for glasses. From there, we'd go through the P.N.E. home, in which everyone wishes to win. Then we'd go through the Agrodome and watch the equestrian, cattle, or pig shows. Then we'd go through the barns and see all the horses, cattle, pigs, and goats all competing to be the best specimen of their breed. Then we'd make our rounds to the games and rides area. Mom and I always played the horse races. This game was like a pinball machine where you'd have slow, fast, speed, fast, slow on the board, and you'd flick the steel ball to race your horse across the wall. All the horses had a name. Mom and I knew which horse to sit at every year, and we always dominated the game and brought home okay prizes. My favourite treat while there at the games were the snow cones. Every year, I always had a snow cone, even to this day, except I've decided I didn't want to be walking around with a blue tongue at my age. We always bought minidonuts every time. Mom and I spent the whole day at the P.N.E. every time we were there. Once, we pretty well exhausted ourselves. We slowly made our way back to the main gates, but not without stopping at the House and Home building. The wholesalers and retailers were showing off the latest in pianos, bathtubs, kitchens, and so on. Then, we're off to the line up for the bus. It was always a venturesome day.

Mom and I were BIG wrestling fans. We'd watch wrestling every Saturday with Ron Morrier. The stars included Don Leo Jonathan, Dutch Savage, Bulldog Brown, Eric Froehlich, Lou Thesz, The Assassins, Gene Kiniski, and, my-all-time favourite, John Tolos. Every Saturday, I'd phone Channel 8 to get ringside seats for two for Monday night wrestling at the Gardens. Mom and I were regulars. It was a great way to release any unwanted energy. Mom and I would be screaming there with the best of them. After several hours of that, our voices were raw. One time, Mom lost her hat. The ladies sitting behind us stole her hat, but Mom blamed me. Mom turned around and grabbed the hat out of one of the ladies' hands, and that became our own wrestling match right there. We felt we won and walked out of there as proud fighters. One Saturday, I actually went down to Channel 8 to watch the TV wrestling and was on TV myself. I thought that was a big deal. Mom and I went to the wrestling matches for years and years. After the P.N.E. summer was over, I was back to school. It was great fun to see all my friends, and enemies, again; like usual, my friends and I were always in the same classrooms for just about everything. Every now and then, one new student would show up. The good, the bad, the smart, and the dumb—we were all there. For openings, some teachers would ask what we did over the summer. I, of course, went to camp while the others, of wealthier, parents went to Europe or other exotic places. Sometimes, we had to write about our summer. Whatever, everyone was glad to see each other in our Sunday best. In those days, you could not wear jeans to school. Mom always had me in a pretty dress, knee socks, and saddle shoes. The teachers were the same as the year before; we just all went to a higher level of education. This procedure would be similar every year for grades four to seven.

In the winter, when ice skating started, we'd have some new faces at Kerrisdale Arena. Of course, Neil, the boyfriend I met at summer camp now came ice skating. Lana, Linda, and I were a team for years to come. With this new found wealth, my expenditures were endless. I went public skating every Saturday and Sunday, and, as a member of the Kerrisdale Figure Skating Club, I went every Monday and Wednesday evening. Lana and Linda were also members. We were really a team for five to six more years to come. I wasn't very good at figure skating but could do some turns here and there. I took lessons at the end of every half hour of the session. Linda and Lana did not take lessons. There was a really cute boy there whom we nicknamed Diddle, Diddle Dee. In our eyes, he was breathtaking. He knew we were nuts for him. He was reserved and stayed away from us. (He just simply avoided us, period). God, if we even got a look at him, we'd go goofy. The three of us never missed a skating day, both at the Figure skating club and at public skating. I remember Linda had this really sore foot when we were skating one Saturday. We skated around and around, and Linda kept complaining about a sore foot. Finally, she went off the ice. I followed her. She had a comb in her boot. To this day, I still laugh about it. I joked with her during our 1967 school reunion about the comb in her skate.

I was very popular with the boys. I remember so clearly that I dumped Neil for Mitchell. Neil was so broken hearted that you'd think he was going to die. Even other kids' parents were concerned at his loss. So was I. I had never experienced a guy getting so upset about losing his girlfriend. Neil never did return to the ice rink, or summer camp. Mitchell wasn't with me for long either, as his girlfriend phoned me and threatened to beat me up if I continued to be Mitchell's girlfriend. Mitchell phoned me later that day and confirmed that our relationship was over. It didn't bother me much, as I always had male company, either as a boyfriend or just plain friend. These events were ongoing.

When it was time to graduate from elementary school, my friends and I all went to Churchill Secondary High. I was a very slow developer physically. All the girls were entering puberty far ahead of me. It was discussed that the teachers were not going to pass me onto grade eight, just because of my slow physical maturity. Apparently, I went onto grade eight. To go to Churchill High was a major walk. I had to cross Granville Street and Oak street and go up eight more blocks. It wasn't the closest joint, that's for sure. Our curriculum was different. New to me was French, cooking, and sewing classes as a course. I already knew the fundamentals in cooking and could already sew. French, I simply couldn't stand or understand to this day. Nor could I stand the teacher. She was a single, loud, screaming woman. When someone proposed to her, we couldn't figure who the hell would want to marry her. Classes with her were horrid. She, apparently, finally kicked me out of her class due to my poor attitude. I got an X in French—I never took it up again. It was my most difficult year. When I finished grade eight, I was passed onto math and science on trial. That summer, Mom enrolled me into summer school at John Oliver on 41st and Fraser. I hated it; it disrupted my summer. Although it was only a month, I passed both subjects and proceeded onto math and science like the others. High school was fun. Now, we could wear jeans. It was passed at the school board that in all public schools in the Province of British Columbia (BC) jeans were allowed in the classrooms. Talk about modernization. I had a tough time in grade eight. My marks weren't very good and, generally, life stunk. When the year finished, I told Mom that I didn't want to go to Churchill for the following year. So, for the beginning of grade nine, I went to Magee Secondary School. The distance was just as far as Churchill High. Magee was considered an academic school, and, considering I wasn't very academic, they didn't think the school would be suited for me. Nonetheless, I stayed there anyway. I liked Magee much better. Although my marks somewhat increased, I still wasn't up to a high academic standard. But I was not failing either. I met Marilyn Koutnik. She was a funny-looking girl and average in school. We became good friends. One thing that was always noted about Marilyn was that every month, she'd have wicked periods and would have to go home early. Only once, while at Magee, I became very ill during class and had to go home. The school phoned my mom. Considering we didn't have a car, I had to walk home. By the time I got home, I was fine. My dog, a part collie and part German shepherd, I named her Lassie, greeted me at the gate. I begged and begged and begged Mom that I wanted a part collie and part German shepherd dog. Considering purebred dogs were only for the very elite, I settled for a crossbred. I search the pet section of the newspaper every day. I even cut them out and pasted them into my scrapbook. The ad was there" PART COLLIE AND PART GERMAN SHEPHERD PUPS, $10.00 EACH. I phoned and hopped on the bus all the way to the east end to pick out the golden-coloured puppy. (Mom specifically said, "Don't pick out a black puppy.") It was something I thought about when, later in the years, I was raising Newfoundlands. I picked out my new friend. The lady called me a cab, and on the way home we went. Right away, I got its food dishes, collar, and leash. I went around the backyard and fenced and blocked off any exits under the fence with pieces of firewood so that my new puppy could not get out of the yard. And, here I have my new friend. I house-trained my pup, and taught her the basic commands: sit, come, stay, and lie down. She was my best buddy. Every day, I could hardly wait to get home after school to see my dog.

Martti Kankanen, Mom's boyfriend, was still in the picture, and I just simply hated him. But I tolerated him for Mom's sake; it was because of him that I could enjoy the luxuries I was enjoying. He even wanted to send me to Finland on my own. That trip never transpired at that time. Nonetheless, money was just flowing. Our house was like little Finland all over again. There was Finnish music, Finnish dancing, and Finnish cooking. Martti was always impeccably dressed (after working in Port Hardy on Vancouver Island in the logging camps as a faller). He dressed the part for city life. He draped Mom in gorgeous clothes and jewellery. When he was around the house, it was always filled with his friends who were also impeccably dressed, with ties, and talking with all Finnish languages. Poker was always played and there were lots and lots of booze, not just beer, but the heavy stuff—vodka, rum, and scotch. Although I never ever saw Mom drunk, she'd always have a glass of Finlandia vodka. Martti drank the hard stuff straight. Finnish music was blaring. Mom would be cooking Finnish meals, which I loved. Martti was a very loud person. He didn't know how to speak in the normal tone of voice. Possibly, he needed to scream loudly at the logging camp. But it didn't change when he was in the house. His loudness bothered me terribly. You'd never know if he was mad or not. When he played cards, everything would be in Finnish. I remember him slapping down cards and yelling the domination of the card in Finnish. Either he was happy for winning or screaming for losing, you'd never know. This lasted for years to come. Just to get rid of me, they sent me to go through summer and winter activities. One Christmas, I knew I was getting a bicycle. Boy, did I get the latest in modern bicycles. It was done all in chrome and blue, with the three speeds in the handle of the bars. It was a classic bike. I got really mad that Christmas that the neighbour had to take my bike and drive it to a gas station to fill the tire; that's how upset I was. I wanted to ride my bike that day, and I did.

Dad, who just returned from the deep sea and his worldly adventures, had called the house for me to come and see him. He had rented a small room in a house—a real dump. He said he missed me and loves me very much. While in town, he tried to see me as much as possible. One time, he came to the school and knocked on the door of the classroom I was in. This disrupted the class, but I didn't care. Dad was nervous; he didn't want to get in trouble with the school. In those days, you could get away with this, but not today. We talked briefly. Another time, a heavy-duty Finnish poker game was going on in the house. Dad phoned the house and was waiting for me at the corner. Mom very discreetly told me that Dad was at the corner. I motioned to everyone at the card table that I was taking Lassie out for a walk. Poor Dad, there he was at the corner. He asked if Martti was at the house, and I said, "Yes." Dad knew I hated him. I felt how it was eating away at him. He came all the way down from Kitsilano to South Granville by bus to see me at the corner for about fifteen minutes. When I returned home, nothing was said to disrupt the card table. Martti could loose it so easily.

At Magee, there were many volunteer services you could do if you wanted to. Marilyn and I decided to volunteer our services to St. Paul's Hospital, a Catholic hospital in downtown Vancouver, on Burrard Street. St. Paul's was a huge, old brick building. Marilyn and I would take the bus down together after school and meet with the nuns. We were supplied with blue smocks and were named Candy Stripers. Marilyn and I enjoyed helping the sick. They seemed to be so happy to talk with us or see us. Our first task, which involved our services twice a week, was getting fresh water for all the patients. Marilyn and I were assigned a floor together. She'd do one side, I'd do the other. After all the patients received fresh water, it was mealtime. Marilyn and I delivered the trays, respectively, to the patients whose name was on the tray. This gave the nurse some freedom and a break. One time, I was assigned to the psychological ward. I was to feed a woman who was bound over her hands and feet. I was to feed her her meal. This was an impossible task as she had some kind of phobia about the dark. Apparently, she had to get home before dark. I was to work with her for one hour. Getting food into her was futile. She would just push my hand away, and say, "You eat it." I did everything in my brainpower to get this woman to eat. Finally, the nurse came in, and I said I was getting nowhere. She told me not bother anymore. It was time to retrieve the hospital trays from the patients. Once Marilyn and I did that and gave the patients fresh water again, and a few conversations with those who really took a liking to us, it was about time to leave. We spent the time from 4:00 until 8:00 P.M. working at St. Paul's Hospital. It was very rewarding. Marilyn and I did this for the next four months. About seven years later, during my aesthetician course, one of our duties, which was done only if you wanted to, was to go to St. Paul's Hospital once a week and help the outpatient women and men to feel good and attractive about themselves. We were to teach them how to put makeup on, and they were very testy in what you said. These patients were very sensitive and no doubt needed reassurance in life. It was rewarding work. As time went on, it was only the teacher and I that continued to go to St. Paul's for these people.

When Martti was in town, Mom was spoiled. They travelled a lot to Vegas and, of all places, Winnipeg. They had a mutual friend in Winnipeg and always took the train there—first class Vancouver to Winnipeg. They'd stay a week or two, only to return to go elsewhere, Vegas or Reno. I was a big enough girl by then to be left alone. I'd get myself ready for school should it be school time. Whatever time of the year, I could prepare myself for the day. When Martti was in our house, Martti could lose it at any time, booze permitting. Mom was always shaking her head at me in a "No" position. "Don't say or do anything." I knew the moment was fridged, not to disturb Martti. It used to bug me terribly. Every now and then, Martti would lose it and would punch a hole in the wall. We had several of them. Then he'd have to fix the hole, which usually ended up looking rather tacky. You'd always remember that Martti did that. But, to cover up for his loss in personality, Martti was generous with the money and gifts. Martti bought himself a new radio. This thing could reach Europe, even Finland. His new radio had so many buttons on it, you could fly this thing. I got his old radio, which was nothing to frown about. I could get a lot of stations, and I really liked it. One time, Martti, Mom, and I went to an exclusive restaurant called Lulu's. Lulu's was on Broadway at Granville in Vancouver. We ordered the finest steaks, etc. Martti and Mom always spoke Finnish in public places. I never knew what was being said. Then, all of a sudden, Martti would lose it, Mom would jump out of her chair, just as our delicious-smelling food arrives, and Mom and I would leave the restaurant, leaving Martti to pay the bill. It was very embarrassing. I still remember it today. These episodes were common: at Marco Polo Restaurant in Chinatown, just about everywhere and anytime. I remember, one year, both Martti and my dad claimed me on their income tax. My dad got shit from Revenue Canada. It was totally unreal in my thinking, but I do remember being told about that one. It was disturbing that my dad got the raw end of the deal; that he couldn't claim me, but Martti could.

School, skating, and camp continued on. The Kerrisdale Figure Skating Club was putting on a show for our parents and family. We had a special routine of various ins and outs and skating techniques that us kids put together to form a program showcasing our figure-skating skills. Mom made me a black-velvet skating skirt which I wore with a black sweater. It looked really cute. Dad showed up at the show; Mom didn't. We had to perform an in-and-out skate around the other kids who were skating straight at us, then swerve around like a half figure eight. Of course, I missed one kid and skated straight. Dad noticed, and so did the teacher. No one was impressed with my mistake. From their point of view, I had lots of room to do the half eight, but, in my eyes, I was going to bump into the other kid coming straight at me. I felt like I ruined the whole show.

Coming home from figure skating on Wednesday nights, I had a choice of the Arbutus bus or the 41st bus to Granville and then down to 64th avenue. On Wednesdays, the 41st bus was first, so I usually took that bus and transferred at Granville. While waiting at 41st and Granville, every Wednesday, at the same time, a woman never failed to walk up Granville Street, as mad as hell with a man right behind her. They were always fighting, to the point that it was very comical. Considering I only took the bus on Wednesdays nights on that route, I don't know if it was a daily routine. But, every Wednesday, the two made their appearance up Granville from one of the many mansions on that street. It was always a topic of conversation when I got home.

One time, Sharon (a friend of mine), her brother, Mark, and I were playing at the corner of 62nd and Adera. There was a house surrounded by bushes, shrubs, and trees. It was a three-story, wooden-framed house that looked like a haunted house. We kids would go into the yard via the front gate that had a spring on it; when we went in and out of the gate, it would snap closed. We played for some time, daring each other to go even closer to the house and running back. So back and forth we went, until, all of a sudden, we were being chased. Whoever came out of that house could run very fast. The three of us ran up 62nd Street where I turned in at Carol's house, only to be caught by this woman. We were in trouble. When I got home, Mom was really mad. She came along with me and walked me back to that house, knocked on the door, and made me apologize for putting her in such an inconvenience. I told her that the house looked like a haunted house, and that we didn't think anyone lived there. It was embarrassing, and I never did that again. Sharon and Mark's mom did not walk her kids to apologize; that was the way there were brought up—no discipline.

One time, Sharon and I were playing Barbie dolls at my house. Sharon was going to stay overnight. Well, we started arguing about who had the best Barbie doll, and Mom broke up the playtime, sent Sharon home, and packed up my Barbie for the evening. I always had to have the best.

While I was at Magee Secondary, a new kid named Sue joined our class. Sue was a reject from Kamloops and was, apparently, living with her grandfather in a posh apartment in Kerrisdale. There was talk that Sue was asked to leave Kamloops. Can you imagine being kicked out of your own hometown? Evidently, she had a baby at an early age and was just a juvenile delinquent. One time, she and I were at 64th Park with the boys. There was a house with a big picture window across the tracks. She picked up a brick and threw it at the picture window, crashing the glass and sending the brick into the living room. I ran like stink. I took an odd route home through the lane, up another street block from home, and just kept running. It was a long time before I went back to the park. Sue really was a bad kid. She constantly stole from everyone. One day, she had bought a hair-dying package and decided to dye her hair in our kitchen sink. This procedure took some time, and, when she finally finished, her hair was blue-black, and she had dye all over Mom's cupboards. Mom was not impressed. That evening, Mom said she could stay overnight. Apparently, she started her period that night and went home taking the bed sheets. She also stole my Mom's expensive watch that was then passed on down to me. That was the last time Sue ever came to my house, or me associating with her. Although she still had some classes with me, I didn't bother with her.

One of our teachers couldn't control any class. When other students got assigned to his class, us kids would throw paper and stuff all over the classroom. We were rather mean, but, of course, I never threw anything around the classroom; I just watched. This poor teacher, of the male gender, eventually quit teaching in the middle of the school year and got a job selling shirts at The Bay, a department store in downtown Vancouver.

CHAPTER FOUR

Little did I know, Mom was getting sick of the neighbourhood, though we spent a good ten years there. She put the house up for sale, though I didn't want to move. What she had in mind was a condo. Oh no, I couldn't have a dog anymore. Mom and I would search the finest area in town called Lower Shaughnessy. We looked at two different buildings and several suites in each building. Apparently, condo living was new in Vancouver and the "in thing" was co-ops. It was popular in New York. A lot of apartment owners of rentals were converting to selling the suits, which, apparently, made a shortage of rental accommodations in Vancouver. Mom chose the suite at #308-1216 West 11 Avenue, Eleventh at Alder to be exact. It was three blocks in from Granville and two blocks from Oak Street. Mom and I had to be approved. I was just the minimum of the age allowed—sixteen. We were accepted. The house on 64th was sold, and I had to sell Lassie. It broke my heart. Mom decorated the new suite very tastefully. I had my own bedroom. Mom bought me a new bed with a white and gold headboard and a white Indian carpet. I had my own phone, television, radio, and matching white dresser drawers. Mom had the hide-a-bed in the living room, which she had custom-made for apartment living. The suite had a balcony that faced south, so we got the sun all day. One more problem to deal with was Martti. Mom, for some mental reason, married Martti the first week we moved into suite #308. Immediately, Martti started yelling and disrupted the whole building. He threatened to cut my face. I called Dad to call the police. He did, but, somehow, I got out of the suite, had raided my piggy bank, and had enough money to get on the bus and go to Dad's place. Apparently, the police did come, and Martti was removed from the suite. When I returned home, at dinner, I told Mom that she had a choice: Martti or me. I said, "Because you simply cannot have this man here. I am sixteen now, and I can go." Mom went the next day and had the marriage annulled. She returned to the name Hillis, and that was the end of Martti.

Daddy-O was lonely and searching for the right woman. He joined Arthur Murray Dance Studio, and, from time to time, I'd go there with him. The dance instructor took me into another room for private lessons. Apparently, Dad was invited to a party. He met a woman named Margie. I didn't know exactly how the relationship started, but I remember being told that Dad had stayed overnight at her place, on the couch, considering Margie still had two young daughters left at home from her six kids. Kathy was my age while Glenda was slightly older than me. Glenda was attending university to become a teacher, and Kathy was still in high school and working part-time at Safeway. Her other children were married and having young families of their own. Her children were educated and have good jobs. Margie did a very good job raising six children, considering their father died when they were young. She moved her family from Kenora to Vancouver and was struggling at various jobs. She said when she got to Vancouver, she had a job the next day. She and Dad were getting close, so she rented an apartment in the West End with a view of English Bay. She did this for Daddy-O. I was always included in the family functions, but it was just Dad, I, and a whole herd of her family. Although accepted, I never felt 100 percent comfortable. Later, I would turn down their invitations, as it was just Dad and I sitting with her family; I wasn't comfortable in such a large setting. To this day, I meet my stepsisters on an individual basis.

But, back to Dad's and Margie's relationship; Dad proposed and had a special ring made for her from one of the stones he brought back from India. The marriage date was set on October 31, 1970. "Daddy-O, how come you're getting married on Halloween?" I asked him. They got married in a small church in the west end, and it was very pleasant. Dad wore a suit, and Margie wore a blue dress with a matching hat. There was great love there, glowing through their eyes. I was dressed in a purple dress with a silver belt and brought along John Beaddie as my date. The reception was at their rented home on 13th Street East. For their honeymoon, they went to Los Angeles and along the west coast. While at the airport, Dad's 26er broke in his suitcase, and booze was running out the back. Margie pretended she wasn't with him. Incidents like this were common and funny.

Now that Dad was married and mom had moved, I had to change schools right in the school year. So, after studying halfway at Magee High, I finished my grade nine at Eric Hamber Secondary School. Eric Hamber was then the most modern and richest of the schools. It was built in a Jewish neighbourhood, and funds were donated to building the best of everything. Eric Hamber was the only school that had a two-storey library. It was the only school on the west side of Vancouver that had a complete track and field and benches available for year-round spectators. I loved that school. Even the lockers were ultramodern. Eric Hamber wasn't particularly close, and I had to take the bus to school and walk home. The walk was right through Vancouver's most wealthy area, Shaughnessy. I thoroughly loved walking through Shaughnessy, and, later, I had girlfriends and boyfriends who lived in Shaughnessy as well. My standard of living definitely improved, and so did my marks at school. I became very popular with the boys and had no problem in making friends quickly and being one of the crew. I became friends with Lorne, Steve, Victor, and Mayda. Lorne lived near the school, Steve lived one block away from me, Victor lived en route home from school, and so did Mayda. I always had a crush on Lorne, but Lorne had a crush on Steve's sister, Lynn, who looked like Vivian Leigh. She was a very pretty young woman. Victor also liked Lynn, but settled for me, as Lynn dumped both Lorne and him and dated George. Later, she quit Eric Hamber and went to a school that offered drama. Victor, Lorne, Mayda, Steve, and I became very good friends for years to come. Mom loved all the kids, but Stevie was her favourite. Steve considered my mom as his mom. Except for Mayda, the others were in one grade higher than I, although we were the same age, considering grade one for me began with a slow start.

That was when the time the boys got their driver's licenses. You were really cool back then if you had a license, not only that, but also a car. Lorne bought a Studebaker Silver Hawk. What a neat-looking car it was, with its tail fins elegantly at the back. Lorne's dad taught driving lessons, so Lorne became a good driver. Lorne decided to teach me to drive. Of course, it was always Steve, Lorne, Victor, and I together all the time. Lynn and I took turns amongst the guys. But, she soon had other friends at her new school, and we didn't see much of her. One day, Lorne told me to park behind this car. But, instead of hitting the break, I hit the gas pedal and went right into the car in front. Steve and I quickly changed seats. Lorne went out to inspect the damage. There was very little damage, so we took off. I eventually learned how to drive, but didn't get my license till sometime later. I did write my BC learners exam, but I thought I failed. Twenty-five years later, when I traded in my Alberta license and went to get my BC license, I was told that I had written the learners and passed many years ago. It made things easier. Poof! Poof!

The Bomac Car Dealership was one and a half blocks from my house. As I found out later, Victor stole one of the new Dusters right off Alder Street. We all piled in this car and drove around Stanley Park, West Vancouver, and all over, and Victor would park the car back on Alder by the lot at night. It seemed that no one missed the car. One day, at dinner, Lorne's sister came running in with Dad and Mom. Apparently, someone stole the neighbour's license plates off their car. Lorne just about choked on his chicken. Our fun with stolen cars was short lived. We knew it was wrong and didn't do it anymore.

At Eric Hamber, my marks increased dramatically. Life was good, and I believe those years at Hamber were my best. Mayda's mom and dad were very wealthy. They lived in a very large mansion on Osler Street. Mayda's mom didn't approve of her boyfriend and kicked her out of the house. Mayda came to live with me for several months, until Mayda and her mom could sort things out. Mayda and I had a lot of fun. We walked to school together and thumbed home. Thumbing home was safe in those days. One day, we made relish in our foods course. I personally hate relish, and the huge jar I made it in looked like puke. While thumbing home, the chap who picked us up was rather weird. When he let us off at 12th and Oak, I left the jar of still-sealed puke relish on the back floor. This guy drove around the block twice, looking for us. Traffic did not permit him to stop, and we laughed.

When I walked home from school during the warm days, I'd go down Osler, past all the mansions filled with Vancouver's old money. My favourite house to this day is on the Crescent. It is a huge white house with a tall fence around it. It was something like the white house in the *Beverly Hillbillies*. It has royal blue awning on the windows, a swimming pool at the side of the house, and a long driveway. The back of this house overlooked the city, the Pacific, and the mountains. To always greet you at the gate were two huge, fawn Great Danes and a small Pekingese; very beautiful dogs. Every time I go to Vancouver, I drive by that particular house.

Back at school, I was exceptionally good at track and field. Being as short as I was, my best sport was hurdles; I could fly over those hurdles. I was also exceptional at the 100-yard dash, and, around the track race, I was always the last on the relay team, to bring our team in first. I wasn't great at long distant running. The only sport I was terrible at was tennis. I couldn't hit that ball; I find the racquet to heavy. Tennis was short lived for me, and I focused on the sports I was good at. I finished grade nine and went onto grade ten. We kids were like glue. Because we lived so close to each other, we were never parted during the summer. I was now too old to go to Holiday Acres. Although Steve had a crush on me, I dated Victor. He had a job, so I was very spoiled. He took me to see every movie downtown that school year. The boys knew I loved dogs, especially collies and German shepherds. Whenever one guy wanted my attention, he'd gain points by oddly giving me enough pictures of my favourite two breeds of dogs.

Smoking marijuana and taking acid was an in thing then. I don't know who got this stuff, but we had it. Steve, Lorne, Victor, and I would take acid and bumble all over the place. When Wreck Beach was becoming the nude beach in Vancouver, we'd frequent that beach. We'd walk down the 100 stairs, walk along the beach, and climb the sand dunes right up to the road. With erosion, I don't think you can do it today. We kids did that game a lot. What a lot of exercise it was, when I really think about it. Mom knew we were underage to be drinking, but we were getting our beer anyway. So Mom would rather buy us the beer and have us drink at home. My house became the hangout. Mom preferred that we kids were safe in the apartment than sitting in some back alley. We respected her and never caused any problems. We played bridge, and Mom would cook meals for us while we had our beer. One time, Victor brought over some marijuana. I didn't smoke cigarettes, or marijuana, but Mom tried one puff. She said, "I don't feel anything." We all laughed. I was just comfortable with the beer. One day, we were having a birthday party for Victor. He had brought over a mickey of dark rum for himself. Mom ordered Chinese food. We kids had a lot of fun. Then, sometime during the early evening, Victor retired to my bedroom. We were playing cards. When finished, I went to the bedroom and found Victor passed out on the floor, floating in his puke; all the Chinese food were freshly floating on the floor. Victor just missed my white carpet.

I said to everyone, "Look at Victor, look at Victor." Well, Victor was out cold. We actually got worried. We needed a game plan, and Mom was into it. Steve was going to phone Victor's dad and tell him that Victor was staying overnight at his place. Steve also told his Mom that he was staying over at my place. We turned Victor over, and Mom cleaned the floor. Steve stayed with Victor while I slept on the couch in the living room. In the morning, Steve and I got hangovers while Victor got up fresh as a daisy and went to work. We were all stunned and continued to sleep in until noon. We laughed. The final time I ever took acid was when Mom was out at a local cabaret. Steve and I were at my house, right out of it. We were both looking at a picture, and I said there are highways going through the living room. Steve and I quit the dope scene. I stuck to beer. Mom would supply it on weekends only and not necessarily every weekend.

CHAPTER FIVE

Dad's brother died in his hometown of Meaford in Ontario, in June 1970. It was a small town on the coast of Georgian Bay. Dad decided that I was to go along, to see my cousins on his side of the family and, of course, Meaford. I had been there before, but don't remember it. At that time, I was old enough to remember any venture he'd take me on. We flew to Toronto and boarded the local bus lines from the terminal en route to Meaford. We passed through the small towns of Barrie, Collingwood, Thornbury, etc. We stayed with my grandmother. This was a very different world. The small town seemed so simple and backward to me. My cousins weren't great citizens of the community either, having illegitimate children at a very early age, continuing to live on welfare, and producing many more kids for the rest of their lives. Anyway, while in Meaford, there was the sadness of a funeral. My Dad is the oldest; Rosena is second in line; Murray, the third; and then Eleanor. Apparently, Murray still lived at home with his mother and did what the locals did—fishing, lumber, and hunting. His dog ended up getting rabies and eventually died. In such a small town, everyone knows everyone. The police put Murray in the Collingwood jail for bootlegging. He was in for just a couple of days. En route home, Murray stopped at a bar and had a few beers before thumbing home. A car hit him and sent him along the road. The car also caught the back of his head and dragged him for a while. The back of his head was smashed right in. That was the end of poor Murray. The family made funeral arrangements at Ferguson Funeral Home in Meaford. After the funeral, there were cookies and cake time at Grandma's, and the people in the town dropped by to console the family, even the town policemen. (I guess Murray was their best customer). Once the fuss was over, and life continued on, Dad proceeded to show me off in and around Meaford. Dad was proud of me and took me everywhere. One adventure was spending the whole day on the Georgian Bay, on one of Dad's friend's homemade fishing boat. It was a big, white boat with ropes and a wheel at the back which released the nets and brought the nets in full of fish. This was their daily employment. Anyway, we ventured out in the morning. There were no bathroom facilities. It floated like a tin can. I was stuck there until 5:00 P.M. I watched while they brought in the fish from those nets, cleaned them right there, and threw the guts in the lake for the seagulls that were following the boat. Boy, did it stink. One fish had a bloodsucker stuck to it. Dad pulled it off and showed it to me. I was not impressed. When I finally got off that tin can, I had to buy some ex-lax. I could never stop talking about that horrid fishing trip I had. My aunt, apparently, went on it once, never to go on it again, having experienced the same thing I did.

Dad took me to the Meaford newspaper-publishing house, and they showed me how the local paper was made. (Most of these people went to school with Dad and stayed in Meaford). Dad took me to the police station and introduced me to the chief who had constantly arrested Daddy-O for having beer or being drunk. Dad showed me the school and the church which he helped build, stone by stone, and various heritage buildings in and around Meaford. Dad took me to Walter's Falls which was named after my great-great-great-grandfather. It was his property, and he built it, so it was named after him. The people who lived on the property had an Irish setter, a very pretty dog of which I have a picture of. Dad also took me to the statue of Beautiful Joe. Beautiful Joe is a dog whose master was very cruel. To this day, I have an updated book on the story of *Beautiful Joe*. I've only been able to get up to the first chapter; it is so cruel. Dad took me to Owen Sound to visit Rosena. Grandma was furious as I saw Mary Lou's kids. Grandma just hated the fact that all her grandkids from Rosena were half-black from the same guy who'd be in and out of jail. Rosena had five kids by the time she was twenty-three. Today, the kids are all grown up, look very attractive, and have kids of their own. That was a short-lived moment.

It was time to venture back to Vancouver. Dad had reservations onboard the train from Barrie, Ontario, to Vancouver, BC. Being as cheap as Dad is, we rode in the coach department for four days and three nights. You really don't get much sleep, as the coach was mostly used for short travels by the locals in each town; it was always noisy. But you would really see a lot of Canada. Dad and I had our meals together in the meal car, and I'd play the games provided by the crew such as bingo. But, basically, I stayed in my seat in the coach section. I didn't see Dad much as he spent his whole time going across Canada in the bar car. Oh well, I was fine just the same. As we were getting close to Vancouver, we were going over the railway bridge in New Westminster very slowly. Dad and I cracked a joke about us ending up in the Fraser River while poor Margie was waiting for us at the train station. It was a "you-had-to-be-there" kind of thing. Once we arrived in Vancouver, I boarded the bus home.

The next summer, Dad decided to send me to Meaford for the month of July. I wanted to go. He put me on the train, but, this time, I got an upper berth. Dad paid for the trip. I shared the seat with another girl who was eight months pregnant. She was around sixteen years old. She said all the girls in her small town were pregnant; it was the thing to do. I was disgusted. She was constantly throwing up, and, one day, she made a real mess in the bathroom, and I ended up going to another car for its facilities, until someone cleaned her mess up. When it was time for her to depart, I wished her well. I also made friends with a couple as we seemed to bump into each other at the same time for meals. Once, we discussed travelling plans. I mentioned that someone was going to pick me up in Barrie and take me to Meaford. The couple was from Owen Sound and was also getting off in Barrie. When I got to Barrie, no one was there for me, so the couple took me to Meaford. When I arrived at my grandmother's, she seemed very surprised to see me. Perhaps she had totally forgotten that I was arriving. I had the bedroom upstairs. The summers in Ontario were warm, and I can vividly remember the thunderstorms there. The storms were always rather low, and the lightning and cracking was loud. I would walk around Meaford, see the shops, and took life easy. Rosena, who I like, came in from Owen Sound frequently to relieve some of my boring days. Grandma was a big boozer. She'd loose it easily and start screaming, swinging a stick at anybody. I remember Rosena brought over a roast beef and cases of beer. All of us were joined at the dinner table. Rosena kept giving me beer so that Grandma won't have too many. I couldn't drink the beer that fast, so I had about half a dozen open beer at the foot of my chair under the dinner table. Needless to say, the beer didn't go to waste. When Grandma eventually lost it, I went upstairs with my beer and left the cleaning of the dishes to my five cousins. After all, I am the guest. One day, I met this young chap and brought him over to my place, or, I should say, Grandma's. We were in the backyard when Grandma came out screaming at him and throwing something at him. Apparently, my grandmother's hatred toward black people was deep. This guy wasn't black, but well tanned. It was embarrassing. Anyway, the guy left, and I went into the house and up to my room. I telephoned Dad and asked if I could come home now, but he said, "Stick it out." I never did stay in Meaford more than a day ever again. I got a ride to Barrie train station and rode back on coach. I don't know why I had a berth going out there and a coach coming back. I held my own. I got a great spot by the window, and it was my spot for four days. I kept myself occupied with books and staring out the window at some of Canada's remote villages, villages where the townspeople depend on the train for their mail and in-and-out transportation. Breakfast, lunch, and dinner were always a boredom breaker. I never missed the time to at least get out of the car for a meal, other than stretching my legs. I would join in some of the evening games, but I soon found it comical in the car I was riding in anyway. In and around Blue River, BC, a young chap ended up sitting beside me. I guess we were around the same age. He had escaped from a correctional institution in that area. He had broken into homes to get his train fare to Victoria, BC. Apparently, he had only enough money to get to Kamloops. He was interesting to talk to, but he had a crummy start in life. He hated his home, mom, dad, and sisters. He started stealing and basically lived on the street. When we were getting closer to Kamloops, he really, really, wanted me to get off with him. Being a very good traveller and somewhat logical in my direction, I said that I was going to Vancouver and I will not get off with him in Kamloops. For some reason, I gave him my name, address, and telephone number. A couple of days later, while I was in school, this guy showed up at Mom's door. He asked for me, and Mom said I was still in school. She was about to close the door when he started to cry. Mom invited him in. When I got home with Mayda, there he was. Apparently, he stole enough money to get on the train from Kamloops to Vancouver. He was en route to his aunt's home in Victoria, BC. Mom checked the bus schedule for the Victoria trip and sent me with him to the Greyhound Bus Station. Mom gave him the $10.00 needed to get a ticket to Victoria.

When I returned, Mom said, "Well, kiss that $10.00 good bye." However, a few days later, Mom got a thank you card from this guy's aunt plus $10.00 in the mail. She and I were surprised, as this stuff doesn't happen very often. From then on, whenever I travelled, I did not give out much information about myself.

Mom phoned the children support system to find out what she can do to help Mayda. Her mother was being unreasonable with Mayda, and Mom was looking after her for free. This couldn't last forever, but she couldn't kick Mayda out either. Several months later, the problem was solved. Mayda went home, only to move out several months later with her boyfriend. Mayda never finished school. She broke off with her boyfriend, married someone else, and had a baby. Her relationship with her mother was still cold. It was like Mayda's mom wrote Mayda out of the family. Mayda's mom's home had quite a history that went with it. They had an old mansion on Osler Street. Apparently, years before them, a wealthy family had hired a female maid to do the chores in the house. The son, evidently, was very attracted to this girl and wanted to have sex with her, but she refused. The outcome, over some period of time, was that the son accidently killed her, burnt her in the fireplace, dumped her ashes down the fireplace, and sealed the hole with cement. In order not to get their son in trouble, the Chinese cook was approached. They told him, "Please say that you did it, and we'll send you back to China with money." It was an attractive package, so he agreed. To this day, the fireplace in the master's bedroom is still cemented in the ash hole.

CHAPTER SIX

Back at Eric Hamber Secondary, I remember clearly that one of the milk and chocolate milk machines wasn't working right. You'd put in your quarter, and three or four milk would fall out. Once the kids caught on with this, everyone in the lunchroom had two or three pints of milk with their lunch. When one teacher came, I laughed because she was probably thinking, "Oh, everyone is drinking milk. That is so healthy." The poor guy who filled the milk machine was laughing himself when he arrived at the school that same day to fix it. Of course, by then, the kids were experiencing sex and, of course, the odd girls here and there became pregnant. I always thought it was sad. Abortion was not introduced to the healthy public then, or, if they were, we didn't know about it; you were going to be a mom, whether you like it or not.

Back in class, I remember my cooking was always very good. I cleaned up and had everything prepared and done in one hour. It was comical, the way some of the kids' meals and baking turned out to be disasters. Throughout the year, all was well in the foods class, except during the last weeks of school, when us kids had to clean the ovens and stove tops. I skipped that class, and the teacher failed me in foods. I thought, "What the hell, I'll take woodworking." The woodwork class was then available to women. I did very well in that course; I already knew the names of the tools and did some pretty good artwork. Our first challenge was to make a jewellery box. I'd veneer the top with various types of wood and lined it with red velvet. Other projects were making candlesticks on the lathe machine. Mine turned out pretty good. We put weights at the bottom inside the wood for sturdiness; it worked. One girl wasn't so lucky at the lathe machine. She had long hair, and it got caught on the machine. It pulled her head so fast to the machine and yanked a huge chunk of her hair right out of her head. She had a splitting headache for some time. It also took some time for that large chunk of hair to grow back. From then on, we had to wear hair nets. It was a good lesson for the teacher, considering we were the first girls to take the course. Later on, automotive course was available. I wish I could have taken that course. In art class, the teacher provided us with a flat, rubber-type sheet that was about one-fourth-inch thick. We were to carve a picture on this, paint over it, and do a silkscreen type of art. I was really proud of my carving. I carved out a Great Dane with scenery to match. I was just about finished when I lost it upon returning to my art class. Rather puzzled, I started all over again, carving out another Great Dane. Once I finished it, my original carving showed up, therefore, I had two. I didn't trust the teacher on that program. It reminded me of the popcorn incident back in grade one. My English teacher said that he would fail me if I didn't write an essay or take a test. I preferred to write an essay; I did it and passed. I guess in those days, you'd push the teacher as far as you can go. I spent half of grade nine, and all of grade ten and eleven at Eric Hamber. Considering the kids I hung out with were in grade twelve and about to graduate, I'd be missing my companions. I decided to transfer to Kitsilano Secondary School for grade twelve. Kitsilano secondary was equally the same amount of travel time from home as Eric Hamber was, except I always took the bus there and back unless I got a ride from a schoolmate. Kitsilano is an old, old school with a lot of history. It is also in a better part of the west side of Vancouver. When Mom and I finished the P.N.E. program, school was in. I liked it there at Kitsilano Secondary. There I met Frank and Judy. They are brother and sister. Frank had a harelip and god-awful teeth while Judy was definitely a slow learner. They lived with their grandmother. Their mother was remarried and living on Vancouver Island. Their grandmother was a sweetheart. She owned a Hungarian Restaurant on Fourth Avenue, just walking distance from their home. There were many times when Judy and I ate there. They had a large, older home that was completely renovated on the inside. We became very close friends, bumming around together all the time. Frank had a car, so, during lunch, we always went somewhere, usually to White Spot Restaurant or the Dairy Queen. We had access to many parts of the city with his car. On weekends, we drove up to Squamish or to Hope just for the hell of it. One time, we were going over three sets of railway tracks around the Squamish area. A train was coming and blaring its horn at us. Being in a standard car, Frank stuck the gearshift in to get off the tracks quickly, and we barely made it. Had the car stalled, we would all be dead. We had to pull over and get our breath for a few moments. We ventured up that highway all the time, never to really have a particular place to go. We didn't go into bars then, as we were underage. The legal drinking age in BC is nineteen. It wasn't a priority, although Grandma and Ma provided us with beer from time to time. Those were the days of incident fun and no debts.

Mom had a new boyfriend named Frank. I liked him. He treated her nicely. He had a house, and Mom spent a lot of time at his place. He bought me a fluffy blouse, but I didn't really like it. Anyway, I thanked him for the blouse and kept it in my closet. He showed his true colours years later. He built Mom a really nice coffee table with a mirrored top. When she died, he knocked on my door and asked for the table back. I told him to have his lawyer call me, and I shut the door in his face. I believe mom saw Martti from time to time. She hung out at St. Regis Hotel a lot. I had a girlfriend at school who worked there part-time. She told us kids one lunch hour, that a couple had ordered dinner to their room, and it was her job to deliver the dinner trays. When the door opened, there were two naked people, one woman and one man, really intoxicated. She was more embarrassed than either of the two. We all laughed at that story. Anyway, she was invited to my place, and it came to my knowledge that the naked woman was my mom. Both she and my mom were embarrassed, and so was I. It was an awkward situation, and, eventually, the whole school knew. Mom asked me about it, and I said the whole school knew. She never did come over to my place again, but she did see Mom at the St. Regis regularly.

Back at school, my life was like that of any normal school kid. Us grade twelves were getting ready for graduation. Someone informed me that I could go down to the sewing room to pick out a free graduation gown. I was greeted by the teacher, and tried on a dress that fit perfectly. I said, "I'll have this one." Apparently, one had to have an appointment and have her name on a list for one of these free gowns; I didn't know that. Another girl had picked that dress. The teacher spoke with me, and I told her that I wasn't aware of the list; that someone told me that I should just go down to the sewing room and I can pick a dress. For a while, there was a moment when I decided that I won't attend graduation because I didn't have a dress. In the end, I got the dress. To get a partner, we all had to go to the auditorium. We were selected by a computer for our gradmate. Considering I am not too tall, I got this short guy. Thank goodness you'd only have to get picked up with this guy and return home with your friends. During the day of our graduation, Mom bought some beer for us. Steve, Victor, and I drank beer, played cards, and got ready for the prom. After the prom, our after-grad party was on a yacht. It was time to get ready for the big evening, but Mom didn't come. I saw Steve later as he joined me on the yacht. By this time, I had drank a lot of beer. I really didn't feel very good at all. I waited for my date. I could hear him a mile away as he drove a standard car and the gears would rocket around and crackle. Riding with him was like you were going forward and backward with great movements. It was comical, but I had to stop myself from laughing. Dinner was at the Biltmore Hotel at 12th and Kingsway. It wasn't a great hotel, but we all thought we were cool. We sat with our date, ate our meals, and danced. I could hardly wait to leave. Then, we all proceeded to the school gymnasium filled with us kids, mothers, and fathers. I still had to sit with my date while I was looking for Frank and Judy. I waved at them when I saw them and looked to see what they were wearing. The principal was up on the stage and was calling up classes in order. Our class was the last class to be called. It was a long evening, just sitting there while I was getting a hangover and feeling rather ill. I kept swallowing; making sure nothing would backfire on me. Finally, the principal got around to our class, and we were called up one by one. Thank God, my name started with an H. I proceeded up the stairs, shook the principal's hand, and I said, "I'll see you in Edmonton." He was from Edmonton.

"Why?" I asked, but that I would never know. It wouldn't be long now before this was all over. Our class was the last to be called, but the first to leave, and I was so relieved. There was only one door to leave from, and all of us, the mothers, fathers, and graduates, would proceed through that door. Being with the very first ones out, I vomited right there all over the place. This meant all the mothers and fathers had to walk around it, the disgusting mess of beer and chicken. I rapidly went to the bathroom to refresh myself, joined Frank, and got a ride home. Frank, Steve, Judy, and I were to go together to the boat. Once I got home, I was really feeling very crummy that I almost cancelled on the boat.

However, everyone said, "No, come along anyway." It was raining very hard all night. Once down by the docks, we boarded the boat. They were checking for booze. Neither of us had any, as I had had enough. Once everyone was on board, we proceeded out under the Lions Gate Bridge, past Stanley Park, and in and around English Bay, West Vancouver, and University Endowment Lands. Should this boat dock somewhere, it would be by one of those places. In other words, we didn't venture too far out into the Pacific. Considering I was rather toast, I slept most of the time. Booze and dope got on the ship anyway; kids were boozed up and stoned everywhere. When night entered into the early morning, people were having sex in the bathrooms, kids were throwing up everywhere, and even one fellow was having a poo on the plush seats. Everyone wanted to get off, but the captain wouldn't let us off at shore. He just kept going around and around in a circle. It was annoying. It seemed we'd never get off this boat. As the sun was rising, the yacht finally docked. Steve and I ventured up to Granville Street while rain was still pouring. We were soaked. By the time we got to my place, I just wanted a hot bath. That was graduation for me.

The following Monday, when we returned to school, the grade twelve kids of Kitsilano High were in trouble. Apparently, there was a small group that destroyed the ship and the organizers and those involved were to go back to clean up that ship. Never again did I hear of any school being able to rent a yacht for graduation. Kitsilano High toasted any future prospects for future graduates.

CHAPTER SEVEN

Dad and Margie were happy, and they decided to buy a house. Considering Dad didn't work much that year, the only bank to loan them a mortgage was Vancouver City Savings Credit Union. To this day, he still has his account there. The house they bought was an older home on East 8th Avenue near Renfrew. It was not necessarily the best area of town, but it was okay. It was situated on a hill, so, from the back of the house, they had a view of the roofs below, from Broadway Street and beyond. When you enter the small living room, their bedroom was off from the living room, the eat-in kitchen was at the back, and the bathroom and spare bedroom are all on one floor. The attic was originally developed as a bedroom, but was now kept as storage. The basement was unfinished, which has a separate entrance. You couldn't go to the basement from inside the house; you have to go from outside the house. Dad made it into a suite. He put in a full bathroom-bed-living room combination. He rented the suite out to one of his coworkers named Fred. Fred was a big boozer and restless with his cigarette. Margie would always worry. Margie decided to join the BC Ferry Corporation and became the supervisor in the office. She wanted to have a common ground with Daddy-O. Every Friday night, I would go over to Dad's and Margie's for a game of cards. We'd have tea, cookies, and bet with pennies and nickels on our card games.

In the summer I would always meet the boat every Saturday morning. I'd catch the Hastings bus at Broadway and Granville and get off at Main and Hastings. (Vancouver's toughtest skid road). The walk down Main to Ballantyne Pier wasn't far. The *West Star* would dock right on time. Daddy-O would be steering this small passenger cruiser. I'd always be waving and waiting for the deck to be lowered. The passengers got off at the passenger deck, and I boarded at the bottom, in the baggage area. Dad would always take me to his cabin to get some stuff. It was always stinky in there, with a bunch of men crammed into one room. Then I'd have lunch in the mess hall. I loved the mashed potatoes and gravy, and the Chinese cooks always loaded my plate. There, Dad would tell me the latest passenger stories. Nearly every trip, someone would die: one time on the dance floor and another missed the steep stairs and landed headfirst into the steel stairs. (He was an employee). Another time, Dad took me to the ship's bow where he showed me his skills in giving the order to the captain—instructions as to docking of the ship. As far as I was concerned, Dad was the best international seaman around. That particular trip was when I was aboard the *Princess Marguerite* coming from Seattle to Victoria. I had a hangover that day and slept on a chair the whole trip, missing the scenery. Afterward, I'd have to board the bus to Vancouver, but I felt better by then. Another time, apparently, I didn't go to greet the boat. I wished I did, as Dad was signaling the mate to reverse engines as the ship was coming into port. The mate ignored Dad's instructions, and the ship continued on into the fish warehouse, knocking it down completely. The passengers aboard must have had quite a sight to see. Apparently, the mate above was trying to get my Dad fired. It went to court. Dad proved right, and the mate was fired. I always said to Dad, "You've got a super job," and he'd say it was not that great. Conflicts would arise in such close quarters, I would assume. Some time down the road, Dad got a job teaching seamanship at North Island College in Campbell River, BC on Vancouver Island. He knew his ropes and knots; he was self-taught. It was said that he got fired for showing up at class drunk, but there was no record of this rumour, only a reference letter from the college for his good work. Dad could have been a captain, except he didn't want to take the eye test; he knew he would fail and possibly lose his bosun job also. Dad was content at just doing what he was doing. When the passenger cruises started for a change in the seventies, Dad took a job up in the *Arctic*, making $50,000.00 a year, which was good in the 70s and 80s. He'd go up to Inuvik and mingled with the polar bears. He got sick and was airlifted to a local hospital for whatever illness. But he seemed to bounce back from whatever illness. He received many "Thank you" letters from his employers in Calgary for his work. Although Dad travelled the poor parts of the world and really saw how people live, during off-season, he and Margie would go to some exotic place. They ventured to Paris, Hawaii, Jamaica, London, Frankfurt, Australia, Haiti, Cuba, South America, Egypt, Israel, and wherever. It was if Dad had a map of the world on his wall, threw a dart, and wherever it landed, he would buy a ticket and go there. Margie didn't go on all of his trips. Sometimes, he'd buy tickets that are for sale in the paper and travel under another name. He could do it and get away with it. (Today, with security so high, this, probably, couldn't happen anymore). Dad and his friend, Fred, drank a lot, and Margie was sick of it. You'd never know if Dad would be okay to attend one of Margie's daughter's functions, such as a marriage or a birthday. In time, Fred was asked to move out of the rented basement, and Dad was given an ultimatum to stop boozing, or it was divorce. Dad quit for five years. Margie is an intelligent woman.

CHAPTER EIGHT

I remember, one day, we were both laughing, as Bill, who I later married, while working for IBM, was sent to BC Ferries Corporate Head Office to clean typewriters. There he showed up in his suit and was shown to the typewriters. Margie recognized him right away. I am not sure if Bill did recognize Margie. Apparently, the other girls in the office were laughing at this guy who had terrible body odor and was trying to figure out how to take the lid off the typewriter. Later in life, he got a PhD. It is a long-standing family joke. Bill and I were greatly in love, and how we met is cemented in stone. Before we were married, we ventured by bike everywhere. Margie's family grew up and had kids, and Dad and Margie's marriage remained a happy one. Dad said he met the right woman, and there was great love between them.

Bill would pick me up on his Kawasaki 500 motorcycle, and we would ride all over town. Or he would arrive at my house at exactly 5:00 P.M., and we'd go out. We were inseparable. We would drive up past Horseshoe Bay and up to Whistler, which is known as one of the world's best ski resorts. Back in the 70s, there wasn't much to do. One Saturday, Mom had invited us for dinner, so Bill and I turned around at a certain point and went back to Vancouver. This one day, we were speeding down the road, taking the turn sharply, when his front tire blew. He was holding onto this thing for dear life. The motorcycle finally stopped. Now, what do we do? It was very near to closing time at tire shops in Vancouver, so what he did was put me and the bike in the bush. I was to stay there until he gets back. I wondered if he'd remember exactly where I was. Anyway, he thumbed to Vancouver, got a tire, thumbed back, and got a ride on the back of an open truck. He had tools with his bike. He fixed the tire, and we rode back to Vancouver. However, we missed dinner. We had some close calls on that bike. I remember a bunch of nuns drove into us. They were just praying to God almighty. Nonetheless, we were okay. Bill had gotten himself a dorm in the old residences of the University of British Columbia (UBC). I believe they were used during the war. His stay there was short-lived as he decided to drive his motorcycle through the dorm and into the showers to wash his bike. He moved to a basement suite in Kerrisdale. While he was there, he bought an old, huge, standard Buick of some kind. This thing was like a tank. He bought a used transmission, and I helped him put this thing in the car. This thing was very heavy. I don't know how he did it, but he did it. Then, he taught me how to drive a standard. Every time I moved the stick shift, I felt like I was stirring a huge pot. It really was too big for me to drive, but I did it. While he had this car, he decided to dismantle his motorcycle. He took it totally apart in one guy's garage; the owner wasn't impressed. The owner of the house was concerned about the gas that Bill left in the corner. Anyway, we painted the bars of his bike with silver, black, and maroon. It looked sharp afterward. We put it back together, along with the gas, and did a test-drive. It was time to get rid of his huge car, so Bill bought a station wagon. It was horrid looking. The gas gauge didn't work along with the other gadgets, and he painted this thing black. It looked like a hearse. When summer came around, Bill, his friend, Leo, from Edmonton, and I all drove from Vancouver to Edmonton, Edmonton being Bill's home. Bill and Leo used some scientific ruler to calculate the gas. They calculated it wrong, and we ran out of gas somewhere outside Jasper, Alberta late at night. They boys thumbed into town, and I stayed with the car. When I think about it, it was rather dangerous and scary. But they returned, and we continued on. Once in Jasper, the boys went into a pub. I didn't go along as I was underage and certainly didn't look like I could bluff my way in. Nonetheless, Bill and Leo did. I waited in the car. Needless to say, they didn't keep me waiting long. Once we arrived in Edmonton, we went to Bill's place, and Leo went to his mother's. Bill's mom was working in Calgary, Alberta, while old lady Rutherford was tending the house. It was her house. She was a gracious old woman from the old Edwardian Age and rare to come by today. Bill and I spent much of the time travelling all over Alberta on his motorcycle. We were a team as far as being lovers is concerned. I loved riding behind the bike. One summer day, just out of the blue, we rode to Medicine Hat, Alberta, and stopped off at his Brentwood College friend's place. His friend's dad was a veterinarian in Medicine Hat, and they owned a bullmastiff, which I enjoyed playing with. Considering we just showed up, they weren't terribly impressed and put us up for the night. We were asked to leave, and, needless to say, we never went back to Medicine Hat.

While returning back to Edmonton, Bill told me to make sure there are no cops around as we were now going to crank the bike up. We were just roaring along when a policeman pulled us over. Bill was so mad at me, saying that I didn't inform him of a cop. I didn't see one, and neither did he. I got off the bike and started laughing. The cop wasn't so impressed either. Bill got his ticket, and we took off again. Bill then went to work up in Hay River, Northwest Territories I had found myself an apartment in downtown Edmonton and got myself a job at the University of Alberta Hospital's Filing Department. I worked nights. It was a boring job and handling those large x-rays was a hassle. You had to make sure you had the right person's x-ray when a doctor requested for it. There were a lot of mistakes in that department that would drive the physicians crazy. I hated that job, and especially the girl I was working with; she slept all night and didn't do much work. When I complained to the supervisor, I got in trouble for finking. That was a good lesson, as I came to the conclusion that she was a friend of someone in there and had great pull. I quit that job as soon as I got a job in the cafeteria of the Royal Alexandra Hospital. I worked nights, serving food and washing dishes. The supervisor was not there at nights, so we all had the run of the place. The people I worked for were great, and the ambulance drivers would come in at wee hours in the morning to tell us the saddest stories, but there were some funny stories, too. One story I remember so clearly was when they had found a body and needed to look for its head. Actually, I had a good job. The pay was excellent, and Bill would drop me off at work and pick me up to avoid transportation costs. As time went on, I was looking for a job as a secretary, since that was what I was trained for. I put an application in with the Government of Alberta and got a job in the typing pool in the purchasing department. I thought this was a big deal; it was my first real job. I met a woman named Marion whom I became good friends with for many years to come. She was a wild woman, around twenty years older than me. She had flaming red hair, and we had a lot in common. She has a small boy, five years of age, named Greg. She and her son's father split up, and that was that. In her day, Marion was very outrageous. She attended a dance at a hall with her friends. The hall was monitored by the police. Someone dared her to steal the policeman's gun. She did and left the building with the gun, bullets and all. When she got home, she received a call from her friends that everyone had been locked in the hall and cannot leave. The policeman was missing his gun, and here, Marion had it at home. In the morning, Marion returned the policeman's gun to the downtown police station and made a report. Apparently, she didn't get in trouble as the policeman was drinking alcohol and had lost his job. Marion felt bad that the guy lost his job, but she was equally relieved that she got off scot-free. Today, I don't think one would. She was a brave woman. She and I frequented all the bars, even some really grubby ones. This one particular night, around closing time, Marion and I left. However, she dropped her wallet. Apparently, her wallet had fallen out of her purse at the Leyland and parked itself nicely under a bench. When she called the Leyland in the morning, it was found. That doesn't happen very often, especially with everything in it. By this time, I was making money, so I enrolled into the Bonnie Lassie Driving School that had a separate building by the Edmonton library. I had written my test three times and passed the road signs the first time. However, I was poor at writing tests. Nonetheless, I loved the driving, and I'd go out here and there with the driver, especially in Edmonton, where they have traffic circles; one needs to know how to drive around those.

When it came to my road test, I passed it with flying colours. Then, I decided that I'm going to buy a car. I bought my first car, a 1977 Plymouth Fury III, two door, and was black in colour. It drove like a tank. I went to get financing for $500.00 to buy this car. Financing was approved, and I owned a car. I would take Marion shopping for groceries as she didn't have a car or a license. We would travel around, meeting friends, and go on long road trips. Marion said I was a good driver, which I have heard from time to time again. Back at work, I had another position and was getting out of the typing pool. That meant I got my own desk and buyer to type for. One could not make a mistake on the quotes, not one, or you'd type the requisition over again. As time went by, I began to dislike my job and Marion and I started to not get along. I had been there almost a year and a bit. I quit on August and returned to Vancouver with Bill. Bill decided to continue on at UBC, but he had taken a break that wasn't that beneficial to him. We rented a suite together on Fourth Avenue. It was a newly-painted and carpeted apartment that cost

$450.00 a month. We stayed there for most of Bill's term, while I got a job for the Bank of Nova Scotia at 41st and Dunbar. That was a perfect location, as it is one of the routes toward UBC. By then, Bill grew his hair and wore it in a ponytail. He also started to smoke pot. He would meet me at the bank everyday, and we'd venture home, eat something, and go back to the university to study. It worked out very well. We were very much in love. Bill had even gotten a marriage license, only to let it expire. Bill bought this huge piece of plywood and made a makeshift table where he could study and have papers all over. He had it in the bedroom. We slept on a foam mattress on the floor. One snowy night, I could see the light and the table shaking. I was tapping him, but he wouldn't wake up. I said, "Bill, there is an earthquake." When I told him in the morning, he didn't believe me, although there were cars that were in the ditch here and there. Once he got to university, he finally realized there was an earthquake and blamed me for not waking him up. On weekends, we'd find a place to motorcycle, too. One long weekend, we decided to go camping in Tofino and Long Beach on Vancouver Island. I never noticed the first time, but I had my periods. No big deal; off we went. Bill packed a tent and the necessary wieners and such for the weekend. We boarded the ferry at Horseshoe Bay and went to Nanaimo and northwest from there. It was a long and windy drive. It started to rain. Although Bill wore rainproof jacket, I did not, so, he stopped at a grocer and bought big garbage bags. He ripped a hole at the bottom and put it over my head and made armholes. It looked really stupid, but it kept me dry. Besides, it was dark out by then anyway. Once we got to Long Beach, we found a spot and pitched up the tent. This was a small tent, which the two of us squeezed into. We spent the weekend in the Tofino and Long Beach area. We were almost the only people there on the beach, as it wasn't exactly 100 above. Bill and I would always have these types of camping trips, but, as time went by, he always had me camping during my period. It took me twenty years to figure that one out. I liked it in the outback, and the drive there was always a challenge. Sunday was return time. We went back to the Nanaimo ferry en route to Horseshoe Bay and Vancouver. Monday morning was school for Bill and work for me. I basically supported Bill during his university years. In time, we decided we were paying too much rent and moved to an apartment with a balcony at 7th and Dunbar. It had a nicer floor plan, but we didn't stay too long there. Bill and I fought during the day and made love during the night. As time went on, I moved out, and moved back in with Mom. Bill joined the Wreck Beach crew in those days, and I hung around the newly developed Gastown. Gastown and its skid road became hot spots in Vancouver during the 70s. I spent a lot of time at the Dominion Hotel's pub. Those were the wild days, when you tried everything out. I worked during the day at a CA Firm and played at night. At that young age, I had no problem staying out late and going off to work in the morning. We considered ourselves the "in thing" at the Dominion. I became a very good shuffleboard player. It was difficult to beat me. However, I was hanging around a rough group of people. They were the type who would kill you in a minute. Some carried guns. There were a lot of different types of dope at your disposal, but I still preferred beer. I remember, one time, Mom came down to join me and my so-called friends at the Dominion Hotel. The police came and asked me for my ID. I just turned and said, "You can ask my mom." The table roared, and the policeman's face turned red. I didn't have to show him anything. Mom would have her booze tricks. Mom taught me to always have the label of my beer facing people, so if someone wants to send over a beer, they know what you're drinking. When my cousin and I were still underage, Mom went to the liquor store and bought a mickey of vodka. We went to a Chinese restaurant in Vancouver's Chinatown, ordered a meal with green tea, and Mom filled our glasses.

Daddy-O took me into a bar in skid row one time and said, "My daughter is eighteen years of age." Apparently, nineteen years of age is the legal age to drink in BC. Dad blushed, but they let me sit there with tomato juice. Those days were wild and dangerous.

While Bill was still hanging out at Wreck Beach crew, meeting and dating others, I moved my nightlife closer to home. I frequented Clementine's, which was once the LuLu Belle Restaurant where Martti, Mom's second husband lost it. Clementine's was bought and transferred by the Stauffer family, who owned the Cave, to downtown on Hornby. Clementine's became my hang out for years to come. It was just walking distance away from home. I had my own seat at the bar. I was respected, and that's the way it stayed. Sheldon Stauffer ran the joint, and the place rocked during Saturday Night Live days. I was there every night and didn't have to pay cover charge on Fridays or Saturdays, nor did I have to wait in line. I just got in. In time, I met the other regulars. We all knew of each other from some other place. One chap who I became friends with, yet never became intimate, was Bill S. Bill S. was many years older than I. He had no respect for women, but he liked me as a friend. He loved naked women, and he used to tell me all about his "fucks." Bill's language only knew that word. He used that word in every sentence he would say, at least twice or three times. That was Bill S.; you got to get used to it. At times, it was very funny. He made sure women worked on him sexually. Some of the things he told me were bizarre. I liked him, and he respected me. He was always brings a lot of fun and, boy, could he drink. He drank the hard stuff, and, when he was boozed, he was over-and-above funny. You could tell when he would get busy as his one eyelid would start to droop. He also knew when to class it up on the golf course. He also liked the races, so, one evening, he, Gordy, and me all piled into Gordy's car, somewhat intoxicated, and took off to the races at the Pacific National Exhibition. I had never bet on horses before, so my first choice was the triactor, a bet of the first three horses in order of placement. I put down $2.00. Bill and Gordy didn't win a thing, but I won the triactor. It was the topic of conversation for some time. Of course, we went back to Clementine's. Clementine's was a gold mine in the 70s. Later, Ken Stauffer bought the restaurant next to Clementine's and called it by his last name. It was great; it had a small lounge, and then the restaurant part. Everything that family did turned into gold. This was a great meeting place for us right after work, before Clementine's opened up much later. It would be Bill S., Gordy, John, and me every day at that restaurant lounge. I don't know where we found so much to talk about, but we all had something every day. Those were happy times for me. Bill and I weren't together, but we knew where we both were. It was time to experience other people. Our group was long standing for many years. It was the same thing every day. During the summer months, I bought a bicycle, and I'd bike-ride from my house, over Granville Street Bridge, around Stanley Park, and back. My other route was straight up 12th avenue to UBC, and then down along Wreck Beach, Spanish Banks, Kitsilano Beach, and then home. Both routes were at least twenty-five miles. I'd do that every day, weather permitting. Then, I went to Clementine's. In the summer, it was nice to spend early evenings outside and not so much in the lounge. We always knew where everyone else was, and we'd join up together some time. I have had two very good girlfriends, Margerite and Kathy, Margerite, who I've known since I was five, and Kathy who I met in my adult years and have lost contact with in the shuffle. Margerite and I lived across the street from each other on 64th in Vancouver. I was her brother's age. She was much older, and I didn't have that much to do with her. She had gotten married, moved to Toronto, and, eventually, had two children. That had become a bum deal. Ten years later, she returned to Vancouver with her children, which were of teenage years and soon to enter university. Margerite had enrolled at UBC to take on a social work course. She had also occupied a town house inside the university campus for single moms. I, then, lived in my apartment on 11th Avenue. She and I just connected. Her mother decided to put us together. We had a lot of outings together. One Christmas Eve, Marg had me over for Christmas dinner. She asked me to stay overnight. For some reason, I really didn't feel like it, although she did offer her couch. I left around midnight and walked along the sidewalk, past the bushes, to the bus stop. I arrived home safely. The next morning, I got a call from Margerite.

She said, "You won't guess what happened last night." I replied, "No, what?" Someone had removed the kitchen window downstairs and entered her townhouse. The kids were sleeping upstairs. Marg was also upstairs, awake in her bedroom. There was more than one person that entered her place. She called her dad and told him to call the police. There was a long mix-up of who she should call. She called the Royal Canadian Mounted Police, but they said she must call the police for UBC Campus. Her dad even called her back, but it wasn't as if she was going to answer the phone. Marg was in panic. There was a lot of shuffling going on downstairs. Eventually, those people left. A long time later, the police arrived. The group had taken the Christmas presents and left through the sliding door. Had I been sleeping on the chesterfield, the entry wouldn't have happened. Another time, I met some guy at Clementine's by the name of Jack. He asked me out on a date several times, but, as time rolled on, he started talking about a girl he met at a Jazz Club who he had been taking out a bit here and there. He started telling me that she lives on the university campus, has two children, and is studying social work. He really didn't have many things nice to say about her. Hmmm...hmmm.... Then, one day, Marg started telling me about this guy she met at a Jazz Club, and that he wanted to take her to the movie, but he told her to meet him inside the theatre. That meant she'd have to pay for her way in. Upon arriving at the theatre, he presented her with a pie, so, the whole time she was watching the movie, she had this pie on her lap. As we started sharing notes, we realized that it was the same guy. So, we decided on a plan. Although I don't remember the exact plan, we both played mind games with this guy for some time, until I finally said, "That girl you're talking about all the time in a not-so-nice way, she is my very good friend." That was the last we saw of him.

CHAPTER NINE

Marg and I decided to go bicycle riding on Salt Spring Island, so, I booked a room that was the only retreat on the island and was supposed to be the best place for comfort and quietness. We packed a lunch, and her brother attached our bicycles to his car and drove us to the Tsawwassen Ferry Terminal. Doug would pick us up on Sunday at a certain time. Once across, we travelled by our bikes through the roads and followed the map to a lodge. And there it was—a large, old-home type of building. We booked in, and they gave us a room right at the top of the stairs. There was no elevator, so we carried our bikes and our light bags up the stairs. From then, we went out to the back overlooking the water, sat at the picnic table, and had our lunch. The place had a bar, but someone had to come and open it up first before I could have a beer. It was rather disorganized. Anyway, we continued on our biking trip and stopped even at a beach. We bumped into someone Marg knew small world. After spending the day there, we went back to the lodge. The dining area was available, but we were the only people who wanted to have something to eat. They did cook a steak for us. But it was really odd being there. Nonetheless, this was our big weekend retreat. That evening, we had our bikes in the hallway. We had this old double bed with iron headboards, a light bulb hanging out of the ceiling, and a sink in the room. If you need to go to the bathroom, the toilet was down the hall. As evening approached, it sounded like the disco was just below us and was just opening up. There was loud music and kids all over the halls who were basically not being very respectful. Marg and I couldn't sleep, and, for some reason, we decided to bring our bikes into the room. By the time we got our bikes into the room, there was no place to walk. Kids knocked on our door, perhaps by mistake, using the halls as a track meet. This changed from comical to no fun. We booked out the next day, so much for our peaceful retreat. We called Doug, Marg's brother, to pick us up early, and that was that. Every time I was in town, Marg and I would meet and inform each other of the latest news. Or, if I'm too many miles away, I do my once-a-year telephone call.

Kathy and I met when I was working at the Vancouver City Savings Credit Union on Pender Street I was the manager's secretary. I always was a manager's secretary when I got jobs before. I also worked part-time at Eaton's, selling men's cologne. I wasn't nuts about my office job, and, to this day, I hate office work. Anyway, Kathy and I loved going to Seattle a lot. We'd go there almost every other weekend. She had a Honda Civic, which was easy on gas. One time, I drove her standard all the way to the United States' border with the emergency brake on. Ooops. Our first stop was always our motel, and then off to Pike Place Farmer's Market on the waterfront. Then, we'd drive around Seattle, over the floating bridges, and stop at various pubs. The motel had an indoor swimming pool. Kathy, being huge breasted, blew away some young, little boys in the pool. They were laughing at her and, eventually, left the pool. Our trips to Seattle were always the same. One weekend, we went over to Bremerton where the United States ships are docked, and we boarded the USS *Missouri*, the ship that became a surrender site on September 2, 1945, during World War II. On the way back from Seattle, we always stopped in Marysville. There, I discovered the neatest Mexican restaurant. It was a gold mine, with delicious food and large margaritas. The place was filled with Mexican music. Then, we went on our way back to Vancouver. We also breezed through the U.S. boarder.

Another time, I went to Bellingham to play racquetball. I set myself up with a club and drove down. On the way back, I stopped in Bellingham and had a beer in a local pub. I talked to the owner of the pub. He asked what my racquet was for, and I said I came down from Vancouver, BC to play. Anyway, I started my way out of the restaurant when he came running out and asked me out for dinner. I went with him for dinner. He was an interesting man. He lived in Seattle, owned the pub in Bellingham, and commuted back and forth. We stayed in touch. Then, one day, he called me in Vancouver and asked me to come down to Seattle for the weekend. He'd fly me down and drive me back. His wife was out of town for the weekend. I said okay. I called Kathy and said, "Kathy, guess what, I need a ride to the airport as Bob is going to pick me up at the SeaTac airport, and I am going to spend the weekend at his house." So I boarded the plane. The flight was very short. Bob was there, and we went to a couple of bars. We were holding hands. He took me all over, like he was showing me off. I didn't mind. While at his place, I slept with him in the master bedroom. He didn't lay a hand on me, not once. He respected my wishes. Although we had a shower together, he was still a gentleman. He took me shopping. I bought Kathy a large make-up kit, with different eye shadows, and accessories. Bob drove me back to Vancouver, but we stopped in Marysville at the Mexican restaurant, and also at his pub, first. Kathy came over to meet him and got her gift. We had lots to talk about. Eventually, Bob drove back to Seattle. We kept in touch for a while, and then we lost contact.

Another time, I was selling men's cologne at Eaton's when a young man named Norman approached me and asked me what time I would get off work. He would like to take me out for dinner. He was from Bothell, Washington, just outside of Seattle. I said sure. He was elegantly dressed, with a white silk shirt and black pants. As we spoke, I learned that he was from some highly-fluent family in the States who were once in the political arena and rubbed shoulders with the likes of Humphrey. He said Humphrey's business card was done in twenty-four-karat gold. Norman was very intelligent, and he would talk about the ventures of being elsewhere. It was like he was fed up with Earth. In his letters, he'd say, "If I told you that I could give you an experience that would forever remove you from 'normal' society, would you risk it?" His one letter to me started it off with:

Did you call me on November 25 as you promised? I wasn't home (and really couldn't be) that afternoon. I am truly sorry, for I long to hear your voice. When (if ever) are you home? I might call you soon. You mentioned that you do not wish to be alone. I, too, share this desire (very much). Are you ever struck by just how absurd this 'all' (life, the world as we see it, etc.) really is? Why do we put up with it? We are stuck into niches by our parents' influences when we were children and by societies' expectations now. I (as I have mentioned before) have no fear of being dead. Why, then, should I fear anything in life? Yet I do, and this is my greatest fault, a fault I hate. Who do I really have to blame for the way I live (or rather, exist) but myself? I feel trapped. I burn with intensity. The energy is expended endlessly, but I am not consumed. I leap from one thing to another. Every delay seems too long, every pleasure to short, and every day expended another, lost to the grave. I exist?I think? I burn; It all seems to be leading nowhere. Is there escape? Perhaps, but I fear the journey. I am weaker than I would like to be and need support. I am lonely now, but would be even worse off if I undertook this by myself. I truly don't know what to think of you. *What is your opinion of me? I sense something tantalizing in your writings. You have the ability to transmit a great deal in very little space. Am I reading too much into your letters? I lust after you, you know. I fantasize about you sometimes, but the fantasy never seems to equal the memory of reality. This might be a good thing. Absence (and abstinence) makes the heart grow fonder. What more can I say?*

Norman (and his telephone number)

His next letter was handwritten. He was somewhat depressed and, hopefully, getting better in a few days. He was requesting that I might find work in the States and move there. His letter said, *"Please write and come down."* Norman's last letter to me was dated February 19, 1980. It said:

Forgive me. I should have written long ago, and I now feel that I have sinned for failing to do so. Sometimes, I am struck by how futile it is to attempt to put my thoughts on paper because they often transcend words. It is much easier to reveal myself when I look into your eyes. I am presently in one of my melancholy moods, and it is at times like this that whatever talents I may have are greatly amplified. I see the world much more clearly now. I wish that you were here so that I could open your eyes as well. I was told once that I had a mission in life— to go forth and speak the truth among fools, to cut from the souls of men the falsehoods upon which they base their lives in. I am beginning to believe that; perhaps, I ought to do just that. The idea of starting a new country is appealing to me more all the time. God, how egotistical can I be? This must sound like drivel to you. On the other hand, what have I got to lose? When we are dead, there is no memory of success or failure. This world is but dust in the wind. Oh, how I want to see you again. I can, for a short time, lean on you. To be released from the constant cycle of study, work, study, work is one of my rarest pleasures. I need a vacation, say about 10 years. Come see me. There is much more I want to say. My book(s) are not coming along very well at all; I often find it almost impossible to think in a vacuum. I need someone to 'bounce' my ideas off of. Somehow, I feel I am on the verge of a great breakthrough.

Signed,
Norman

P.S.
I want you. As usual.

Then, as time went on, I didn't hear from him. But, one day, a call came in for me at Eaton's that a very rich, fluent family in the States was wondering if I knew where Norman was. Apparently, they had gone through his room, found my name and address, and had known that Norman had ventured up to Canada to see me from time to time. I received a letter from his father, dated October 24, 1980. It said:

Dear Ms. Hayes,

You do not know me, but I think you know my son, Norman, whom I understand you met while he and his friend, Jerry, were visiting Canada about this time last year. The reason for the letter is that our son, Norman, is missing from home. If you had any recent contact with him, please call us, collect, as soon as possible (and the telephone number). We fear for his safety, and his mother, grief stricken, is almost in total collapse. If you can provide any information, please do so.

Signed,
(Norman's father)

I called Norman's father directly and informed him that I haven't seen or heard from Norman for some time. They said, "Thank you." To this day, I do not know if Norman is alive and well. I was shocked when I read this letter and have kept it in my photo album with all of Norman's letter's.

CHAPTER TEN

The year of 1971

It is Easter break, and all of us kids are off from school, doing what we know best—flirting. My boyfriend was returning from Brentwood College, an elite private school for young men. Brentwood College is on Vancouver Island, just half-hour north of Victoria, British Columbia. Roland Wood, or Rolly, as he was called, lives in Vancouver's old money area called Shaughnessy. He lives in a gray stucco mansion, walking distance from my home. The Woods have it all: fine silver, crystal, maids, cooks, and were owners of one of the mines on Vancouver Island which they acquired after the Second World War. It had various names. Today, it is called Myra Mines. It was a nice sunny day in Vancouver, and I was walking up the hill to Rolly's place. As I turned into the circular drive, I saw the most gorgeous man ever. He was just getting off his Kawasaki 500 motorcycle, six feet, one inch, tall, slim, and had that face. That was Rudolph Valentino's clone. It was instant love! But I was Rolly's girl. I got to know many more Brentwood boys that week, and all of us gathered together daily, playing cards, drinking, partying, and beach bumming. My house was the center of focus for the Brentwood boys. My mother loved them all, and our door was open anytime of day for us kids. Mom knew we were all underage to drink in the Province of British Columbia, and she knew we would get it anyway, so she bought us beer, and we drank at my house as she felt it was safer that way, and she'll know where we all were. From then on, on any holidays coming up, the Brentwood boys were at my house. As we all got more familiar with each other, we got more daring. Dope was in; Rolly brought over some marijuana. My mother tried some and she said, "I don't feel anything." But marijuana wasn't the only drug we tried. While I was Rolly's girl, I still had this eye for this gorgeous man named Bill Hayes. Rolly's parents owned this beautiful cottage on Pasley Island, just on the other side of Bowen Island, BC. It was a private island for the rich. All us kids would go over to Pasley via the *Bowen Island Ferry*, drive across Bowen where the family powerboat would be at Tungstall Bay. From there, we would venture across the strait to Pasley. Once we arrived at Pasley, the resident manager made sure our boat was secure and safe, and our bunch all coupled off and walked across Pasley to Rolly's cottage. We would usually arrive around dinnertime, so, we pulled out the beer and steaks. We would relax and watch the sunset. The next day was crab fishing and cruising. Considering I was Rolly's woman, I was not to lift a finger, ever. Rolly didn't believe that his woman should to do any manual work; that was left for the rest of the women, which put me in an odd position. Nonetheless, nothing was said or revealed as to my upper-class position. We all came from the same type of cloth. That evening, everyone settled in his or her respective beds. Of course, Rolly and I had the main room filled with the most luxurious of cottage gear. The bed was king size, with this huge goose down comforter that was apparently used by Rolly's dad during the Second World War. This comforter kept us warm. The next agenda was a bacon-and-egg breakfast around our modern campfire built out of stone. That was out of this world and was the finest relaxing pleasure us kids could endure for a school break. Of course, I didn't have to wash dishes. After breakfast, Rolly went to retrieve the boat, which we had to board via rocks down a short slope in front of their cottage. At this point, it was only the four of us: MacGregor, a flashing redheaded chap, his weekend girlfriend, Rolly, and I. The men were in charge of the crab-fishing nets, which we placed that morning. That morning, we ventured to Gibsons Landing, BC, a very popular hotspot, where the movie *The Beachcombers* was filmed during its heyday. Going over to our favourite spots, we were in full speed. We kids were very daring. We roared across the strait, make believing our powerboat was a professional racing boat. I remember we docked at Gibsons, and then ventured back to check the crab cages. We caught some huge, lovely-looking crabs. Back at the cottage, the remaining crew had the campfire going. They would be able to go out on the boat the next day. But, of course, I ventured out every day as I was the owner's girl. I remember so clearly, the boys cooked those crabs in boiling water. Those creatures were screaming for dear life. If this is the way crabs are cooked, I'm not sure I like it. Anyway, though I am not a seafood lover, I tried a few pieces. It was the most delectable, scrumptious crab I ever tasted. Needless to say, you couldn't get it any fresher.

While on our school break, Bill Hayes and his date also went with us. That was when he lost his virginity. No big deal; we were all doing the same thing. Our break was over. Back to the mainland for me, and back to Brentwood for the boys. Rolly would come over more often than the guys, and just him and I would go over to Pasley Island for weekends. Rolly was a tall, thin chap with severe acne problem. When Rolly was attacked with pus, he was *attacked*. He always had huge pimples all over his face—just his face. If you overlooked that, he wasn't such a bad-looking guy, and he was very rich. The Brentwood boys were preparing for their graduation. It was held at the posh Victoria Golf and Country Club. I was Rolly's girl. The boy's didn't come over to the mainland. We girls had to venture over to Victoria. I went over with Rolly's parents. We all booked into the Empress Hotel. All my expenses were paid. I bought myself a beautiful, dark purple dress with a shiny silver belt attached to it. The material was the finest, and I just felt so pretty in it. So, off we went to the Golf Club. I knew a lot of the Brentwood boys, and it was funny to see us all dressed up. We usually saw each other in jeans, or naked. It was an elaborate affair, with dinner and dance. When the evening came to a close, Rolly's parents let him have the car, so a group of us went out. Bill and his date, the same girl that he lost his virginity with, came along as well. We cruised around Victoria, doing the graduation stuff. Later, around 4:00 A.M., I went to my hotel room that I shared with Rolly's parents. I was very quiet and embarrassed. In the morning, they didn't seem to mind. Nothing was mentioned as to the time I returned. The remainder of our graduation was again spent on Pasley Island, with the same crew that always joined us. We repeated the same fun and games. As summer was arriving, the Brentwood boys went to spending their time in Vancouver, at least the ones who lived there. Some went back to their roots, others prowled around for the right university, and some just sat on their ass, waiting for their parents' inheritance. My house was the focal point of hanging out again. Bill Hayes was one of the chaps looking for accommodations in Vancouver. He finally found a room in a house near the university. Bill had received an honors scholarship in physics. He chose to go to the University of British Columbia. As my relationship with Rolly was deteriorating, my interest in Bill was flourishing. Rolly's dad was demanding most of his time, teaching him the family business. I still had one more year of school to go; Bill was waiting to start university. All summer long was open for us. Bill and I became inseparable. Rolly, to this day, blames Bill for stealing me and hasn't spoken to Bill since. It was very heartbreaking for Rolly. I later heard he inherited a million and married a German girl. My mother liked Bill; he came from a very rich, old money, political family in Edmonton, Alberta. He is the great-grandson of the first premier of Alberta, Premier A.C. Rutherford, the Gentleman of Strathcona. Premier Rutherford expanded the south part of Edmonton, as we know it today. The mansion, which he built on Saskatchewan Drive, overlooking the river, is now open to the public for viewing. It is built with the reminder of great wealth and opulence, modern before its time. The University of Alberta campus also has their main library named after him—Rutherford Library. Premier A.C. Rutherford had two children: Hazel and Cecil. Cecil went on to study law and became a Q.C. while Hazel became a housewife. In his earlier years, he would ice skate on Saskatchewan River, where he would meet Helen. Helen, being a tiny-built lady of great promise and elegance, married Cecil. They lived for a while with his parents, Premier A.C. Rutherford. As time went on, they built a house on Edinboro Road, not too far from the premier's house. In those days, it was just about the only house there. That property, in today's standard, is very large. This set the standard for Windsorpark. This is Edmonton's old money area today. Helen had one daughter, Margaret, who lived in grace and favour. Margaret studied at the best universities and, eventually, married. She had one son, William Cameron Hayes.

As the school year approached, I transferred from Eric Hamber Secondary to Kitsilano Secondary. I spent only one year there—grade twelve. Bill would meet me at school, depending on his schedule, or at my house every day at 5:00 P.M. He would pick me up on his motorcycle, and off we'd go somewhere. Bill enrolled in the Bachelor of Science program and specialized in physics. Because of his high marks, he was alotted a cubicle on the top floor of the science building at UBC. This was only available for the smartest students. As we got to know of his competition, one of his acquaintances allowed me to use his cubicle which was next to Bill's. I took an interest in psychology and sociology, so Bill got me books out of the university library. At the same time, I also did my regular homework for grade twelve. As Bill was focusing his attention on me throughout the year, his marks dropped drastically. Mine improved; Bill was a very good and patient teacher. I asked him, "Why want to be a physicist? The only job for you would be in NASA." His second year was a disappointment. We, at this point, now lived together, and I worked at a bank to support him. Well, his marks were so low at the end of the year that he decided to enter the University of Alberta in Edmonton instead. I followed him to Edmonton. He lived in a student residence; I rented a furnished apartment and got a job in the Purchasing Department for the Province of Alberta. Bill decided that I should get into the university program; he paid for me to take psychology during the first and second term. We were not close at this point; he went his way to discover other women while I ventured to discover other men. I enjoyed the dating at U of A and passed both terms with an average score, definitely not scholarship material, but I passed. I did very well in clinical psychology than I did in social psychology. This particular education furthered me in getting 100 percent on my cosmetology course that I would take several years later.

I was renting a room near the university when Bill proposed to me. July 16, 1977 was our marriage date. Bill was now residing in Vancouver to continue his studies at UBC; the University of Alberta was not for him. Being dirt poor, we had no ring. We walked to the justice of the peace's home and got married in his living room. Bill's behavior was unusual. While I was excited, Bill sat on the couch like a king and didn't say a word. He was also mummy like and made it look like I was forcing him to marry me. Anyway, it was done. I've married my prince. We flew back to Vancouver. However, little did I know, the Vancouver Police were looking for me while I was with Bill. Once settled in our basement apartment in Shaughnessy, Bill and I took to married life. Neither of us had any money nor a job. I remember being out of the house one afternoon, when I returned, Bill said that the Vancouver Police was there to inform me that my mother died on July 26; we were now in August. I was supposed to identify her body at the coroner's office in the basement of the Vancouver Police station on Main Street. Mom was an avid traveller, so it wasn't unusal for her to be not around. Apparently, she was returning home from Seattle. She met a chap on the Greyhoud bus, and they both checked into the St. Regis Hotel in downtown Vancouver. She had a heart attack in the hotel room. Considering the chap may have been a married man, I think he freaked and ran from the room, leaving Mother unattended. And she died.

Finally, Bill got a job with IBM and was sent to Toronto for training. Wives were allowed to tag along, so I spent four weeks in Toronto during the summer of 1977. Bill and I really enjoyed Toronto. It is a vibrant city, and we had lots to do. With Bill gone during the day, I had all the time in the world to see Toronto. We stayed at the posh Prince Hotel in Don Mills. I would learn the bus and subway routes from the hotel to downtown, and I fulfilled my day exploring the sights. I was always back at the hotel room to meet Bill at the end of the day. One thing I really wanted to do was see New York, so I booked a flight from Toronto to New York. I left as soon as Bill left the hotel room. I've never had a bath and put on make-up so fast before, and rushed to the Airport. I arrived in New York soon after. What a neat city it seemed to me. There were lots to do there, especially if you were very rich. When the day came to a close, I flew back to Toronto, just in time for Bill to return from IBM. He asked what I did that day. I said I went shopping, but I didn't tell him what city I was in.

When Bill's course was finished, we returned to Vancouver. At this point, we were both living in my mother's condo, one of the first in Vancouver as a legal co-op. I was fortunate. I had a paid-off condo right in a sought-after area in the 1200 Block West 11th Avenue at Granville. Plus, I had $6,000.00 in the bank. That was not too bad for a twenty-three-year old woman. Bill and I were still enthralled with Toronto, so we decided to move there. Considering we both had Alberta driver's licenses, we flew to Calgary and bought an old Green van, drove down through Montana, and along to Seattle, Seattle being one of my favourite cities. We travelled around there and bought the most beautiful Alaskan malamute puppy from a breeder. This pup was silver-gray and black, and his markings were gorgeous. As a dog lover, this was my first pup since I moved into that co-op eight years earlier. We named him Orbit. We ventured back to Vancouver and loaded up the van with all things we thought we'd need. I loaded up my mother's beautiful porcelain dishes, glasses, and some of my treasures. After all, I'm now a wife and was prepared to run the house and entertain as fine as we could afford. Bill loaded up the van with all his electronic devices, wires, computers, and so on. Bill was building a synthesizer as he was totally convinced that he was going to be a rock star, and Toronto is the place to be. I went along with him, as you simply just don't know. Bill could not write, read music, nor does he particularly have an ear for music. Music was one subject I always had A in. I was supposed to sing, go on stage, and the synthesizer would do the rest. I was in the background; Bill had it all planned. It was around October of 1977 when we started off across Canada in our van. It was my first attempt driving across Canada, though I had been across by train and plane many times before. While going across, we slept in the van and just kept going, taking turns driving. However, when we hit Ontario, the storms were outrageous, and I seemed to be doing most of the driving. Bill did a lot more sleeping in the back than I did. It took several days to venture through Ontario. The roads were bad around the Thunder Bay area, and the days were short. It wasn't much fun. When we arrived in the Toronto area, it was a blessing. The next project was to find housing. We found a little white house with a picket fence around a very large yard to rent. It was perfect! The rent I was receiving from my Vancouver co-op was paying the rental of this house. All we needed to do was find work. Bill was so involved about being a rock star that he had set rules. He had the master bedroom, and I had the spare bedroom. The living room was set up as his working/electronic room. He set everything up on this huge piece of plywood with four legs that took up most of the living room. There was no way the living room would be set up as a living area, with a couch, chair, and TV. I began to get discouraged about the living arrangements. Newlyweds don't live like this; separate bedrooms! I would cook for him, but he had total control of the dog. I was not to feed it, play with it, or groom it. In my mind, Bill was changing; he just wasn't the same guy. While we were somewhat short of money, our outings were few and far between. However, Bill wanted to see the CN Tower. It hadn't been open for long, so we went. Once on top of the tower, we were refused entrance because Bill did not have a tie. He got really, really mad, criticizing the phoney class structure Toronto has. We never did go back.

Back at home, Bill continued soldering wires, playing around with the gadgets he was creating. He had decided that I could not come out of my room unless it was to cook for him, use the washroom, or solder wires for him as per his instructions; I would gladly solder wires just to get out of the room. But, one day, I made a real mess of my soldering. It went all over the circuit board, and that was the end of my soldering days. Bill got mad. I was now confined to my room only to read Freud and Yeung. I was to be quizzed on all this. This went on for months and months, and I began to cry in my room daily. This was not married life. Supper was always to be made ready, but, one day, there had been some moldy tomato soup in his bowl. Rather than throwing it out, Bill stood over me for half an hour, screaming at me to eat the soup. I refused to eat it. But he said that mold is what penicillin is made out of, and it is good for me. I left for my bedroom. Some morning, Bill would monitor if I were using hot or cold water to brush my teeth. When he discovered I used hot water one day, I got screamed at. As time went on and I was shut in my room; I decided to go back to Vancouver. I booked my flight, and Bill drove me to the airport. I was devasted. My deep love for Bill was real and pure, but I could not endure this treatment any longer. I had a very quiet flight home, a couple of beverages, the airplane food, and movie. This was the first time I was on a 747, but it didn't excite me. Upon arriving in Vancouver—my hometown, where I was born and raised—I didn't have a place to live. I had rented my apartment out to a university student, and I ended up at the YWCA for two days. I hated it there. Soon, I found a self-contained apartment above the stores on Broadway at Oak Street, overlooking downtown and the mountains. It was back in the area where I lived and near my apartment and friends. My self-esteem was gone, and I needed a lift in life. I was no longer paying rent for the house in Toronto, so Bill had to make do himself. His grandmother always sent him money, although Bill tried to get some out of me. One thing I always seem to have was money in my purse.

It was now entering 1978. Bill was freezing in Toronto, and I was living just fine in Vancouver. I decided to join Elizabeth Leslie Modelling School when January began. Two nights a week, us women were taught etiquette, walking, speech, dress, make-up, and colour tones—just about everything to be that perfect woman. I met some super people there who I later chummed with. Around this time, my renter moved out, and I moved back into my co-op.

I assumed Toronto wasn't such a great place for Bill; he told me he was coming back to Vancouver. I didn't know when exactly, but he was coming. My hangouts in those days were Stauffer's Café on Broadway and Hemlock during the day and Clementine's Disco next door at night. The two places were owned by Ken Stauffer, the founder of the Cave in Vancouver, a very hot spot for present celebrities and newcomers. Disco was in with Saturday Night Live, and all of us same crew basically lived in both these places. I probably spent a good ten years parked there. Sheldon Stauffer was Ken's son. He ran the club while his dad ran the restaurant. I had my own spot at the bar, and I was well respected. I always came in there myself and left by myself. I was no doubt one of the boys anyway. No one caused me any trouble, but, in those days, the seventies, there was dope. However, there were no fighting and shootings like what we experienced in the 90s. Bill knew where he could find me. That year, I decided to change my career. I really hated secretarial work and decided to take an aesthetician course. I enrolled with in the Cosmetology School of Canada. It was a six-month daily course. My father paid for the cost—$1,000.00—a lot of money in those days. I thoroughly enjoyed this course.

One of my treasured experiences was to go to St. Paul Hospital in the evenings and work with the psychologically whacked-out day patients. These men and women had gone through some trauma, mostly marital, and no longer felt beautiful or attractive and were totally down. Our job was to give these people a lift. You had to be so very careful; they could snap at any moment. I enjoyed working with these people, especially when I can see progress. I was working twice a week. All the patients showed up every week. Progress was being made. As time went on, I was the only student with the teacher that wanted to continue this program on. So, basically, the other girls got tired of the evenings. It was just the two of us now, but it was well worth my time and effort.

Halloween was coming up, and all of us students painted our faces with artistic designs and went walking downtown to Granville Street. One day, we were out for lunch. We stopped and had lunch at the restaurant on top of the Bay department store. The design one of the girls put on my face was one that I'd put on every Halloween. I studied very hard and, in six months, received my diploma in this field.

One day, I was walking up at Broadway and Hemlock when here along came Bill in his suit. Needless to say, I was happy to see him. We went to Stauffer's for lunch and beverage and repaired our marriage. Bill decided that I should have a ring, so we went and bought a band with a few rocks in it, which you'd need a magnifying glass to see them. Anyway, I wore it with pride. But, as time went on, it was obvious that we grew out of each other. I wanted to go another direction. Bill wanted to study; I wanted to party. I threw my ring out of the window. He went off to UBC to study for his bachelor's degree. Although we were in the same city, I went off dating other men and looking for work.

After looking around for a cosmetology job, I realized that the pay was poor. I was making more money as a secretary. I lucked out and got a job as a receptionist at Vancouver City Savings Credit Union on Pender. It was the only branch downtown and the only branch that was closed on Saturdays. This branch was close to Eaton's, the Bay, and Woodward's, Vancouver's top-leading department stores. While at the bank job, I typed for the manager and addressed people. I enjoyed that, but my boss was all full of himself. As time went on, I kept noticing an older man staring at me whenever he came into the branch to make deposits for his company. Finally, he came over to speak with me. His name was Dan Evans. He was a real gentleman. His office was just below the bank. He was in the mining business with the stock market. We became good friends, but never intimate. He was working on a project called Pride Resources. In those days, there was a curb exchange, and he was working on getting this on the curb. Other than wining and dining with me frequently at the Panarama Roof on top of the Hotel Vancouver, at the Georgia Hotel, and Hy's, he was teaching me his trade. It was very interesting learning the stock market. He wanted me to type his prospectus, and there was a time limit on this project. His typewriter was the same as mine upstairs. He brought up his work and print wheel, and I typed it in-between my regular work. No one knew but us. One evening, I went downstairs to continue typing. We'd call it a day, go out for dinner, and continue the same thing the next day, until it was done. I didn't make any errors; I was very proud and still have my copy today. In learning the stocks, I borrowed $500.00 from my branch to buy stocks in Pride Resources. It was ten cents a share. Dan even took me to the Vancouver Stock Exchange for viewing. I was impressed. As time went on, I sold my shares due to a gut feeling and doubled my money. I was very proud, and it had been a great lesson. Dan and I were good friends. He gave me a specially-made jade and silver axe brooch—a piece from his mine. Today, I still have this treasure—a token of our two-year friendship. One day, I got a phone call from him. He said he had severe throat cancer; he died.

I got a job at Eaton's during Thursday, Friday nights, and all day on Saturday. Sunday shopping wasn't introduced then, but this was perfect. Every Thursday and Friday evening, I would just walk two blocks from the bank to my retail job. I realized I had a technique for selling. My job was to sell men's cologne right near the main entrance. I sold more cologne on those three days than a regular full time clerk.

I received an award for my sales; I simply loved retail. Considering I only had to pay $55.00 a month for my co-op fees, I was rolling in the money. I still joined my regular crew at Clementine's and Stauffer's. It wasn't that I was missing anything while at work; no one went too far. On summer days, I'd go bike riding around Stanley Park and UBC. This was almost daily, as long as it wasn't raining. Vancouver's seawall is one of the most picturesque in the world. You can really loose yourself in its beauty.

Then it was time to divorce Bill. We had separated for a while and had gone back and forth for too long. I could no longer stand his marijuana smoking, to name a few. So, I filed for divorce, but under Bill's instructions, he'd rather file because when he becomes rich and famous as a rock star, it would look better that he divorced me. It didn't really matter to me; I just wanted to get out. In those days, you had to have a reason. So, I said I committed adultery. I needed a man to help me, so I called a friend, Rick James, and asked him, "Would you like to come to Bill's lawyer and say you committed adultery with me on Halloween night?" He agreed to this, and I bought him a beer. He said the lawyer just tore him apart, so Rich told the lawyer that he wouldn't do this again. By 1980, I was a free woman at age twenty-six. I dated here and there. I was getting discouraged with my receptionist job. The bank manager who I typed for was a very young, immature chap. I grew to hate him. He'd go out of his way to make things as uncomfortable as possible. If you were a customer and he didn't like you, it was known that he would return certified cheques N.S.F. In one week, three of us handed in our resignations. Shortly after that, he was fired. I believe he went to become a real estate salesman. From there, I went onto a one-girl office program with three guys running a computer company. Around that time, I joined the Supreme Court Racquetball Club. It was on top of a parking lot in downtown Vancouver. It was where I learned how to play racquetball and met Vancouver's new money. Lots of prominent businessmen played there and opened up a new flock of dates. I was busy all the time going here and there. Debbie was the accountant at the club in those days, and she mentioned that the accounts were being done at the computer company I worked for. My job was to input the figures of the club into the accounting package. One day, instead of saving, I wiped out the whole program—absolutely everything. I got very worried. I've lost my job and the club's accounts. It, apparently, got corrected. I didn't loose my job, but it got around the club. While working one day at the computer company, an older man came into the shop, a suit-and-tie, big-shot businessman from Toronto by the name of Richard Freedman.

CHAPTER ELEVEN

Big Shot? Not really, but that was the image he projected, and I fell for it. He came over to my desk and said he was divorced. I replied, "So am I." He appeared a little taken back. He said he'd like to take me out for supper and won't accept no for an answer, so, I said "Okay." He said he would pick me up at 5:00 P.M. at work. Sure enough, Richard showed up in a rented Lincoln Continental, and we went off to a fine steak house called Hy's, the place to go in those days, and still is. With my newfound freedom, I was now being dated by men with fine cars and money to spend, and they invited me to fine dining. I loved every minute of it. It was a sure cry away from the moldy tomato soup Bill tried to force down my throat. Those days were over. Richard was a gentleman. We talked about Vancouver, Toronto, his telephone business, and my interest in dogs, the Canadian Kennel Club, and my various hobbies. After dinner, he dropped me off at home. He asked for my telephone number, and I gave it to him. I was in seventh heaven. Richard called me at work the next day and said he was flying back to Toronto, and that he would call me again. And he did. It started out to be biweekly, then weekly. Then, he started coming out to Vancouver monthly. Something was happening here. When he was out here, he always rented a luxurious car and stayed in a hotel—never with me. I was always wined and dined nightly while he was here. By now, I have tried just about every fine steak house in town and had narrowed them down to my favourites, according to taste and service. Richard was a birthday kind of guy; he flew out from Toronto for my birthday on December 7 and treated me to a weekend at Harrison Hot Springs, an attractive resort smack in the mountains of BC. That was where I had my first experience of a full massage. Richard and I were put into a very hot whirlpool tub and got rubbed down for an hour. This was a luxurious and a nice birthday present. I was also introduced to Richard's cousin, Gordy, as he is known. Richard and I went up to his mansion in North Vancouver. Gordy was a self-made millionaire. He created Brittania Jeans, sold it, and made millions. That evening, we were all to go out with Gordy, his fiancée, Richard, and myself. I thoroughly enjoyed my evening, and Gordy didn't mind showing off his wealth with his Bentley. By this time, Richard and I were already intimate. I remember that day well; it was at my apartment, on the red shag carpet. That was the first time I had been with a man so many years older than I, eighteen years older to be exact. I was just totally attracted. Richard kept coming back and forth from Toronto. As time went on, Richard would come over to play cards with my father, John, his wife, Marg, and myself. I can't remember the exact card games, but I do remember that my dad wasn't impressed with a man so much older, plus, he was Jewish. I assumed my dad felt it was just a phase I am going through. Richard did spoil me with clothes. When he came out, he'd come with a suitcase filled with petite clothes. His brother-in-law was, apparently, in the clothing business in Montreal, and Richard picked up all the samples after they were worn down the runway. Evidently, Richard had good taste for style and my size. One evening, he called and said he would be coming to Vancouver with his just-married daughter, Cheryl, and her husband. Tour guide? Hmmm, this seemed fishy. Richard stayed in a hotel. The next day, the four of us ventured to Seattle, one of my favourite cities. We spent the day there, had dinner, and returned back to Vancouver that evening. I was now getting suspicious. I think Richard lives with a woman in Toronto and I was going to find out my way. When the week was over, Cheryl, her husband, and Richard flew back to Toronto. In my attempt to become Sherlock Holmes, I called the Toronto directory and got a number for a Richard Freedman in Toronto. I called that number, and a woman answered the telephone; it was Richard's place. My suspicions were true. I was hurt and mad. I confronted Richard, and we had an argument about this. It was my right to know what was really going on. That ended that! Now, what do I do? I made plans to move to Toronto, not necessarily to be with Richard, but for a change. Toronto is the center of the Canadian Kennel Club and is the center for dog lovers, dog shows, and everything that I really specialize in. I put my head together and phoned a lawyer friend of mine at that time. He was originally from Toronto and was barred from practicing law in the Province of British Columbia for running an illegal adoption scam. He was in the papers, TV, and radio and really got some government officials angry, one being Grace McCarthy. I gave him a call. He said I could stay in the suite he just rented since he hasn't moved in yet. It was totally vacant. Great! I'll get to Toronto and he will let me in his apartment. What a view. His suite was overlooking downtown Toronto, and I could reach out and touch the clouds. The building was called the Manulife Tower at Bloor and Yonge. This was, in 1982, in Toronto's heyday. Money was flowing all over. Toronto was the place to be. When I wanted entertainment, I just went a few floors up and sat in the posh lounge, just staring at downtown. My next step was to find housing. I purchased a map of Toronto and rode on both subway lines from one end to another. I fell in love with the subway. What a super efficient way to get around such a large city. I also took their streetcars from one end to another. I got a good sense of where I didn't want to live. Eventually, I found the perfect place—a room with a balcony at the top of an old mansion in Rosedale. This room had a view of Bloor and Yonge and downtown for $55.00 a week. I still stayed in touch with my rich lawyer friend after I settled in my own place. As I am open to try just about anything once, my lawyer friend asked me if I would join him at Ramblewood in Guelph. Ramblewood was a nudist colony and sex trap. I thought, *Why not?* Women could get in by themselves, but men had to have an escort. I was game, and we went every weekend, until I got a call. We would venture off to Ramblewood in his Mercedes along with the finest wine; it was a bring-your-own-booze place. I believe his wine was $1,000.00 a bottle, and we had two; he always left the price tags on his liquor. It was $50.00 each to get in Ramblewood. All my expenses were paid. Once there, you would be given a locker to lock your clothes and purse in. I had never done this before and was actually surprised who was there. There were very old couples sitting there naked on a couch and some younger people in the hot tub. Upstairs were different rooms with toys for your sexual pleasure. You can just pick anyone you liked and go here or there. Apparently, these older, retired people travelled from camp to camp. One couple was from Florida. Another couple looked like they were in their eighties. That was an experience I chose not to do forever. As my welcome wore out with my lawyer friend, it was time to move on. Of course, by this time, I had a phone and found a job. I went to our government employment office and got an interview with Paul Tuz, president of the Better Business Bureau (BBB) on Bloor at Shelbourne. This was a huge, old office tower for the Confederation Life Insurance Company people. The religious TV program *100 Huntley Street* was two blocks away. Paul Tuz decided to hire me at $1,000.00 a month. I started the following Monday. While I was in Toronto, I had my apartment in Vancouver rented once again, so, I was financially doing well. My position at the bureau was at the enquiries. There was a special group of people for complaints, catalogue sales, accounting, legal, and secretarial. My next goal was to get a social life, so I joined the Parkview Racquetball Club adjacent to the Inn on the park in Don Mills. I brought my racquetball gear with me. I joined, but it wasn't cheap. It was the elite club in its day for racquetball and squash. After work, I went there straight to play every day. I was beginning to become a very good player. The men at the club were also rich and available. I loved working at the bureau and had made some long-time friends. Life was great. I started dating a few men who wined and dined me all over. I went to Niagara Falls for a weekend with the possibility of having a heavy affair with my date. All my affairs were heavy. He was a nice guy who sold wholesale products for the carpet industry, chemicals, and so on. Apparently, he still lived at home with his mother and sheltie. I thought it was odd for an older man to still be living at home, but, apparently, he was saving money. After three months of living in Toronto, my phone rang; it was Richard. He had known I was in town and got my phone number from either Bell or my father. He desperately wanted to see me. Apparently, Jo-Anne, his live in partner, kicked him out of her house. That was it. After ten years, Jo-Anne wanted him out. He asked me out and picked me up in his Audi. I was impressed with his car; I love luxurious cars. Anyway, we had supper, and he explained his situation. I basically explained I was doing well and not particularly interested in starting a relationship with him. Nevertheless, we parted that evening after having a good time. But Richard didn't quit. He called all the time, so I went out with him. We were rebuilding our relationship; it simply happened. I told Richard that I played racquetball at the Parkview Club. He knew the club as he sold a telephone system there and knew the key people. Richard decided to join, and he upgraded my membership to Gold, the same as his. He bought me the best racquetball racquet that money could buy, showered me with the highest quality of equipment, and dolled me up in the best runners and matching outfits. I had so many outfits, so I didn't have to wear the same outfit twice a week. Our relationship was flourishing. I continued my job at the BBB and met Richard at the club every evening. Sometimes, he'd pick me up at work. As I became a good player, I had lots of games and became the doll of the place. I was a happy camper. I had everything I needed, except a dog. Richard decided that it was time that we move in together. He rented a three-bedroom apartment for himself, his two sons, Ronnie and Mitchell, and me. Ronnie was around eighteen while Mitchell was 16. This was new to me, very different indeed. But, it worked. Ronnie and Mitchell could see there was great love between myself and Richard. Ronnie, Mitchell, and I all got along. Our first trip was to Montreal by train to visit Richard's mother and father. My friends at the bureau phoned in sick for me, so, early Thursday evening, Richard and I boarded the Via Rail at Union Station to Montreal. We had a suite on the train. It was an overnight train, so we arrived in Montreal the next morning. Once we arrived, we stayed with his sister and her husband in Cote-Saint-Luc, a dominantly Jewish area in Montreal. His sister didn't seem to mind us sleeping together. For some reason, I was accepted. During the day, we travelled to Montreal's famous eateries, one being Schwartz's. Bagels and bagels were everywhere, being baked in brick ovens right before your eyes. That evening, Richard and I went over to his parents' apartment, a huge apartment near downtown. His dad was a dentist, still practising, and his mother was a housewife. I remember her being the typical Jewish mother. She always had something to say, and in a loud way, with the typical Jewish accent. Richard's father rarely said much, and, when he did, she would butt in anyway. All in all, I was accepted, and that meant a lot. Nothing is more uncomfortable than being not accepted by your lovers' family, as they can make life difficult for you. In Bill's case, his grandmother never had a feel for me. I am sure she influenced Bill from time to time, which didn't help our relationship, or marriage. Anyhow, it was a great weekend. Richard and I boarded the train Sunday night and arrived at Union Station Monday morning. Back to work. Only my friend at the BBB knew I went to Montreal.

I started to become quite a very good racquetball player, so Richard paid for me to have lessons with Heather McKay. At that time, she was the World Champion in racquetball and squash. She was hired by the Parkview Club to teach. I saw her play both games in competition; she was so good you couldn't take your eyes off of her. As I improved my game, I joined the Parkview Racquetball Tournament. This was in conjunction with their three other clubs and other independent clubs in and around Toronto. One weekend, I took the Greyhound bus, played at Niagara Falls, New York competition, and won my first trophy. I was getting excited with this game. When I wanted to do something, I had to do it well. Back at the Parkview Club, I had games, games, and more games. We had a raffle and trophy night one night, and I was voted Miss Congeniality.

Richard liked to get out of Toronto at least once a month, either for a week or a weekend, depending on business. On one long weekend, he took me to Lake Placid, New York. This wasn't long after the Winter Olympics, so you could see the treasures and memories of that great event. Our drive was picturesque and all new to me to view. Richard had been to Lake Placid before, skiing. We arrived at a nice motel, got settled, and did some sightseeing. We had dinner, went to the lounge, and then to our room. The next day, we went way up the ski slope on the chair lift. It made BC's Grouse Mountain look pretty small. It was scary if this thing fell. Richard was actually paranoid and told me not to move so much in the chair. Once we arrived at the top of the mountain, we hiked a bit and looked at the gift shop. One thing Richard and I have in common is our love for malls, stores, restaurants, and spending money. We saw just about everything we needed to see for that long weekend. Then, we were back to Toronto, and I was back to work. My job at the BBB was fun; I really enjoyed it there. Richard continued with selling telephone systems. He sold a system to *100 Huntley Street*, the religious TV program coming out of Toronto. I went with him to their set; it was interesting how they did their television program. Richard was an avid golf player. He was a member of the Aurora Golf and Country Club in Aurora, Ontario. This club was about three quarter hours north of Toronto. I spent all summer long with Richard driving the cart. I couldn't see the thrill of golf, but I was occupied. Well, it was time to take me to the Bahamas. Bahamas! Really! Richard asked me to get permission from my job to take a week off to go to the Bahamas. I did and got the time off. I was surprised as I hadn't been there that long. Possibly not long enough to get holidays, but off I went. It was pretty down there in the Bahamas. We were in the best hotel, in a lovely room overlooking the water. This was great. Richard and I travelled the shops that were set up like individual tents along the street, and the people were peddling anything and everything. Of course, Richard was on the golf course. He brought his own golf clubs. I didn't want to join him; I took a tour bus around the island with all the other tourists. One thing: I was a terrific traveller. I can go anywhere by myself, unafraid. I have a great sense of direction and can always find my way back. Another thing: I always wanted to go horseback riding down a sandy beach. One of the brochures in the hotel showed a ranch, horseback riding, trail, and beach. That's it! I wanted to go there, so Richard and I went there. He was supposed to go and wait for me while I went riding, but he changed his mind. I thought he looked kind of funny on horseback, being a little overweight. Anyway, I told the guide that I know how to ride, and I wanted a horse that moves. Well, I had this plug that had a terrible temper. I had to be at the back of the line, one horse length behind the horse ahead of me. If this horse was to act up, I was supposed to hang on. Anyway, Richard could tell I was pissed off. We got to the beach. Everyone else's horse was galloping along the beach, but this plug, which I was kicking with all my strength, was just walking an odd trot down the beach; I was so annoyed. That's it, I hate the Bahamas. Richard didn't laugh; he knew I was annoyed. Why couldn't I have gotten a better horse? I was sure I voiced my opinion. Anyway, after a week in the sun, it was time to go back to Toronto, back to work for both of us. But, when I arrived back to snowy Toronto, you could tell I came from somewhere warm.

Nonetheless, back at the club, Heather had me booked in and around Toronto, playing in tournaments. I won three more trophies, and Richard was proud. Life was good. Richard decided that the apartment that the four of us were in was too small, so he rented a house in a very good area—in Mount Pleasant. We had to be interviewed by the owner. Richard signed a lease with the option to buy. We all moved in, and I loved it. There was much more room. Richard's friend gave him a Calico kitten, and he named her Neco. A pet! Now, I was really loving this. Ronnie was an excellent cook and was focusing his future to be a chef. Mitchell loved dressing up as a clown and entertaining children. Mitchell was a splitting image of Richard; Ronnie looked much different. Cheryl, Richard's daughter, also resembled her dad a lot. Richard was getting comfortable at the racquetball club, and there were a lot of available women with money. Richard had his favorites, and, at times, I'd get mad. He had a roving eye, and I didn't like it. We started to fight about this. I brought it up, but Richard denied it every time. Nevertheless, I still became uncomfortable. I believe one's senses are always right. With his business, he attended business shows. One was coming up in Chicago at the McCormick Center. I was to go along. Once again, I asked my supervisor if I could take three days off. I got permission, so off we went. I had never been to Chicago or to a business show before; I was enthused. Upon arriving in Chicago, we went to our hotel. I was so impressed with this city. Richard took me to Hy's Steak House that night, and I worked the booth with Richard. I didn't know anything about his business, but I was a good showpiece and handed out pamphlets. Richard hated to be alone; he always needed someone with him—always—but I don't. Those four days went fast. I learned a lot. Then, back to Toronto we went, back to work and racquetball. Well, not long into a new year, Richard wanted to take me to Los Angeles to meet some of his suppliers, so I asked for permission from my job to take a week off. I got it, so off to L.A. we went. I had been to L.A. before, and it is one of my favourite cities in the world. I love Beverly Hills, Santa Monica, the studios, the restaurants, the weather, and the craziness of the place. We checked into our hotel. The next day, we were to meet the owner of a telephone research and designing company. I had lunch with the executives and toured the plant. I was learning so much, but, when I look back at it, I was also Richard's showpiece. Never mind; I was his woman. We continued our fine dining and touring of L.A. Richard had a meeting in Orange County, so, that day, he let me have the rental car. I took myself to Disneyland. He knew I could travel alone and find my way around with no trouble. I spent the day there and met him, at a set, time for dinner. My day went well; so did his. We still had a few days left, so we decided to rent a car and drive from Los Angeles to San Francisco, along the Pacific Coast. What a beautiful, breathtaking trip it was. We stopped at various restaurants and shops along the way. Oh yes, Richard brought his golf clubs. We stopped at the famous Pebble Beach Country Club. What a windy course it was. You could also see the great wealth around that area. We stayed overnight in Monterey and had dinner at some fancy restaurant that was also on the list of makers of dinner for the president of the United States. Then, off to San Francisco and we booked into our hotel. Richard got very angry as they put us in some crummy room right beside the entrance of the hotel. He made such a stink that we got moved to the best room in the hotel with skylights, and so on. This hotel was on Fisherman's Wharf. The next day, we travelled the shops and restaurants, and I purchased what I liked. I wanted to go on a helicopter ride over San Francisco and Alcatraz. At first, Richard didn't want to go; he was not a risk taker. But, he came along anyway. I made sure I got to sit up front, right beside the pilot. That's the way I am; I hate the back of the bus. That was a twenty-minute ride, and I loved it. But, I think my man just wanted to get off. Well, it was time to leave San Francisco for Toronto, back to work and racquetball. We always travelled business or first class and always spent our waiting time in the Maple Leaf Lounge or whatever lounge the airline had for the first class travellers. The flight was several hours long, and we started to argue and argue well. I moved my seat to somewhere else on the plane. I thought I was being smart. Richard thought it was funny because he knew we'd have to meet to wait for our baggage in Toronto and go home together. When we travelled, we basically got along beautifully. Back at home, we started to fight a lot. Our fighting became physical. Richard hit me a lot, and I took it for a while. I was always bruised on the right shoulder and arm. It seemed to happen weekly. I remember one day, he choked me, and I thought I was going to die.

One day, we started arguing in his car. He slapped me in the mouth hard enough to kill my front tooth. I had to get a root canal; that tooth was dead forever. Richard paid for my dental bills. However, our arguing didn't stop, so, one day, I phoned my former husband, Bill Hayes, in Edmonton. He wanted me back, and he said we would start all over. He went and bought me a ticket to Edmonton, business class, one way. Richard went to work, and I phoned the bureau and said I won't be back. I just simply left. My good friends at the bureau knew that Richard and I had problems. Bill picked me up at the Edmonton Airport in his brand new, two-door, black Corvette. Wow! That car was gorgeous. At that time, Bill was living in his mother's elite home in Windsorpark and teaching at N.A.I.T. (Northern Alberta Institute of Technology). I drove Bill to work every day and had his car all day; he didn't want to leave it in the parking lot of the school for vandalism reasons. Then, I'd pick him up after work. After a couple of days, I knew Bill and I would never be husband and wife again; we are nothing more than really good friends.

I called Richard; Richard wanted me back. He phoned me, and I phoned him. Richard bought me a ticket from Edmonton to Toronto, business class. I left after one week and left Bill with a $300.00 phone bill. Back in Toronto, we decided to solve our problem. We both went to a psychiatrist. We went twice a week; sessions were either singular or joint, depending on the focus of each other's stories. Those were one-hour sessions at the doctor's going rate. Richard and I were tested. He said that we were so suitable for each other. He had not had a test so close for two people. The psychiatrist decided that Richard needed the counselling, so he was to attend a group session at the psyhchiatrist's home twice a week. I drove Richard there and picked him up afterward. It was almost like Richard wanted me to be comfortable, like saying that that was where he was going. In the meantime, I had my apartment for sale in Vancouver. It took several years to sell it because it was a co-op, and you couldn't get a mortgage for a co-op. The apartment was vacant and furnished, and the realtor showed it when he felt someone suitable would be a cash buyer. It wasn't an easy sell. As time went on, I was still uneasy about my relationship with Richard. His birthday was coming up, so I got together with his sons, daughter, and his daughter's husband about having a birthday party. Cheryl and her husband would come in from Guelph, Ronnie would make the cake, and I'd prepare supper. I went and bought balloons and blew all these things myself. I hid them in Ronnie's closet until I was ready to hang them all over the living room. Ronnie thought I was nuts. Of course, coming back from Edmonton, I no longer worked. Although I was still accepted to come back to the BBB, I decided not to. I had money, and I wanted time off. January 13 came along and I hung up all those balloons all over the house. Richard came home and was taken by surprise with the trouble we all went to. We all had a great night. But I was still unhappy. I asked Richard if he would fly me back to Vancouver. He agreed, but I was supposed to come back. I said I would. I packed everything up. I went home, but I had no intention of coming back.

CHAPTER TWELVE

Once back in Vancouver, I ventured out with friends and frequented a place called the Elephant & Castle Pub & Restaurant in the Pacific Center. It was one of my many stops every day. When I went out, I usually sat at the bar and didn't say very much. As time went on, I noticed a very good-looking man sitting down the way. It seemed we had the same schedule. He never said much either. One day, I had no choice but to sit beside him, and we started up a conversation. *Nice guy*, I thought. We started a relationship. I also got an offer on the co-op. Now, I am flourishing. Some changes were happening here. He was very French, with a very deep French accent. His father was Polish, and his mother was French. His name is Yves Maciagowski. Unfortunately, he had a different life than mine. He was working hard in the mines in Yellowknife, surrounded by heavy drugs and hookers. At the time I met him, he was living in a skid road hotel on Granville Street, being influenced by the heroin users and hookers. I liked him, and I believed he had just fallen and that this wasn't the real Yves. Some time after that, I got an offer on my co-op, one I couldn't turn down, so my place was sold. Considering I had not planned on returning to the West Coast for several years, I bought a ticket from Vancouver to Honolulu, Los Angeles, Las Vegas, and Vancouver. You had to be in three major cities other than your hometown and stay for many days. What a deal. Off I went to Hawaii. I stayed at a hotel on Lewers Street, not far from the Don Ho Show. In fact, it was just across the street and down a bit. My room faced the water. It was beautiful. When I landed, I was overwhelmed by the heat, the openess of the airport, and the slight breeze. I had just bought a new Nikon camera, worth $1,000.00, back then. My day in Hawaii was usually spent travelling and going to the malls, restaurants, and pubs. One pub was the Rose and Crown. I liked it there. I am not a big suntanner; walking in a light top and shorts is about all the sun I prefer. I wouldn't usually travel in a bathing suit down the beach, or Main Street.

One day, I was really hungover, and, I decided, rather than walk anywhere that day, I would take a day bus ride around the island. I went by the Dole pineapple factory, museums, castles, Pearl Harbor, the Monkey Bar, Hawaii Football Field, mansions, and famous buildings. Hawaii certainly has a different history. One day, I rented the flashiest red car ever, with a convertible top window. That car was spanking brand new; no one had driven it yet. I was the first to power around in that car, a standard. At first, I was going to rent a Mercedes for $250.00 a day, but the girls at the rental office really pushed this red car to me for $150.00 a day. I didn't know what kind of car it was, but it was like a Porsche. I drove that thing all over, and the men were waving at me. I was in heaven. I basically repeated all my trips by car as I had done by bus earlier in the week. Everything was the same, except I felt much better! Well, my Hawaii trip was coming to a close, so off to Los Angeles. From Hawaii, I boarded Wardair, in a huge plane to Los Angeles. It was a very rough flight, and I can remember, in the coach class, the seats were so huge that I couldn't place my feet flat on the floor. That was one flight I remember well and didn't like it. Once in Los Angeles, the hotel bus picked me up. I was only staying for one night, but I really wanted to see Las Vegas. Once in Vegas, I checked into the Holiday Inn on the main strip. I was so impressed with all the craziness of Vegas. One sad thing though, I arrived at Vegas when they had a strike, so there were very little shows playing. Oh well, I loved the one-armed bandits. I won money in my hotel casino; it was around $300.00. That was a lot for me. I enjoyed Las Vegas very much. As my two-week trip was coming to a close, I left for Vancouver, stopped there one day, saw Yves, and left for Toronto.

I moved to Toronto with $45,000.00 in cash in 1983. I stayed with my girlfriend from my BBB days, Joan. She had rented a house on the west side of Toronto and was expecting her first child. While there, I still kept in contact with Yves. He would call me from time to time and send me red roses. I hired a real estate agent. Already knowing where I want to live in Toronto, I picked East York. I searched and looked at various houses. I wanted to make sure that the down payment and monthly payments were low. I found a place for $55,000.00, side by side, two-story, brick house. Now, I can get my dogs! Possession date was three weeks away. I paid for Yves to come to Toronto under the condition he quit the heroin. He agreed. He wanted to get out of that low-life as well. I bought myself a car: an old, green, four-door Ford Granada. It was working and was suitable enough. I picked up Yves, and we stayed at Joan's for about two weeks. As time went on, we settled in my new house. My BBB supervisor's cat had kittens, and I was going to get one. My first pet arrived. Yves named her Menou. He said all cats are named Menou. She was a cute and smart tabby. She had a home! The next thing to do was to paint and furnish the place. Yves painted, and we went shopping for furniture. I bought a couch, bed, and dining set. All my personal belongings were being shipped from Vancouver at a cost of $1,000.00. I really didn't have that much, so I though that was expensive. I was always smart with my money. Yves and I took several months off, but then, it was time to find a job. I found one before he could. I was hired by Dunham-Bush, an old company in Weston, Ontario, as a secretary. This was clean across the city for me to drive, but I got used to travelling in Toronto, where going to work one way took at least an hour, the norm. Dunham-Bush was an American-based company and hired a lot of professional engineers. If you weren't an engineer, you were a salesman or secretary. Some people had already been there for twenty years.

Each morning, I'd have tea and read the paper, and, every Friday, I would check the lottery numbers. I always bought Wintario for a dollar. One Friday morning, on August 1, 1985, I won $5,000.00. My boss allowed me to go to Yonge & Bloor and down to the Ontario Lottery and Gaming Corporation office to pick up my prize. But, they said I was too excited and told me to go to Park N Ride and take the subway down. That seemed logical, so off I went. There were three of us in there: two women and one man. We all won $5,000.00

from various tickets, and we were all discussing what we were going to do with it. The other woman was the most homely thing you could ever imagine. She had an outdated 60s look and was somewhat unclean looking. When she said she was going to use the money for her wedding, the guy and I looked at each other with the same question in mind and were holding back our laughter. Thank God I was called up to pick up my prize; no identification required.

When I returned to my car, someone had hit it and left a note. That was all I needed! You mean there are still honest people out there? The car got fixed. It just needed some bodywork done. It made my weekend great. Our neighbours on Cosburn were nice people. There was a woman whose husband worked for Canada Wire and Cable, in Leaside. It was not too far from our home. The man told Yves to apply there. It took Yves a year to find a job. I supported him with his cigarettes, bus fare, and whatever he needed and wanted. Yves did apply several times, had several interviews, and finally got a job there. He almost got a job with Air Canada, except he didn't have a driver's license. But that was okay; he's got a job. Although his job was mining, that was a good city job as far as Toronto was concerned. I worked during the day, and he worked nights, so we didn't see much of each other. He would call me every morning at work and ask how things are going. I usually saw him on weekends. The schedule worked for us. I had a newfound wealth of $5,000.00. That was a lot of money, and I could spread it around far. I bought two of the best in colossal kennel and cages, a tack box, and the best dog-grooming supplies. I had new windows added in the house where needed, a new kitchen put in the old wartime kitchen that I had painted an ugly purple, and, most importantly, I had a trip to visit my mother's family in Finland. I booked myself for two weeks on September 1985. Little that did I know that trip would prove to be a very important trip for me for years to come. Of course, if I can fit in a schedule around dogs, I will, So, I wrote the Finnish Kennel Club in Helsinki and asked about various shows in and around Helsinki. I would miss the All Breed Dog Show in Helsinki, but I would be there for the Finnish Newfoundland Club Specialty show in Espoo. I wrote the puppy advisor and informed the person that I was coming from Toronto, Canada and will be at the show. I wanted to learn their Dog Show ways.

I had booked my flight for Helsinki on July 4, 1985, at a cost of $1,009.00; I had used my savings for this ticket. I would leave August 30, 1985 and return September 14.

In those days, there were no direct flights from Toronto to Helsinki. One had to change planes in Montreal. I arrived in Helsinki and went through Customs. I was so impressed with the floor in the airport—all solid wood. I thought, *in Canada, this type of floor would be wrecked the first day.* There was wood, wood, and wood everywhere in Finland. My cousin, Tuula, and her husband, Pekka, met me at the airport. They were my English-speaking relatives, and they would show me around the southern part of Finland. Tuula taught several languages in the jail, and Pekka was a mechanic for Finnair. They had a Mercedes. Wow! I get to see Helsinki in a Mercedes! They live in

Kerava, a suburb of Helsinki. They had a very large house made out of wood on at least a one-acre lot full of trees. I was nervous about meeting relatives and being in a foreign country so close to Russia. Tuula liked her beer, and so did I. She finally had a partner. Pekka wasn't much of a drinker, although he'd have something. Tuula and Pekka had taken holidays to accommodate my visit. The next day, we travelled to downtown Helsinki and the market. I fell in love with everything Finnish and realized that my roots are here. I was impressed with everything. The fruit and vegetables at the market made our fruit and vegetables in Canada look rotten. I remember a cauliflower was fluorescent white, not with brown spots I see at home. The size of the tomatoes and potatoes...no wonder I had so many potatoes at home. Tuula and her daughters, Lisa and Anna, would make their Finnish dishes, and I can remember saying just about for everything, "I remember Mother cooking or baking this." I picked up the Finnish names quickly and had an ear for their dialect. Every home in Finland has a sauna. Every morning and evening, you'd have a sauna. Tuula and I would go to the sauna in her basement with what she called our "Sauna Beer." We always had a cold beer. Pekka made for me, by hand, the famous birch branches that you whack on your skin in the sauna. At first, I felt funny whacking myself, but once you start smelling the aroma it gave off, you would be in heaven. By now, I could run the sauna myself, from turning it on accordingly, to controlling the temperature, and to the length of time I could stand being in there. No wonder the Finns have such lovely skin. One day, Tuula and I went to the shopping malls in downtown Helsinki. There were the most elegant of shops with the finest in Finnish wares. We went into a leather place. The leathers felt so soft, and the quality made our fashion look tacky. Although I had lots of spending money with me, I passed on buying a leather coat. I bought a fine, leather black purse, leather belt, reindeer leather change purse, and small gifts. Then we went into a fine porcelain kitchenware place. I was so impressed with the black dishes that I bought four of each plate, cup, saucer, soup bowl, and serving plate. I also bought matching cutlery set in black. To this day, my relatives add to my set. Arabia is the set. I also bought items made by Fiska, Marimeko, (fine cloths and wood) Iittala, and Finnish crystal. I also collect fine tablecloths and cloth napkins. Now, I really have a lovely set that you could not buy in Canada, not even to this day have I found a similar set anywhere.

I was now to go up north. My cousin up north would meet me there. She was going to be my English translator. I flew to Koupio from Helsinki, about halfway up Finland. My cousin was attending university there. I stayed with her at the university residences, met her boyfriend, Vesa, and got settled there. Leena is my second cousin, the daughter of my cousin, Taisto. Leena and Vesa showed me around Koupio. Leena was then taking driving lessons. Soon, I learned their system. That evening, I went to a university party. While everyone else was dancing, I became a wallflower all night. I was oddly dressed and had a funny accent, so I just sat there, drank my beer, and watched. The next day Leena, Vesa, and I went further north by train. My cousin, Taisto, worked on the train, so Leena could travel free. He collected tickets. Upon arriving in Paltamo, there was a big welcome, Paltamo being mother's birthplace. (She was born in a sauna). I couldn't believe I was standing on the very grounds where my mother could have possibly stood on and where a major war happened once upon a time. I tried to picture Russian and German soldiers all over the place. The next day, we went over and met my mother's sister. This would be Taisto's mother. She doesn't speak English. We drove up a gravel country road and turned into a long driveway with a wooden, red, old house by the lake. Out came my aunt with the traditional headscarf and dress, thick socks, and tights. She started to cry; she never believed she would ever see me. Apparently, I looked exactly like my mother, as I was constantly reminded. Inside the house, I saw this beautiful wooden floor, a traditional spinning wheel, a huge brick oven, and family photos everywhere. My aunt had a full spread of food ready, and she also had some of her spinning work for me. Up north, those who live in the bush live off the land. All Finns had gardens full of every type of vegetables; most importantly, strawberries. My uncle, Frans, came across the lake on his boat for this visit. There were two living siblings of my mother. Apparently, my relatives owned all the land around the lake. Getting from one place to another in the early years was by boat, but now, you can drive around. After we ate, Leena, myself, Taisto, and Frans went across the lake for a very special trip. I was going to the house where my mother was born and raised. This was very emotional for me. We arrived at this large, old, wooden red house that was painted white around the window frames, a popular colour in Finland. I asked why most houses were red. They said their winters are so long and all they see is white, so they painted their houses with bright colours. It made sense to me. Inside, the rooms were particularly small. The living room and dining room didn't have a divider. It was like one big room with kitchen, table, chairs, and TV. The flooring was wood with pieces of carpet here and there. The walls were painted by the looks of many coats over the years, and the wallpaper was old and dirty. We stayed for several hours, and I heard earlier stories. I noticed Mom and Dad's wedding picture at my aunt's house. It was time to take the boat over to Frans's house. He had a special supper there—and beer—so we all went to receive the same hospitality I've been receiving since I arrived in Finland. I was Frans' favourite now and would be until his death. My two weeks in Finland was going sadly fast, and I was now to return to Kerava. Pekka was yet to take me to the Newfoundland Specialty. It rained that day. I was the guest of honour; it was announced over the public address system that a visitor from Canada came. The puppy advisor basically went through the rules and regulations of their shows with me. I was in heaven! I also had lunch with the Swedish judge. As bored as Pekka may have been, he didn't show it. My cousin, Tuula, and Pekka took me out to a restaurant where they served reindeer meat. This was the tastiest meat ever. Once again, I'm not sure about our own Canadian beef that we so much bragged about. We travelled by car around Helsinki one more time, seeing Koff, the beer distillery;

the McDonald's that just opened there; the churches; the Presidential Palace; the opera houses; and the government buildings. Soon, my trip came to a close. Tuula and Pekka took me to the airport as tears were flowing. Then, I was back to Toronto.

After a trip like that, it was hard to nourish your way to their way, especially at work. But that is life. Everything was normal at home. It was now time to get my dogs and start my hobby. I formed a kennel name, Windsorpark, in 1985 with the Canadian Kennel Club. February was coming up, and I wanted to go to the Westminster Kennel Club Show in Madison Square Gardens in New York City. I asked my boss for the Monday off so I could fly down there for the day and see the working group. I got the day off, so I boarded a plane, which almost ended up not landing in New York because of a severe snowstorm. We almost landed in Washington, D.C. The plane tried several attempts to land, and finally did. Good! I was in New York for the dog show; I had no interest in seeing the White House. I took a cab from the airport. The cab was slipping and sliding all over the place. We almost crashed into a school bus on some bridge, and the school bus crashed into the bridge's railing. The cab just slithered past the bus. It was an expensive cab ride, and I got out a few blocks before Madison, just to save money, and walked. I paid for my ticket at Madison and bought a catalogue. I was so impressed because the cream of the crop of show dogs could only get this far in the show world. Suppliers from all over lined the arena walls with the latest in dog gear. This was also a benched show, which meant that all Newfoundlands would be together, all pugs together, and so on. All the rows were named for a breed, with a security guard at each end of the rows. The show area was carpeted, and beautiful flowers and plants surrounded the ring. The world's top judges and handlers paraded around and, most importantly, there were North America's top dogs. I was enjoying myself; another dream come true. Before I could blink an eye, it was time for me to return to Toronto. Later that year, in '86, my father bought me a week's pass to Expo '86 in Vancouver; I was able to get a week off and spend time with my friends. Of course, I centered my trip on the Newfoundland Specialty Show held at BC Place. I actually missed Princess Diana's trip there, but my Dad had taken some pictures.

Going home was refreshing, but I considered Toronto home. I had lots of new things to share with my doggy friends who haven't been to Westminster or Expo '86. I had always wanted a collie, but I was taken by the size of the Newfoundland dog and Great Pyrenees. I bought a Great Pyrenees and was dissatisfied with it. I sold her and bought my first Newfoundland from a breeder in the west side of the city. As I was learning the business, and as time went on, I found that that Newfoundland was no-show quality. I was turned off with Canadian breeders, as they put such restrictions on their litter, such as non-breeding contracts, breeding rights, and so on. So, I went to the U.S. for a pup. I bought two dogs from a breeder there, but they turned out to be duds; all these Newfoundlands had severe medical problems. I spent $1,000.00 in one month at the vets; good learning lesson for me. My whole world was centred on dogs. They are my great love and passion forever. I groomed and showed my dogs and got to know the people, the handlers, and the show circuit in and around Ontario. I spent a lot of money travelling for my dog hobby, but I wasn't making any money. It was now going onto three years living in my place, and I was allowed two dogs in that area. I felt it was time to find other accommodations, an acreage. So, I looked on weekends with Yves for a spot. I found one—a gorgeous, white, brick house right on Highway 48, across the street from the school in Beaverton, Ontario. It was almost three acres, had a finished basement, and with a fireplace. The upstairs had the most gorgeous oak flooring. I put an offer on the house for $110,000.00, with conditions that I can build a kennel, get a mortgage, and sell my present home. There was no problem, and the contract was signed. I phoned my girlfriend, Janice, from the BBB, who was now a real estate agent, to list my house. For the house I paid $55,000.00 for, three years later, I sold it for $120,000.00. However, I had to renew my contract for my old house. It wasn't an easy sell, but it got sold, so off Yves and I go.

Yves didn't drive, so he decided that he'd get a room in Toronto and come up on weekends, until he got a driver's license. Nothing really changed because I didn't see him on weekdays anyway. He knew how important it was for me to get my dog hobby going. I rented a Budget Rent A Truck, and Yves and I loaded up our belongings, dogs, ourselves, and drove up north. It was at least one hour north of Toronto. We got settled over the weekend. I was so happy for my dogs because they could run, run, run. Yves got himself a perfect schedule with the bus system, so he had no problem travelling back and forth. All was well, except I needed a job closer to home. I got a job in Richmond Hill for an alarm company called Pyrotronics, later to become Cerberus Pyrotronics. I was a secretary for the main salesman (manager) by the name of Gerry Landmesser. I did the secretarial things like bringing him coffee and bowing down to all his wishes. Personally, I hated secretarial work; I found it so demeaning. At times, I felt I knew more than the boss, was less paid, did all the work but, at times, looked down upon. Nonetheless, it paid my mortgage, so I had to suffer with it. Back at home, life was good. I joined a dog-training course in which the instructor was a Finnish lady named Marja Higginson. This course was held in Sutton, Ontario, about fifteen minutes south of where I lived. I also hired a professional handler by the name of Chris Holman. He was a lawyer and bred boxers. His live-in girlfriend, Carolyn, bred Bull Terriers. I hired Chris to show my future "Best in Show" Newfoundland by the name of Ch. Mudge's Bonnie Bay Clipper. He was one of the best specimens of the breed I've seen in Newfoundlands for some time. I bought him from a breeder in Calgary, Alberta. Some of the long-time local breeders were jealous that I had him. He was my foundation stock for my breeding program introducing Windsorpark Kennels—my kennel—finally. I had everything I ever wanted now, my dogs.

I really enjoyed my new home, but it was still a drive to work. Yves and I were getting along, and he proposed. But I said, "Not this year." I really liked

Yves. He was good to me, but I didn't want to marry him. He said he would wait.

Every Christmas, my relatives in Finland would always send cards or gifts. I was saddened to learn that Anna died on June 20, 1986, nine months after I had visited her. She lived a long, hard life. Being in Beaverton and travelling the distance like I did, I now needed a new vehicle. A girlfriend from the office who lived close to me had her vehicle in Sutton Ford for repairs, so she was driving a demo truck. I was really impressed with her truck. It was all white, with racing stripes, fully loaded, and I wanted it. It was a 1987 Ford Ranger XLT half ton; perfect for transferring my dogs to shows. There was a joke going around the office that said Gerry's secretary has money; she's bought a new stove, fridge, dishwasher, a house, and, now, a new truck. I got financing through Ford Credit. I put $2,000.00 down and owed $14,000.00 over a five-year period. My credit was AAA.

I had since forgotten about Richard. Apparently, he didn't forget about me. I just shut him off cold; he had no idea where I was. Years had gone by since I felt humiliated by him. I received a letter to my address in Beaverton. I knew the handwriting, Richard's. Hmmm, I was surprised. I read his letter. He wanted to see me desperately, I guess to give forgiveness. I though about it for a couple of days. He had his cousin in Vancouver phone my dad to get my address and phone number. I called him and arranged to meet him at a posh restaurant lounge called Timothy's on Yonge Street in Newmarket, Ontario. The drive was equal for both of us. He was happy to see me and vice versa. We solved our problem. He had gotten married, and I basically told him that I am doing just fine. He asked if I needed anything, and there was something I do need—a cap for my truck. Apparently, he was in the middle of selling Car, Truck and Cap Company a telephone system. He said he would work a deal with them in getting me a cap. And he did. He bought the top of the line cap, with fancy windows, lock, and boot. This was very impressive. It finished the whole look of my truck. I thanked him, but not with sex. That he would never get from me. I went back and told Yves that my former boyfriend bought me this cap. He said, "That was nice. Can you go back and ask him for a dining room set?" Richard and I kept our friendship.

I was looking for a good foundation bitch at this point. My friend, just out of Chicago, had a bitch which had excellent hips—very rare in Newfoundlands. She'd sell her to me, plus do the breeding with her Landseer male. I agreed. I finally have a Windsorpark litter. When the breeding was done, I decided that rather than ship Brandy (the Newfoundland foundation bitch), I'll drive down to the Chicago area and pick her up. I left Beaverton early in the morning and basically had to drive around the great lakes. I made it into their area shortly after supper. All was well. I liked Brandy's gait; it was perfect. But I didn't like her head type. Oh well, it didn't matter. I had all the necessary paperwork with me for transferring a dog over the border. After seeing the sights, I left with Brandy a few days later. I was now getting into my third year in Beaverton. It was around 1987-1988. I was enjoying life, my dogs, and Yves, but I hated my job. I found that in every office job, there is someone there who would really hate you, and you would hate them, usually from the same sex. One day, a handful of us were in the lunchroom having lunch, and I cracked a joke. Well, this woman just screamed at me from the other side of the table and called me rotten. I'll never forget looking at her ugly face. Apparently, she had been a long-time secretary of my boss. She went in his office like a roaring idiot. Who knows what she said? When lunch was over, my boss called me in and had an attack of schizophrenia. I really couldn't figure out why he was so mad at me for cracking a joke. It, apparently, got around the plant, and everyone felt sorry for me. It was rude and out of line. From that point on, I hated Gerry Landmeeser. It was tough to work with someone you hate. But I stuck it out. Usually, in every office, there is a blow of some kind. It's forgotten in time until someone else has a big blow.

I was getting ready for my puppies. I had the basement all set up as a nursery. I had a proper cage with an orange plastic tarp. The cage could be opened for two people to squeeze in and help. Brandy was also separated from the males; she had her own room right under my bedroom. Brandy was just busting, and she could not walk up stairs any longer; she was just so heavy. I used to let her out on her own through the basement backdoor. While in Beaverton, I met a girlfriend who was especially good on working with horses, dogs, cats; you name it, she'll fix it. She helped me out. She didn't want any money, just a pup. It was late, around 3:00 A.M. I heard Brandy bark. That was it; it was time. My boss at work knew I'd center some holidays on her whelping, so when I could call in, I did. I went downstairs and saw my first pup—a male Landseer, with the most perfect markings: black head, black saddle, black rump, the rest white, with a few ticking in the front. That's it; he's mine. I kept a list of times, weight, and markings of each pup. It seemed to take some time between pups. Brandy was having a very difficult time whelping. This dog was not well, and she was stuffed with pups. I called the veterinarian to come over. One pup was stuck in Brandy's birth canal. The vet showed me how to go into the birth canal with my hand. I would get into Brandy's canal and feel around. Soon, I would be able to tell if I had the head or bum. If I had the head, I would carefully put my finger around the head and pull from the ears very so slightly. Once the pup came out, Brandy was too ill to do anything. I ended up having to break her sack, get the puppy breathing, cut and tie the cord, and find it a station by its mom. This went onto the next evening. That was not normal. Brandy also had no milk. I had pulled out approximately ten puppies, and there were more. The vet called, and I said that there has got to be a problem. He agreed, came, got Brandy, and off to the vet's clinic we went. Brandy had one pup stillborn in my truck. Apparently, there was two more stuck way up into her rib cage. One died, and one lived. I stayed as long as needed. The pups at home did not have a mother; I became their mother. I called the office and said I wouldn't be returning until Thursday. I had to find someone to help feed these pups while I was at work. I made formula, bought bottles, and fed all these pups by hand: four feedings a day and four feedings at night. I was consistent with the feeding times.

Once I finished the last pup, it was ready to start all over again. I was bushed. The first two weeks were severely important, and I was going to make sure these pups had as good chance as they could. Brandy was in the vet's, recuperating. I decided to get her spayed. I didn't want to put her through this again. This was her last litter. I contacted the chap who sold me Brandy and mentioned her difficulties. I think he knew and just conveniently shipped her to Canada at a big US price tag. I didn't get much luck there, but I learned something new about the dog business. I went to pick up Brandy and was disturbed to see her at the vet, lying on the cement floor next to the garbage. What kind of a vet place is this? I brought Brandy home. She had no interest in the pups, so I relinquished her job and let her relax. I was the pups' mom. As soon as I opened the door, these scrambling pups came to me. It was so cute. I had seven Landseer and three pure black pups. All my Landseer pups were nicely marked. It was a nice litter, but there was much work to do. Of course, it was my first litter, and it was a really tough one. It didn't turn out to be a normal litter. But I certainly learned that if I should have a difficult litter again, I'll know what to do.

In the dog business, you have to like poo—lots of poo, when you have a litter. It is so nice when you can let them outside. I had a winter litter, so my pups were in and out when really young. I used to put them out the basement window. I fenced off an area from the window. The windows were very large for a small pony to go through. The funny part about this is when the pups got older, they still would come in through the window. They weren't scared at all; they just jumped in. The pups were old enough now to get their tattoos. A unique shop in Toronto called The Piranha Shop tattooed litters at $5.00 a pup. I loaded the pups and started off to Toronto, but I stopped by Pyrotronics first. Everyone came out and grabbed a pup, and all the pups were carried all over the office. Even the president had one, but my boss chose to stay out of the fun. It also gave people who are not dog people an idea of the work I had. Having a litter from birth is so sweet; you get to know all the pups' different personalities. I kept two and named them Windsorpark's Sterling Czar and Windsorpark's Lady. Both were Landseers, one male, one female. My plan was to breed Lady with Clipper. Sterling was my showstopper. I was now getting a line going, finally, and it does take time; it took years. Yves was continuing coming up on weekends; our relationship was fine. However, the drive from Beaverton to Richmond Hill was becoming costly.

CHAPTER THIRTEEN

My relationship with my boss, Gerry Landmesser, deteriorated. I hated it at the office, so I started applying for jobs in Newmarket, Lindsay, and Orillia, Ontario, far closer to home and easier on gas and time. I got one interview in Lindsay, but it was not permanent. I got an interview with a company named Dixon Ticonderoga, a very old, established company. They make our famous Pink Pearl erasers, crayons, pencils, and all sorts of writing instruments. It was on an old building, with creeking floors, but the old, unique building was worth preserving. I was interviewed by Ian Hayes and Paul Dalziel. Ian Hayes was the marketing manager, and I'd be his secretary. Paul Dalziel was the Personnel Manager. My job would be to quote prices to the school boards all over Canada, type the quotes, and send samples of requested products or anything new. Of course, I said, "I can do that." I had a second interview a week later. I really didn't think much about it; a second interview is normal. But, when I had a third interview, I was beginning to wonder if I had the right clothing on. Each time, I wore a different dress, thank God. If I remember right, Ian asked if I was married or if I have a boyfriend. Different type of questions for an interview. I got the job. I was so happy to get out of Richmond Hill and Pyrotronics. I'll save at least $100.00 a month on gas. I took a week off in-between jobs. When I started, I was introduced to my coworkers before Ian got me settled in my new post. This was May of 1988. My first month on the job, I didn't feel I was picking up the calculation for quoting the pencils. I asked Ian a lot for help. He helped and covered up any mistakes I may have made. I also typed for Kevin, a younger chap, married with children, and making a way in life. He was okay, but he wasn't a favourite amongst the girls in the office; he was very arrogant. Whatever, I enjoyed the downtown Toronto atmosphere. Ian left for holidays for three weeks with his live-in girlfriend, Julie, a very French girl. They went to Florida. Apparently, Julie had a sister there, and Ian was trying to get a green card and move to the U.S. Considering we were an American-based company, Ian had hopes for a transfer. He was gone for three weeks in July. It was a long three weeks, and I made some goofs. Oh well, it was covered up and corrected. Nonetheless, I thought for sure that I'd lose my job. Ian returned and assured me I would not lose my job. Someone was retiring so we held a party at an exclusive dining lounge in Newmarket. It was very pleasant even though I hardly knew the person; it's one of those got-to-go things. Ian was sitting and staring at me in a very obvious, uncomfortable way. I tried to avoid his stare. I thought it was late enough so, after dinner, I got up to excuse myself. I said, "Thank you. I had a lovely time," and so on. As I was leaving, Ian jumped up and made a spectacle of himself. He approached me in a loud manner, jumped up, and said I wasn't leaving, I was going to the Tudor Bar. I was absolutely taken back and embarrassed; everyone was looking at us. I left and went home to Beaverton; Yves was waiting for me.

Monday morning, I could tell Ian was still embarrassed. But no one mentioned anything, and it was forgotten. However, I began to think, *I think this guy likes me. No, he's my boss. Get that out of your mind, Anita.* It was ridiculous. You don't mix business with pleasure. Soon, I forgot about it. Life was good. I finally understood how to calculate and quote without making a mistake. My dog hobby was keeping me occupied in and around Ontario, and Richard and I remained friends, with the odd lunch and telephone calls. One Friday, Ian asked me to join him after work at the Tudor Bar in the Upper Canada Mall in Newmarket. I said "Okay." He took his car, I drove my truck. He wanted to show off his brand new 1988 New Yorker Landau, what a gorgeous car. Anyway, I met him there. He was such a gentleman. I drank Labatt Lite while he drank Labatt or scotch. It was a nice evening, and we went down to the Aurora Motel on Yonge for more conversation and drinks. I basically let him know how important my dog hobby is to me, my home, and little things people talk about on their first meeting or date. He told me about himself, his girlfriend, former wife, Linda, and family. I was getting pretty drunk, and there was the idea that I should get a room upstairs in the motel. Ian paid for my room. He walked me to my room, and I called Yves that I'd be home tomorrow. Ian had gone into the bathroom. When he came out, I was naked. The look on his face was of surprise. He took his clothes off, and that was the start of our relationship, I think. I returned back to Beaverton the next day. All was fine, but I was terribly embarrassed. On Monday, I was very sure I'm going to loose my job; I slept with my boss. Oh my god, I've never done this before, and I was somewhat worried. Monday morning arrived, and I was very shy and ashamed. But when I saw Ian, he was the same; nothing was said. He asked me to join him at the Tudor Bar for lunch; I'd take my truck, he'd take his car. We fully discussed our weekend together. No one else knew but us, so there wasn't anything to worry about. We dropped the issue. Back to work, we went separately. Later in the day, Ian asked me to join him at the Tudor after work. Once again, we went our separate ways, said good night, and so on. (I would always laugh inside. "Good night, Ian," when in actual fact, I was meeting him in three minutes). This started to become a routine for several months to come. On one lunch hour, he gave me the most gorgeous gold earings. He had bought them in Florida and just gave them to me in August of 1988. Ian started draping me with lovely jewellry. I wasn't originally attracted to Ian. I liked tall men. Ian was short, had a mustache, and, in my mind, not that great looking. He had to work for my interest. We continued the business as business; no one noticed a thing at work. But off work, something was happening between the two of us. We went shopping one day, and he bought the loveliest silk camisoles—one black and one white—and other sexy night items, plus two new bras—one black, one white.

Ian was now commuting to Beaverton and Aurora. One evening, he just went for a drive to Beaverton, came in for fifteen minutes, and left. Another evening, Ian and I were in my truck parked on the parking lot of the dealership where he was waiting for his car. He and I got busy. He took my nylons off and put them in this coat pocket and put my glasses in his inside coat pocket. We got so busy that I forgot my wears when I started my drive home. The next morning, I needed my glasses. My dad was staying a month or two, and we were going to Meaford for the weekend. Yves was going to look after the dogs as usual. I didn't know what to do. I couldn't phone Ian, what if Julie answered the phone? So I called Kathy, the receptionist at Dixon. I explained to her that Ian has my glasses and asked if she could call him and ask him to meet me at Upper Canada Mall at 11:00 to return them. My dad, by this time, was somewhat drunk. Anyway, I met Ian there, and we had a few beers. This was the first time Ian met my dad who was totally drunk. My dad was loud and was nailing him with questions like: "What do you want with my daughter?" and all that fatherly stuff. It was embarrassing, to say the least. Anyway, I got my glasses, and Dad and I headed out for Meaford. First stop was old Bill Cargo's place for more beer, then off to Owen Sound to visit his sister, Rosena. All in all, it was an okay weekend.

Ian and I continued our meetings at lunch and after work, which was now daily. Ian decided that it was time to get rid of his girlfriend and my boyfriend. Our relationship was working quickly and overtime. Ian knew what he wanted. But getting rid of people in a nice way isn't easy. One does hurt the other. Ian let me wear his three-diamond and eighteen-karat gold ring, a ring that he had set with his mother's wedding stones. I only wore it around him, not around Yves or at work. Back at work, Kathy was the only person who knew Ian and I was now an item. Kathy didn't tell anyone. It was getting into Thanksgiving of 1988, and Dad was still with me. Ian decided that that was the weekend everyone—Yves and Julie—gets out. He had a plan. Julie was to go. She did, but not without a fight. I was to go home and tell Yves to pack up his stuff and I would drive him to Toronto. Once I got Yves all packed and into my truck, I was supposed to phone Ian. We would pass each other on the highway, flash our lights, I would continue to Toronto, and, later, Ian would spend the weekend with my Dad and me. We were going to eat the turkey and potatoes that Yves had already started. This was cruel. Yves went to my dad and said, "Anita is kicking me out." My dad just walked quietly into his bedroom, without saying a word. My dad felt bad. He liked Yves; everyone did. As I was driving Yves back to Toronto, we were relatively silent most of the way. I saw Ian going north; he saw me going south. We flashed our lights. Yves had no clue what was going on. Once back in Toronto, Yves unloaded his personal wares and proposed marriage to me. He wanted me; I was his woman. I was hurting him terribly; he was choked.

I went back to the ranch. The whole drive was around one and a half hours for me. The Thanksgiving dinner was ready, and Ian presented me with the most gorgeous diamond engagement ring—a pear-shaped diamond surrounded with twenty smaller diamonds. This was in October 1988. The ring was worth $5,600.00. It was the nicest thing anyone has given me; it was so breathtaking. My dad just went "Ohhhhh..." My dad liked Ian, and Ian liked my dad. We made a call to Ian's dad, Clifford, in Montreal, and he welcomed me into the family. I thought that was very nice, considering he hasn't met me yet. But I guess he knew over the phone that Ian and I were happy. I was introduced into the Hayes family. Oddly enough, my first marriage was to William Cameron Hayes, and my up-and-coming marriage was to Ian William Thomas Hayes. I didn't have to change my credit cards or drivers license. That was different. During that weekend, it was decided. Because of my dogs, he'd move in with me. What are we going to do with two houses? We would sell mine, and I'd move into Ian's home in Aurora, Valallah Heights. Ian wasn't impressed with my Newfoundland dogs; they had to go, but Menu can stay. I can't give up my beloved dogs, I just can't. So we came to a compromise; we'll get a dog that we'd both enjoy. A collie was the choice. I knew a Finnish breeder who apparently had puppies. When they were ready to go to their new homes, we'd pick up Ben. I wore my engagement ring to the office. When people asked me about it, I just said, "I always had this ring. I just thought I'd wear it rather than keep it in my box."

Regardless if whether my coworkers bought that story, no one mentioned anything. Kathy knew Ian and me was an item, so rather than have two vehicles travelling the same distance every day, I asked her if it would be okay to park my truck at her place during the evening and if I could pick it up and drive it the one block to Dixon. That way, Ian and I could go to Beaverton in one vehicle. She didn't mind. Ian shut his house down for several months. One day, Ian's boss commented, "Why does Ian have snow on his car when there is no snow in Aurora, and Anita doesn't have snow on her truck when there is snow in Beaverton?" Very clever. Possibly, our secret won't be a secret for long. He lived with me and all my Newfoundland dogs for several more months. It was coming into Christmas, and Ian asked me to ask for permission off to join him in Jamacia. I was to ask permission between Christmas and New Year. This could not simply be done. I just joined the company, and I am asking for time off, especially at Christmas time; some people of twenty years didn't get that time off. But I got off. I told them I was going to Vancouver to visit my family there. Ian and I went to Jamacia and stayed at the Sandals Royal Carribean adults-only club. He gave me a very special present: he had specially made a gold Newfoundland dog- shaped pendant on a gold chain. Behind it engraved was "Clipper: My Best in Show Dog." Ian loved jewellry; he should have been a jeweller.

CHAPTER FOURTEEN

We boarded the plane to our hot spot. Sandals was a new place. Apparently, it got a little damaged from the tidal wave that hit Jamacia a few weeks earlier. You could see the devastation still there, and the poverty. Here we were, going to an exclusive sun club. The cab driver said we could drink in the car. Really, well we were at home with that. Ian booked a suite on the top floor of a two-story housing area overlooking the bay. It was beautiful. Our main plan was to lie around the pool and relax. We didn't want to get involved with the games that were available to win a sandals necklace; we just did nothing but relax around the pool. Every morning, we went to our same spot by the pool and basically stayed there all day. We were in and out of the pool, in the warmth, and having beer delivered at their slow pace. While in Jamacia, Ian took me to a very posh restaurant over looking Montego Bay. Apparently, Princess Margaret had dined there. The view was breathtaking. Evidently, Ian had taken his first wife, Linda, there on their honeymoon, and we were sitting at the very same table. He said Linda vomited here. I promised Ian I wouldn't vomit. My meal was lovely, and I was enjoying myself. The next day, we went to see downtown Jamacia. I was horrified of the stink and poverty. It was scary. One black guy wanted a dollar if he'd show us around. The cab driver informed us about the scams downtown. I was uncomfortable down there, but we had to persevere and wait for our cab to return an hour later to pick us up at the very same spot where he dropped us off. There was an old donkey on show. The Jamacians wanted a dollar to take a picture of this donkey. Ian got two beers, and we sat on a bench right opposite the donkey, where the cab should come to pick us up. Ian was risk taker; he was going to take a picture of this donkey. I said, "No." They'll break the camera if we didn't give them a dollar. While we were sitting, drinking our beer, Ian held the camera on his lap and snapped a picture; it turned out okay. He was always taking more risks than me. All I wanted to do was go back to Sandals. Finally, the cab came. We went back to our room, put on our bathing suits, and went back to the pool; the hell with downtown Jamacia. Near the close of our trip, we joined various outings at Sandals, such as live bands and dancing. We got a table with other people and thoroughly enjoyed our evenings; it was all so romantic. Well, it was time to go back to Toronto, so we joined another couple who was also on our flight. We went to the Jamaican airport, what a zoo. I've never seen such disorganization. People were pushing and scrambling all over the place; it was awful. I and some other girls told our mates that we were going to the bar, and they should get the boarding passes. An hour later, Ian and one of the girls' mate joined us, totally flustered and really needed a beer. It was a zoo, and we almost didn't make it to that chartered flight. I am not in a hurry to go back to Jamacia; I got tired of the hayman, their music, and their slow way of serving. Back to Toronto for New Year!

Beaverton was in a snow belt, and the weather could get annoying. My dogs were being boarded at Chris and Carolyn's, and so was Menou. We did pick up Menou and left the dogs there for another day or so. It was New Year's Eve, and we were invited to Ian's neighbours, Stan and Irene. It was a secret the two men had for some time, when Irene found out she got mad at Stan. Anyway, it was a successful New Year.

Ian and I headed back to Beaverton. We had a lot to drink, and, early that morning, Menou was crying at the top of the staircase leading to the basement. Menou's litter box was perched up on a table away from the dogs. Apparently, Menou couldn't get to the basement as it was fully flooded. At least two inches of water was flowing in. The sump pump broke. Where do you get a new sump pump in the country on New Year's Day? What a mess! The basement was fully carpeted, and the rug began to really stink. I phoned up a carpenter and begged him to find a sump pump and help stop the water from coming in. He did, thank God. It took the three of us two days to clean the water and several weeks to dry it out. I had to take the house temporarily off the market. We were back in Newmarket, back to work. It was obvious now that Ian and I was an item. We both came back with tans; I hadn't gone to Vancouver. That meant we did not have to hide anymore! No one really cared and thought our relationship was meant to be. Ian and I thought for sure we'd both get fired. Interpersonal relationships in an office environment are simply not done. My dad decided to come out to Beaverton again, but also to take a trip to Meaford and Owen Sound. He has a sister there, Rosena. Apparently, Dad was already in Owen Sound and we were going to pick him up. Ian and I stayed at the Holiday Inn while Dad was at Rosena's. In the morning, the phone rang, and my dad asked to speak to Ian. Evidently, Dad had a wild drinking night, wrecked Rosena's trailer, took a cab, was obnoxious, and the cab driver took him to the detox center. We were to pick him up there. Well, Ian and I were both equally hungover. Nonetheless, we went to pick up dad. Dad was so embarrassed; he didn't say one word the whole trip back.

Ian was a good salesman, and Dixon had a branch in England. There was talk of sending Ian and me over to England for two years to get the operation up and running and increase the sales. Apparently, there was a sales show over in London a week before I was supposed to go. Ian worked the show. And some of the girls in the office were actually jealous; I had only been with the company for ten months, and I was having a paid trip to London, England, business class. My job over there would be looking for accommodations and banking facilities while Ian's responsibilities were to learn about England and to sell in the northern part. He has English in his background, as his grandfather was English. I was free to go as his wife. Immigrating would be no problem. Finally, I was to go to meet Ian in London. This was so exciting! I arrived in London early in the morning. I was supposed to take a taxi to the Swallow Hotel where I would meet the CEO and Ian for breakfast. I was in my best professional behavior; this would be an opportunity of a lifetime and a great experience. I had tea and small talk. Ian was supposed to work the show this day, so it was suggested that Ian take me to our room, get freshened up, and also attend the show. Their show rules were very different from North American rules. You just don't go into people's booth and help yourself. Dixon had a very impressive booth, and I knew we'd have a few days in London for this show. Being a lover of the British Royal Family, Ian was so excited to show me Buckingham Palace. We took a cab there, and I was just taken away by its history and the great wealth that is inside. Also, a team of the Queen's Guards was on horseback, trotting by. Ian and I walked all around the whole palace. I was so overwhelmed. We stopped at Harrods, had lunch, and shopped around. Harrods was a very busy and crowded place. I, of course, had to buy something. I bought their bubble bath. We were informed that we were to go to Peterborough the next day with the manager of the English division of Dixon. We would drive up from London to Peterborough. Considering we were tourists, he drove us through the ambassador's area, an area with great, big, tall fences with mansions on the other side. Farther into the country, we experienced the beauty of old England. We stayed at the Swallow Hotel in Peterborough, a far more modern motel than its London outlet. In work during the days, my job was to find housing, banks, and do the housewife role. I did my homework. I am sure the CEO was impressed; I just didn't use the time for nothing. One evening, Ian and I found a real old pub walking distance from the hotel. There was actually a man putting coal in the fireplace there, really old stuff. The English beer was a little heavy for me, but we'd drink anything anyway. The British have very strict drinking laws. I remember Ian helped himself or showed the bartender how to pour a drink. Ian gave himself more than an ounce. The bartender freaked. He got the hint; this bartender could have lost his job because of Ian. I was sure he hated Ian. Working during the day was basically introducing Ian to the ropes. It was apparent that this boss had no interest in hiring Ian; he found Ian a threat. Back in Canada, we had a lovely home and car, and this chap wanted to lower our standard of living by giving Ian a less luxurious car than his other sales representatives, a lower wage, and lousy benefits. This was not going to work. Ian and I discussed this fully. Why should we live less here? We were better back home. We both worked hard to get this far; we were not interested in going backwards. The week went fast. Ian and I took the train back to London and spent the last two days seeing other sights: Tower of London, the Crown Jewels, Westminster Abbey, and so on. Not much was said about relocating to Peterborough anymore. It was a closed program. Back at home, I finally sold my house. I was to move into Ian's house in Aurora. I made over $100,000.00 on my sale, so I paid off Ian's house—$70,000.00. I paid for the new fence and bought furniture. Julie had taken some of her furniture and some rooms were left vacant. It was easier to get rid of Yves, but Julie put up a fight. She was going for Ian's house. To compensate for this, he wrote a contract with, several pages thick, to Julie, and paid her off with $6,000.00. This cleaned Ian's cash flow right out. Ian had to sell his beloved Honda Gold Wing motorcycle to pay Julie. But it was worth it; better than splitting the house. It would have been a really messy affair Ian didn't need. Our London trip was in March, and Ian set our wedding date for July 14, 1989. It was no secret at the office, so Ian and I went to work together. I had sold my Newfoundland dogs, and Menou moved in Aurora with us. Menou hated the car and had a very difficult time travelling; she was just simply scared. Our collie pup was ready to come home. We went to pick up Ben. Ben became Ian's dog. Ian loved Ben. There was definitely a close attachment between them and to myself as well. While Ian and I were planning our wedding, Dixon was planning to get rid of us. We didn't know a thing at that point. Ian's brother, Robert, suggested that we plan our honeymoon around his travels as well. Not a bad idea. We would have a Hayes reunion in Lahr, Germany. Ian's other brother, Dr. Ralph Hayes, his wife, and children were living there. Clifford, Ian's dad, would join us over there from Montreal. This would be the first time for me to meet the Hayes family. Robert would fly in from Montreal with his daughter to Paris. We'd meet Robert in Paris from our Toronto flight on July 16, 1989. (I had married husband number one on July 16). That was just the first planning; it was not confirmed just yet.

Ian and I were picking out types of wedding invitations, wedding this and that, and the guest list. Only top executives at Dixon were invited. My dog handler, Chris Holman, would be best man and Irene, our neighbour, best woman. Chris, also being a lawyer, was drawing up the prenuptial agreement. That was when Ian and I had our first really big disagreement. There was no way I was signing a document basically saying that if the marriage goes toast, Ian walks away with three fourths of my money. We never did make an agreement, and we never had a money problem ever since. All these years, I had looked after myself, paid my bills, did shopping, made travel arrangements, and survived. I wasn't rich, but not dirt poor either. I always had the things I needed. The wants are always there, mind you. Of course, all upcoming marriages have the real things to take care of; Ian decided that he will be looking after me. He will pay all the bills, all my credit card bills included, my car insurance, my car payments, everything. We had a joint chequing and savings account. Ian was a life insurance kind of guy, so he got out $100,000.00 for me in case of his death and $100,000.00 for himself in case of my death. He insured his New Yorker: he insured the stove, the fridge, and always bought warranties. He was just one of those kinds of guys. Neither of us had hidden money elsewhere. No discrepancies there. Ian decided to send out wedding invitations in three parts, like a big-surprise store opening; it worked. It was very imaginative, and every guest would get a coaster with our names on it and the wedding date. These coasters were made of heavy brass and leather, with gold letters in the center, presented in a black-velvet pouch. We thought it would be much nicer than pieces of wedding cake or a book of matches. Each day, we thought of new things to do or add to our big day. Back at work, Dixon decided that I couldn't work with Ian anymore, that they will offer me a receptionist job with less pay. I wondered what they were going to do with Kathy; I guess they would promote her. I wasn't happy with this offer, and everyone was already several weeks into negotitation with what to do with me. Ian decided that I should quit and stay at home, relax and enjoy being a new bride, and we can go on from there. After all, our house was paid for. Our house being paid for was a slap in the face to the president of Dixon. Tim was always jealous of Ian, his good salesmanship, and bubbly personality. To have a paid-off house bugged Tim. I guess men can have an affect on each other the same way women can in a tightly-closed office environment. Our invitations were ready, so I went to pick them up. Ian and I planned on a four closed party at the actual ceremony and the reception for our friends at our house. I would make the sandwiches and food the night before. I also bought wedding decorations for the living room and dining room. Our invitations were mailed. The top executives of Dixon and a group of close friends were invited. Life was good, and Ben was growing fast. Ian and I were just excited about our wedding. One evening, we decided that we would go over to Europe for three weeks. The first couple of days would be in Paris, then Germany, Finland, and Sweden. This trip would be divided equally so we can spend a reasonable time with all our relatives. This trip cost around $6,000.00. I paid for this trip. Remember: this was without having to book hotels; we had places to stay. It was a good chunk of money back in 1989, but this was our honeymoon! As usual, Ian went off to work daily. He always dressed himself in the finest suits and silk ties. You could tell we were two very happy people together. One morning, Ian returned home around 10:00 A.M. I knew what happened, Ian was let go from Dixon. This was a big blow to Ian; he never really recovered from that affair. Apparently, Ian was given three weeks to stay on at Dixon while he looked for other employment. This would not affect our honeymoon. This was a clever way of not letting it be so obvious that it was wrongful dismissal, or having to pay Ian a lump some package. Ian would show up in the mornings and leave Dixon around noon every day. We decided which was now best for us. Because of this tragic financial loss, Ian and I couldn't really afford to go on our honeymoon. My last savings was for our trip. I suggested, "Why let Dixon ruin our honeymoon? We should go and worry about money later." Nonetheless, I wrote the top executives at Dixon that our wedding was off. In other words, he was saying, "You're no longer invited." That was a good move. Ian was getting depressed daily. I suggested, "Why bother returning to Dixon? After all, that's what they want. Let's just focus on our wedding and trip." He agreed. He didn't show up at the company, and he was coming around. We had plans of selling the house and moving to Mississauga where Ian can go back to this other writing instrument company called Faber-Castell. Ian did very well there. In those days, he was making $70,000.00 per year. We would focus on that plan after we get back. Ian and I would drive around Newmarket, and, every once in a while, we'd bump into someone from Dixon. Everyone other than the top executives thought we both got a bum deal, and we did. Wedding day was approaching. I bought a lovely navy-blue dress, nothing particularly fancy, but attractive. I also went searching for navy-blue shoes; they were hard to find. I realized it was summer time. It was hard to find navy-blue shoes, so I settled for these plastic navy-blue shoes that was the right colour. They certainly weren't worth wearing for any other reason except that I needed that colour. Ian said we should be colour coordinated. He was wearing a navy-blue suit and silk tie. Chris, Irene, Ian, and I travelled together in Ian's New Yorker to the City Hall in Newmarket, just the four of us. Can you believe Irene was teary eyed? It was a quick service, just what we wanted—something simple. We were then married. Ian had a photographer waiting outside for us. We took some beautiful pictures in and around the grounds of the city hall. Back to the house, Irene was helping me with the food; most of it was already prepared. As the evening was getting on, our guests were arriving. Ben was in his cage, so he wouldn't get fur on people's outfits. It was a nice reception that lasted until 4:00 A.M. Ian and I were both hungover and tired. When, on the fifteenth, I saw the mess, and I told Ian we should have hired a caterer. The smell, ashtrays, took a burden on my head. Ian helped me to clear up everything. It took several hours. I decided that because we were going away for three weeks, I should also thank all the guests for the gifts. So I wrote everyone "Thank You" cards while with my hangover. At least, when we get back, that project is done and not weeks later. Once we completed them, we went next door to Irene's and continued partying. We all had lots in common; we like socializing. Ian always likes his cold one; I was his live-in partner for life.

That evening, we drove Ben up to Marja's, Ben's breeder. She was going to look after him while we were gone for three weeks. Irene and Stan will look after Menou and the plants. We had an early evening because on July 16, I will be flying to Paris, France with my husband. We boarded our plane. Ian brought on our handycam, and this would be the first time he was going to use it. (I also mentioned that, many years ago, I had married Bill Hayes in July 16.). He wasn't interested. Because we were flying business class, we had access to the first class lounges all over Canada and Europe. Ian and I always enjoyed our beer, anywhere. Our flight to Paris was your normal flight with movie, drinks, dinner, and sleep, if you can. Once we landed in Paris, we had a three-hour wait for Robert and his daughter coming in from Montreal. Clifford was already in Germany. Sitting in the Paris airport was different; we kept seeing the same hooker working in the place the whole three hours. I wondered how many people pick up hookers at an airpoirt. Is she booked in the airport's hotel? In Paris, being a major travel spot, I saw the most interesting of people.

Finally, Robert arrived, and we took a cab to our hotel near the railroad station. In fact, it was just across the street from the railroad station. It was booked by Robert; it was very cheap. Robert had been over to Europe before and knew where to go. Ian and Robert also spoke French. The four of us went to all the spots in Paris. Each day was a new day for some sightseeing. I was overwhelmed. Don't forget: we were newly married. (My diamonds just sparkled). I was one happy little girl. Ian always called me honey or his little girl. We were going to grow old together!

The weather was very warm in Paris. You wouldn't need any overcoat or sweater. Robert had a big bout with cancer and beat it, so this trip was an award trip for him. He was always around 200 lbs, but, now, he was down to 140 lbs. He definitely looked like Ian. Ian was the baby out of four: Peter, Ralph, Robert, and Ian. Peter was the only one who did not join us overseas. He was in Daytona Beach with his wife, working at a 7-11, and was much of a recluse. Ian's mother, Ena, passed away some time ago. Robert's oldest daughter was around sixteen, and Robert wanted her to see Europe. The youngest girl will get her turn next year. We would all meet for breakfast and decide on our daily plans. That day, we went up the Arc de Triomphe. From way up there, we saw all of Paris, the wayward way people drove, and the Eiffel Tower. We took our time and walked down the famous street where Hitler conquered the French and claimed victory. I loved the outdoor cafés. Ian and I stopped for a beer and lunch. We just sat, watching people. I was amazed that the French eat while they walk. Everyone had a bottle of water or a sandwich. Also, you had to pay for the use of the toilet. Not only that, I had to figure out how to flush the toilet. The toilets on the street stunk. The toilets indoors stunk as well. They were built closed in, no airflow. I almost puked while entering these places and was flabbergasted that you had to pay to pee. Ian and I walked all the way down and up the other side and stopped for beers here and there. By the time we reached the top of the road, we had to use the washroom. I laughed. Downstairs we'd go, men on one side, women on the other. There was a big window on the men's side, and I could actually see Ian peeing. As we met in the common area, Ian motioned to me not to pay; we were running for it, up the narrow staircase to the street. We did! No one came after us. We thought we were cool. Ian knew French, and he also knew how to get back to our hotel by subway. That was a great help because I was lost. The next day would be on the Eiffel Tower. Here we went up the big, old, steel tower. It was jam-packed with people, and it was very hot that day. It was even uncomfortable to be outside. I remember Ian walking on the metal flooring that seemed to be just sitting unnailed on the floor. It moved, and Ian jumped so high. I got scared to walk on that, we might fall through. We were actually glad to get down from that tower. I wouldn't make a big effort to go up it again. We also took a riverboat ride along the Rhine and saw some of Paris's historical buildings and churches. We saw one church that we just had to add to our itinerary. On the nineteenth, we went to the Louvre. There was a three-hour wait to get into this museum. The Mona Lisa is in there. Ian and I travelled through this place as if we were on a track meet to the beer at the other end. However, we weren't all that impressed with the museum. We left Robert there and carried on our own way. I found Paris a dirty city. Ian and I sat at one outdoor café around rush hour. We had pasta, as we both love pasta. At around 5:00 P.M., the city seems to back the sewers and water was coming upward from the sewers. What a smell. And there we were, trying to enjoy dinner with that smell. Opposite from where I was sitting, a male was thoroughly enjoying his mussels. I can't stand seafood, or its smell. This guy was eating his mussels to the point where you had to watch but couldn't because he was so gross. He had those empty shells piled high like a mountain on a spare plate. I had to stop looking at him or I'd puke my own dinner. I said to Ian, "We've got to leave this place." We went down the road to another outdoor café. There was certainly no shortage of café's in Paris. I noticed these, long, thin breads in a basket by the door of this shop/restaurant with various fruits and a menu. Ian and I had a beer. I noticed a dog came and peed on the bread, and someone else came over to buy the bread. This bread was not covered; it was just there. Then, right in front of us, a bagman, with a dog, laid a straw mat down on the sidewalk in front of us and went to sleep. People just walked around or over him while his mutt was guarding him.

Robert had bought a car in Paris, and, as our trip closed there, we drove from Paris to Lahr, Germany. Robert knew the route; he had done this before. All smokers were in the backseat. Robert and I had the front seat. It was a beautiful countryside. You could see an odd castle, way up in the hills, here and there. Ralph and his Chinese wife knew we were coming. Apparently, we arrived late, and supper was burnt. We didn't notice; it all seemed okay to me. Ralph opened their fine wine, which you can buy all over Europe, to toast me into the family—a big welcome. It was very, very nice. This was my first meeting with the Hayes family: Clifford, Eileen, Ralph, Robert, and the children. Ralph is a physician for the Canadian Forces base. He rented a huge house amongst the trees. This was a five-bedroom house, rather modern for Germany, I assume. Ian and I had our own room, Clifford had his own room, Kim had her own room, and Robert had his own room. Being in Ralph's place, there were rules. *Do not keep lights on unnecessarily. No smoking*. We must conserve water, so Ian and I had to have a shower together, turn on the tap, get wet, lathered, turn it off, and back on again. All tin foil and Saran Wrap was saved, paper bags were disposed. I followed all the rules, but Ian broke one—the smoking. The next day, Ralph loaded us all up, and we went to see a fifteenth century castle. Clifford stayed at the bottom of the castle, but we younger people walked up and up the worn stone stairs to the top. It was breathtaking, knowing the history of this castle and know that someone lived here at one time. Then we walked down and back to the car. I joined Clifford and got to know him. That day, we walked through this old German town. It was magnificent, with its flowers and the way they paint their homes, with great pride and so very clean. Even the public toilet was spotless and, thank god, free, but I still couldn't figure out how to flush it. I actually came out and asked the lady behind me how to flush the toilet. Was I embarrassed? No. The woman could tell by my accent that I wasn't German. We took many pictures and stopped at an old war park where machinery from the war such as tanks and guns were on display. Then, we had lunch. Eileen made sandwiches for us all and brought some beer. Ian brought his handycam along. No one else could touch this gadget, only Ian. Unfortunately, through the whole three weeks, Ian was only in the first part of the video for a few seconds. Eileen had lovely suppers every evening, and, every day, we went somewhere. Ralph even drove us down the *autobon*. I thought that wasn't so great; it was just an old four-lane road. Our trip in Germany was coming to a close. Ralph wanted to take the family to a restaurant where they have deer. The deer, actually, were bred there, and you could pick the one you like. It was different to see all those animals running around when you knew you were going to eat them. We all sat at a picnic table at the restaurant's outdoor patio. It was a lovely meal. We had good conversation, except little Fraser was acting up, and Eileen had to leave her table to settle him down, only for her to pick at cold food. Kids.

Robert and his daughter were going to venture south while Ian and I were going to Frankfurt to catch a plane to Helsinki. Clifford was staying in Germany for another week or so. Ralph took us to the train station in town, where we board a train to Frankfurt. Landing in Frankfurt was interesting. I had never seen so many tracks of train. I remember Ian and I were running like stink to catch the train, from the downtown station, that would take us to the airport. We made it by only seconds. We were puffing away on that short ride to the airport. The tracks were all numbered, so we had no problem. Had we not ran, we would have missed that airport train. First place to go to was the first class lounge. There, they handled your ticket and baggage. Ian and I travelled light; we just had one carry-on bag each. We had none of that waiting-for-a-suitcase stuff. After all, we were staying with relatives and could do laundry at each place. Once settled in the Maple Leaf Lounge, we had a beer, relaxed, and discussed our next destination. We had several hours' wait there. No big deal; we're on our honeymoon. Once aboard, Ian was really doing his cam-recording of the flight. Then, we took off. Hello to everyone back home and hello to Helsinki. *Here honey, Helsinki, my wife is very excited now*. My cousins, Tuula and Pekka, were waiting for us at the airport. We would spend the beginnings with them. We arrived around 9:00 in the evening and were a little intoxicated. We sat outside, on their patio, and had more beer, Finnish beer. Now that my Finland trip was already familiar to me, this would be Ian's turn for Finnish hospitality. Tuula and Pekka let us have their main bedroom, and, of course, Pekka had cut the usual birch branches for us both and started the sauna. Considering I had sauna experience, I showed Ian the ropes. We sat down there with our sauna beer. Ian couldn't get used to the heat and the steam. It took him several days to endure the Finns' bathing system. The next day was driving around Helsinki. Of course, the market, and pretty much everything else, had been shown to me in 1985. Ian was really impressed with this country. We were to go to Paltamo to see the rest of my family. Leena was our translator there. We took the train from Riihimaki to Kajaani. We actually saw the Russian train parked next to ours. We were both bug-eyed. This train trip took most of the day—eight hours from Riihimaki to Kajaani. Tuula and Pekka would meet us up north by their cottage later in the week. I saw all the trains that were leftovers from the war on the side of the track. I kept thinking how my mother had been on these trains. Once in Paltamo, Leena greeted us. It was just walking distance to their home. We got used to sign language, and Ian picked up the language for ping-pong. Taisto had an old, crooked table in the backyard, and Ian played there frequently. Ian was also impressed as Finland is known as the Land of the Midnight Sun. The sun doesn't set in the summer, so all of July, the sun shined. At three o'clock in the morning, the sun is already bright, and Ian couldn't get over this.

All my relatives had wedding presents, cakes, and elaborate Finnish dinners for us. Ian fell in love with Finland. We spent a day fishing and swimming, and it was always everyone together. Now that everything was covered, we were to meet Tuula and Pekka at their cottage up north. They picked us up and off we went. They were already there with their two children, their collie named Nellie, and their rabbits. Our sleeping area was the small cottage a few steps away from the main cottage. Their refrigerator was a hole in the ground, with dirt, and there was an outhouse. I can't stand outhouses; I'd rather do my thing in the bush. The only sanitary place was the sauna. Pekka was making us birch branches, while I was waiting for the sauna to heat up. Ian and I just relaxed; our jackets zippered up to our chins. The mosquitoes were plenty and huge. No one informed me about these pests. After the sauna, we went to bed. I couldn't stand it; it was cold right by that lake. I really wanted the trip to end. It did, several days later. Because Tuula's car was full of kids and animals, Tuula gave us their key to the house back in Kerava.

We boarded the train for Kerava. Once we arrived there, we decided to stop at a pasta restaurant called Ravintola ProvenCale. There were only a few people in the place, but it was very beautifully decorated. It was quite a classy place. The owner was from Italy who married a Finnish girl. We were really getting the real stuff. The menu was exciting, lots of different pastas and pizzas. I kept one of the menus for my photo album. We told the owner we were from Canada. During our wait for dinner, we had a glass of Koff, a Finnish beer. It was served in a tall Koff glass, a very pretty glass. At the end of our meal, we asked the owner if we could take the glasses back to Canada. He said we could. We caught a cab to Tuula's afterward. They were most likely behind us by car. We decided to relax in the sauna. Ian was now a good camp guy; he could get it rolling. And I got the beer. Ian was getting used to the heat, but, now, he wanted to do the cooling-off period, I guess pretending we were going to jump in the lake. So, he figured we should go outside, cool off, and return to the sauna. Actually, he probably just wanted a cigarette. And off we went with our beer to cool off outside. I grabbed a small hand towel on the way out. There we were, naked on the front porch of my cousin's home in Finland. The bugs were going into the house, so Ian closed the door. It was a peaceful evening except, just like that, rain started to pour, and I mean pour. I had a shower cap on my head, and the droplets were bouncing off. We went to go inside, but the door was locked! Oh, my God, what do we do now?! We're naked outside! Ian told me to walk around the house to see if there was an open window, so I walked through the mud around the house and saw that there was no open window. Then, we remembered that one of the neighbours had the key to the house because they were feeding the hamster. But which house? That rain was really coming down. The houses were not that close by; it was a walk. Ian decided that I should go to the door naked. We argued as to who was going to what house for the key. It was decided that it was better that a naked woman should go to the door than a naked man, so I squeezed this hand towel over my body. It just barely covered my breasts and other private area. Off I went into the mud and up the dirt road, rain bouncing off my shower cap. Ian was calling, "Are you okay?"

I knocked on the door, though I wasn't sure if this woman or man speaks English. A woman answered the door, and the look on her face was of shock. I said very carefully that I am Tuula's cousin from Canada and was locked out of the sauna and asked if she had the key. In perfect English, she said, "No, I don't have the key. The other neighbour has the key."

I asked her, "Would you be so kind to get the key for me?" I couldn't face another house. This lady was kind. I walked with her to the driveway, and she went and got Tuula's key. When I got back, I was very wet and muddy. Ian opened the door. We were now laughing so hard, Ian was actually rolling on the floor. Just as this was all happening, my cousin Tuula, Pekka, and their kids came home. They could hear us laughing from outside. We had covered ourselves by then, and, when they came in with the luggage, we told them the story. Everyone just burst out with laughter. Then, we took pictures. If there was anything on this trip, nothing could top our sauna story.

CHAPTER FIFTEEN

Our Finland trip was coming to a close. Ian and I had spent two weeks with people, lots of people. Tuula decided to take us to Stockholm, Sweden. Tuula, her daughter, Lisa, Ian, and I boarded a luxurious cruise ship, the *Viking Line*, from Helsinki to Stockholm. While boarding, I was swinging my arm and hit my diamond on some steel. I mentioned this to Ian, and he said we'd look at it when we get back to Toronto. This trip was breathtaking. It had everything on board: casino, dining, and shows. Ian and I were in seventh heaven. It was a Finnish ship, the staterooms were very clean, and you could sleep overnight and arrive in Stockholm in the morning. We all went to the shows, and I slipped off to the casino. They had scratch tickets and other interesting video lottery terminals. While we were having breakfast, we enjoyed the beautiful islands around Sweden. We were getting closer, about another one and a half hours. I loved Sweden. Being a monarchist, I was taken away by the palace where the king and queen work and have state dinners. The government buildings, the elite shops, the transit, and our hotel were very new and modern in downtown Stockholm. We all walked, walked, and walked for three days through the fine parts of Sweden. Tuula even took us to the Royal Armoury at the Royal Palace. While we were getting our tickets, Ian was fidgeting with the handycam. The guard there was very harsh and concerned; he thought Ian was going through the Armoury with his camera. Actually, Ian was just rearranging his camera, unaware that the guard was fuming. Finally, my cousin spoke Swedish to settle him down and told him that we had no plans to use the camera in the Royal Palace. We carried on to seeing the treasures of the past and present Swedish Royal Family. Anything royal just gets me bubbling. I was in heaven, enjoying this trip. Our finances were getting low. Thank God, back in Germany, Robert lent $1,000.00 to Ian brotherly love. Sweden is a lovely, picturesque city, but, of course, I like Finland more. Our trip to Sweden was coming to a close. Tuula went back to Helsinki, and Ian and I boarded a prop plane from Sweden to Berlin. On this trip, we were surely alone. The plane we were on was relatively small, with just a few people on it, although full. There was a real funny chap sitting not too far from us named Hans. He entertained everybody. He was a schoolteacher in Berlin. We made friends with him. He asked us where we were staying. We told him we were staying at Penta Hotel Berlin, a five star hotel in downtown Berlin. He said he'd join us for a beer down there in the next few days. He did, and he told us where to go and what to see. We kept in contact with Hans for a year or so after our trip. Our trip to Berlin was very emotional for me. My mother spent the war years in Berlin, helping the Germans. As I walked the streets and saw the old, half-bombed church, I knew my mother had been in that church and walked these streets. My mother was even in a crowd and saw Hitler. During this trip, my emotions were my own silent ones. Ian and I went to KaDeWe, a shopping department store that would make Harrods look like a second hand store. This store was spic-and-span. Germans take pride in their heritage and goods, and this store, and its service, leaves a good impression to its country. Ian and I got visas to go over to East Berlin; that was my first time ever inside a communist country. All foreigners go through Checkpoint Charlie, but, if you are German, you can enter at any gate. I advised Ian not take the video camera; all our honeymoon pictures were on that tape, and I didn't want to lose it. We had another camera, and that was good enough. There was a line to go into East Berlin. It was really something to see the Berlin wall, all white on one side and full of graffiti on the other. Berlin has an incredible history. The German soldier gave each person entering 25.00 East German Marks. You had to account for every penny upon returning. As Ian and I walked through that side of Berlin, we could really feel that communist feeling. There were bread lines, store lines, and women and men in outdated clothing, mostly black-slip dress for the women and men in outdated suits. I went into the lingerie department in one store, and the bras and stuff there for women were so outdated that I'd use them as rags. Most of the products were from Russia. Well, our main goal was to have a beer in East Berlin, so we stopped at a restaurant/pub called Sofia. We sat at the bar. The young waiter there spoke English. There were guards in every part of the place we went. I was constantly telling Ian not to laugh or speak so loud. Our bartender told us that he was born and raised in East Berlin, and that he, by their standards, had a very good job. If he should get a $1.00 tip all day, that was very good. Ian gave him some Canadian cigarettes, and he gave Ian some communist cigarettes. He was very discreet; one should not do this, apparently. We asked this guy a lot of questions, and he was very happy to tell us what it was like to live on that side of the wall. He was very knowledgeable as to what went on in the west side. I was very, very uncomfortable in East Berlin; it felt like we were constantly watched and could get arrested for a simple thing. The beer cost ten cents a liter of beer for 10 cents. There was no way one could drink $25.00 of beer, and there certainly wasn't anything I want to buy there.

After spending the day there, I wanted out. Back through Checkpoint Charlie, Ian hid some coins in his sock. I didn't know it at that time, but, when I found out, I got annoyed with him. It was crowded at the checkpoint. There was a big window, so the westerners could see relatives on the east side who were trying to get legally out. The western Germans were swearing at the guards on the east side of that window. All I wanted was to get out of East Berlin. Finally, we traded our funds. I was never so relieved. I told Ian, "Ian let's go back to the Penta Hotel and have a beer." The cab driver took us around and showed us where Hitler's bunker was; I was lost for words. Now, time to relax at our hotel. A travel agent in Berlin booked us a room in Frankfurt for our final night in Germany, the last day of our honeymoon. He asked us if we wanted an antique hotel, and we thought it was okay. He also booked our train ride from Berlin to Frankfurt. That train ride was scary also. It actually stopped in East Berlin. There were guards who got onboard to check the train. A guard with a German shepherd started at the beginning of the train with a poker, looking for anyone who might be hiding under the train. The dog went from the front to the back of the train, and the guard gave the dog a cookie after coming out at the other end. (Needless to say, their German shepherds are beautiful over there). Our hotel was near the railway station in downtown Frankfurt, in the roughest area possible. Ian and I lugged our baggage for several blocks. We were starving, but didn't stop because of the atmosphere of the area. We couldn't find anywhere to eat. Once we got to our hotel, we got the best suite in the place. Actually, I think we were the only people in the place. Our room was antique all right—a huge room with all kinds of old stuff. It was elegant and had a balcony. Well, we thought we'd go downstairs for an elegant dinner in the last night of our trip, but they had no restaurant. So, we sat out on the lounge balcony and had two beers each. They served us on silver trays. Too bad this place had no food; we were really hungry. So, we went to bed hungry. We were up early in the morning and were off to the airport. The cab driver who drove us to the airport had a brother in Toronto and asked us to say hello to him. He lived on the same street that I lived on when I lived with Richard on Glenforest Road—small world. We parked ourselves at the Maple Leaf Lounge at around 8:00 A.M. and had a beer. We had about a two-hour wait. That's all part of vacationing—the waiting.

We saw our flight coming up on the screen, Frankfurt – Toronto. We were going home after the most beautiful honeymoon ever. Once in Toronto, the first thing Ian did was open a beer and held it up like the Statue of Liberty. We went next door to Stan and Irene's to share our three weeks of pure fun with them. The next step was to pick up Ben, and our family was complete again. Now, going back to reality took several days. What are we going to do for work? Where do we want to live? And so on. Well, the world was open to us; we could move to Finland, England, Germany, Mississauga, or Calgary. Calgary? Paul Dalziel, the Personnel Manager who hired me at Dixon, had relocated to Calgary. He made $500,000.00 and bought a beautiful house there, bought two wicker businesses, and two new cars—all cash. Ian and I were going out to visit my father in Vancouver that August of 1989, and we were invited to stay with Paul and his family in Calgary for a couple of days. So, our first stop was Calgary. Ian and I were impressed with the city; look what you can buy in the way of houses. Paul offered Ian a job as manager at his Marlborough Mall wicker store. Why not? It would be a great experience for Ian, and he was a salesman. So, we went looking for a house, a new one if we could. There was a house just finished by AMR, the builder just two doors up from Paul's. Ian and I went to see it. This house was it; it had our names on it. It was our dream home, and there was a view of the Rocky Mountains. This house was close to 2,300 square feet. As you enter the white hallway, you would view a large, spiral staircase. To the right was a cathedral ceiling covering the living room and dining room. Everything was oak trimmed, which Ian wasn't used to. To the left was the powder room, the laundry room, and the den or library. Farther to the back of the house was a family room with gas/slate fireplace, a kitchen nook, and a gourmet kitchen any woman would dream of, with a huge center island. There was also a telephone table. There were lots and lots of cupboards and mirrored closet doors. The basement was a full walkout basement. The upstairs featured three bedrooms, and the master took the whole back of the house with a suite and Jacuzzi, his and her sinks, his and her closets, separate shower and toilet. There was also a main bathroom with two other bedrooms. The view from the Jacuzzi was of the Rocky Mountains. This sold Ian on the house. The outside of the house was light-brown stucco and shake roof; all this for $210,000.00.

We bought it with cash. We took lots of pictures to show to my dad in Vancouver and our friends in Aurora. Ian had a job, and Anita had her house. We went to visit my dad and went back to Aurora to put Ian's house on the market. When we returned to Toronto, Robert called and asked us to come to Montreal for a visit. So, Ian and I drove to Montreal with Ben. This gave Ian an opportunity to show me his home of birth and see Clifford again. Robert had news for us; his cancer returned, and he is dying. I broke out in tears and gave him a hug. It wasn't the most pleasant of visits. He asked us what we would like. I suggested to Ian, "I want the *Playboy* and *Penthouse* magazines." He had finished years going back to the 50s, 60s, 70s, and 80s—a very valuable collection. That would be ours. We spent several days with Robert then ventured back to Toronto.

Our neighbours were sorry to see us go, but that's life. We found a good home for my cat because she would not make the trip; she hated cars. I gave her to a sweet older lady who was a cat lover. Menou had a good home. This was in August of '89, and the market was dropping fast in Toronto. Ian originally had the house listed for $300,000.00, but no bites. I believe we finally sold it for $240,000.00, less our realtor fees. After paying cash for our home in Calgary, we didn't have much left, minus $5,000.00 more to have Mayflower to move all our furniture. But that was all okay. Ian wanted to do all the packing; he did all the glassware and was very thorough in this delicate stuff. It certainly was a good way to get rid of junk. Anyway, by the time this was all finalized, it was October '89. Our neighbours had a big going-away party for us. Irene was in tears as we were waving goodbye and saw Ian's New Yorker for the last time. (My truck was shipped by train). So, here we were, Ben, myself, and Ian. The trip started off okay, until we started to get into the isolated, depressed parts of Ontario. A huge snowstorm blocked traffic on the highways for many miles. It was snowing so hard you couldn't see the very front of the hood. But Ian believed we should keep going. The snow squalls were dangerous. We went down and up the old route. Ian had a beer while driving; so did I, being in the passenger seat. We had to stop overnight. We rented a crappy motel room in Kenora, Ontario. It had very little hot water, but it took dogs. We had a time limit to close this house. We couldn't be slowed down here. Anyway, we woke up early and headed out west. The roads were wicked, and the days were long. Driving was slow moving. Ben didn't want to go out to pee or poo; he held himself. As we were carrying on, the road was closed between Marathon and Thunder Bay, Ontario. The Ontario Provincial Police closed the highway; we were stuck in Marathon, Ontario. The OPP flagged us to turn into town. We were sliding and slipping along the road, and, just as we were doing this, a guy in a huge truck smashed into our car—twice. He almost pushed us into the ditch. Ben flew between the seats and onto the front floor. But he was okay, poor little thing. Ian jumped out of the car and was furious; he was just jumping around, screaming at the guy. It was Ian's new car. An OPP constable drove our car back out of the ditch's way. I couldn't get out of my side of the car because of the ditch. The OPP got us out. Anyway, during all this, we were also lucky to get the last motel room in this town: a corner room, main floor. We booked in. Ben finally had a big pee and poo in the room, and I saw Ian laughing again like I saw him laugh hard in Finland with the sauna story. At least, Ben was relieved. He was such a sweet pup. We spent three days in this room. Ian and I didn't venture anywhere; we couldn't. He slipped to the bar and bought beer, and, every day, we watch the weather report and phoned the OPP to see if the Trans-Canada Highway was open yet. Ian was getting disturbed. Where's Mayflower Moving Company with all our furniture? In a ditch, too. Finally, they opened the highway. We could see the devastation along the way; there were semitrailers in ditches and cars that had to be towed. Ian got a towel from the hotel and pushed it into the hole where our car was damaged. Our trunk was ajar, and the snow was blowing into it and the hole on the left side at the back. Here was this new car, looking like this; in our minds, it was embarrassing. We tried for Thunder Bay that day, but we ran into another setback. Ian forgot to put winter-windshield washer fluid in the car, so the whole container was frozen. Ian pulled over to break the ice with a screwdriver, but poked a hole right through the container. So, as we were driving along, he'd stop to throw snow on the windshield to clear the mud off. It was a Saturday in Thunder Bay, and the service department was closed. I don't know what negotiating Ian did, but somehow, somewhere, the Chrysler dealership there got us up and running about five hours later. Ian and I were really behind schedule. We thought that if we were going to miss the deadline, I'd go into Winnipeg and fly into Calgary to finish the house deal. Nevertheless, we managed to drive straight through to Calgary; it took twelve hours. We called the builder from Medicine Hat and said we were just about there. Once in Calgary, we remembered our directions and found our dream home. The builder met us at the neighbour's and in we went. We were very tired, but happy. We had no curtains. Paul recommended this Chinese fellow who did his windows, so we hired him. We had beautiful flowing drapes in the living room and dining room, Levallor horizontals in the bedrooms, and verticals in the family room and kitchen nook. We were a glass house of windows for three and a half weeks. Our furniture arrived, of course, on a snowy day in October. Ian and I carefully unloaded our special wares, and I dressed up the kitchen the way I wanted it to be. A week later, my truck arrived by train. Ian started his job at Wickertown in

Marlborough Mall with Paul. Ian really liked retail. He was very good at salesmanship, and so was I. However, Paul was unable to pay Ian a good wage; we were struggling. We paid $3,000.00 for drapes and $1,400.00 for a solid-oak table and chair set. Ian just wasn't making enough money. Paul understood, and Ian and I decided to put our heads together and think of something else to do.

We were both smitten by the idea of being self-employed; it was the way to go. While we were in Calgary, we received a call that Robert had died. That was in November of 1989. Ian went back to Montreal for the funeral and came back with his dad, Clifford. Clifford stayed with us over the Christmas period. He had his own room and bathroom. He was no trouble; he cooked his meals, did his own laundry, and entertained Ben. He liked to watch his television shows. Once Clifford was settled, Ian and I focused on our business. Paul was very helpful; he told us about the gift shows in Edmonton twice a year and suggested that we should go. But how do we get in? Ian went as Paul's employee and I as his wife. This show was in February of 1990, we had all the time to figure out what we want to do. Ian and I were playing cards one day, and he said, "Let's sell candles." Candles, really? The realtor gave us wine, a set of candleholders, and candles for a gift, which were seated on our kitchen nook table. That's how we became interested in candles. We decided to do our homework! We visited every mall in Calgary to see the area we would like to be in. We did a market research in Alberta and visited candle stores within the Province. Ian put together a portfolio and sold himself here and there. He went to see the leasing manager in Southcentre who showed us a few spots. Bankers Hall, downtown, was one and a corner in Southcentre Mall at MacLeod Trail in Anderson. The spot was presently a month-to-month lease and was used as a children's clothing store. It was boarded up in an odd way. It seemed perfect for us; the space was just the right amount of size to sell our product. We were across from a major bank and next to Eaton's and Alberta Government Telephones; not the greatest spot, but not a bad spot either. We were recommended by Paul Dalziel to employ his lawyer, Richard DeVries, to form the company, Richard being a good corporate lawyer. We called our company Candle & Flame Creations Ltd. Ian was president, I the secretary, and Richard as treasurer. Shelly Hayes, an employee of Paul at the Wicker Store was going to leave Paul and join us once we got established. Ian signed a five-year lease. We were to renovate that corner. We hired a retail designer, and she drummed up a perfect looking storefront; the shop was going to look like a boutique from the hallway. We were going to have a large window in the centre and folding doors on either side of the window that folded into slots in the wall. There was one small storage room to the right and a cash desk. The colour scheme was hunter green and light yellow. Ian borrowed $25,000.00 from his dad to get this operation up and running. We also went to Edmonton and did our buying for our company; we didn't have business cards yet. The operation was so new, we couldn't really book an order but take names, catalogues, and do more research at home. Ian and I came back to work at home on locating candle wholesalers. Most of the local suppliers came to our Woodbine home, and we set up orders; delivery was COD (cash on delivery) to our home. We became good business friends with several local wholesalers who gave us a good beginning. One supplier was going to supply a cake with our name on it. Out-of-town suppliers came to visit our shop when they were in town. We really did decorate our shop well. We had a professional window dresser, and we changed our window every so many weeks, especially if it was around Christmas or Easter. We had oil lamps. All kinds of candles were delivered to our home. We unpacked the goods, priced them, and repacked them. Thank God we did. Otherwise, it would have been a lot of extra work. We had a deadline. The mall regulates shopping hours and monitors if you open late or close early; you can get fined. Ian and I worked day in and day out putting the glass shelving together. I polished everything; my job was very good, it was rearranging the goods. I have a talent for making something look attractive. I mentioned to Ian that we didn't have enough products to fill the store, and I was right. When we opened, we looked a little understocked. But that quickly changed, Shelly even came down to help us arrange. She was a great worker and wanted so badly to work for us. However, we couldn't hire her just yet. The day to open—June 2, 1990—was arriving. I took a picture of Ian turning on the cash register that was so carefully bought. Everything we did was well planned. Our doors were open, people came rushing in, and Ian had his first sale. We're in business. The hours were long. Our schedule was Monday to Friday, from 10:00 A.M. to 9:00 P.M, Saturday was 9:30 A.M. to 5:30 P.M., and Sunday was 12:00 noon to 5:00 P.M. At the beginning, Ian and I would both work the store together. Ian would open at 10:00, and I'd show up at noon to relieve him. We got each other beepers. He would take off to a restaurant in the mall called Zaros. We always went to the lounge. I would work with Ian for as long as possible. At times, I'd go home for the evening and cook for Clifford and return to give Ian some company until 9:00. It became a ritual that every evening, Ian and I would go home and jump into the Jacuzzi. We'd be in that tub by 9:15. We lived just a few minutes from Southcentre. It was, apparently, time to hire Shelly. We possibly couldn't work seven days a week. Shelly was the most super person, married, nondrinker, and honest. She would work Sundays and Mondays for now, more hours later. Southcentre would have two sidewalk sales a year. One was in July. We weren't open long enough to have sidewalk material, so we put out some of the good items. The sidewalk sales were fun. But you really had to watch it; people would rob you blind.

One day, Ian was standing by our table. A young woman was being rude and tossing a valentine-shaped box with beeswax candles and a flower in it. She just kept tossing the box; it was beginning to bug Ian. She said, "What's the purpose of the flower in the box?"

Ian replied, "It's decorative, like the diamond on your nose." Well, she just flipped out and left. Good.

Life was good; everything was wonderful. It was decided that Clifford should sell his Montreal home and live with us. With Robert gone, there was nothing for him to do in Montreal. He loved our company and Ben. So, Ian listed the house. When the house got sold, Ian went back home to pack items that Clifford kept for 100 years, so to speak, like bank books from 1939. Clifford saved everything and paid the $5,000.00 to have all his things shipped out to Calgary. I remember the day when all this junk came and filled our huge basement right up, and the smell of all this old stuff. Oh, well. One day, Clifford could amuse himself and go through his boxes.

Our home was complete. We cruised into our first wedding anniversary. Ian was a gift giver. He constantly bought me diamonds, opals, gold, cards, flowers, and silks. He repaired my diamond ring that I chipped during our honeymoon. He replaced it with a larger karat of diamond and had the other diamond set into another ring. He also upgraded my wedding band in karats. I had my own money and could spoil him with material items. One item he loved was the coloured TV I bought him, a small portable one. We used it on our back deck quite frequently.

The Woodbine *Grapevine* was the neighbourhood newspaper that was put out by the residences. They needed a sales representative for advertising. I applied for the volunteer job and got it. I was to go to the businesses in Woodbine and solicit for their advertising. It was a fun job. I did that post for three years. I really felt I was part of the community. Also, the Collie Club of Canada needed a membership chairperson. I applied for that post and got it. I did that for five years. Although I have only one collie, I still kept active in the dog business. My job with the Collie Club was to look after new and present memberships. The Collie Club in Alberta also opened new friendships for me and Ian. We participated in all their functions and volunteered our services. We were known as the cute, happily-married couple with no problems. The Collie Club was having its first sanctioned match in Calgary, and Ian and I were asked to volunteer in setting up the concession. We did this for a whole day, just standing around, selling donuts and coffee to all the dog lovers of Calgary. A sanctioned match is a match where you and your dog learn dog-show ways and rules. I met Sue Thompson there, and we became good friends. I also met the president of the club, Irene, who posted me the membership-chairperson job. It was just a fun day. July is Calgary Stampede Month. Neither Clifford, Ian, nor I had been to the Stampede. Ian couldn't go because he worked the store, so I bought tickets for the chuckwagon races, rodeo, and front seats for Clifford and me at the Calgary Stampede Parade. Clifford love parades, so I spent the whole day Stampeding with Clifford. I even bought Cliff a straw cowboy hat, so he'd look the part. Ian and I were both dressed to the hilt. Ian bought me Stampede dresses and more stampede dresses, and stampede wear for himself. Of course, we had the best cowboy hats and boots. We're Calgarians. Clifford tramped along all day, and Ian came to pick us up by the grounds. Boy, were our feet sore. Into the Jacuzzi I was going and slept well after that.

One evening, Ian turned to me and said, "Dad doesn't look very good. He'll be dead by Christmas." I thought it was quite possible. Clifford decided that now that he was a Calgarian, he would rewrite his will. So, Ian and Clifford went to our lawyer, Mr. Ron Peterson, to redo Clifford's will. Clifford decided that everything would be shared equally between Ian and Peter. Should any of the boys die, half would be left to their wives. Clifford left out Ralph. Clifford said Ralph had a lot of money, but there was more; Ralph accused Clifford of molesting his daughter while in Germany. Ian and I didn't believe this, but it left a great hatred between Cliff and Ralph for life.

Ian had rules about our relationship. We never went to bed mad. All our solutions and problems were always discussed in the Jacuzzi, and Ian and I always kissed each other every night and said, "I love you, see you in the morning," and went to sleep. That solution worked for us. Mind you, we did fight, too. Ian did have a roving eye; that was what our fights would mostly be about, but nothing too serious. Life was cruising along fine. Christmas of 1990 was coming up, so Ian and I went to Edmonton in August to buy our product for the upcoming Christmas. This would be our first store Christmas. This would be making money in time. We were getting to know people, the regulars at Zaros and so on. Very rarely would Ian and I go out at night; we loved our home and enjoyed being at home. We met Arnie at Zaros. He was an engineer. John was a chartered accountant, and the waitresses were all nice people. Everyone got to know us as a happily-married couple. Ian and his roving eye would piss me off at times, and we had a good fight one night. We were in the Jacuzzi, and I started bitching about a woman who seemend to be chasing Ian or vice versa. Well, Ian got out of the tub and yanked me out. My nipple caught the jet and ripped it three quarters off. Blood was everywhere. I just said to Ian, "Never mind, I'll just fold it back up and hold it until it heals."

"No way!" Ian cried, bouncing around like a rabbit. He was so upset. It was around 2:00 A.M. Ian drove me to the Rockyview General Hospital's emergency room. I was there for hours. Finally, this doctor came, froze my nipple, and sewed it back into place, poor little thing. The next day, there were flowers everywhere and "I love you" cards.

Clifford asked me, "How come Ian bought so much stuff?"

I just told Cliff, "I guess Ian felt like it." I was very close to Clifford; I was the little girl he never had. He didn't question me. Clifford loved Christmas, so we bought a big Christmas tree, he and I decorated it. The whole family filled the tree floor with lots and lots of presents. Ian asked me what I wanted. I said I wanted a sewing box, a really fancy one, as I was doing a lot of cross-stitching. Ian and I were working many hours and didn't get a lot of time at home, so Christmas was special. We put out the silver, crystal, and turkey with all the trimmings. Christmas was coming finally for the store. Ian and I did $15,000.00 in November and $30,000.00 in December. We got so excited when we did our first $1,000.00 day. But it wouldn't be enough; it would not pay for our suppliers and keep us going right into the next summer. So, in

January, we thought we'd keep the candle store as a hobby for me, and Ian would get a full-time job, until the economy gets better. The store wasn't making money, but it was too new to toast.

One evening, a call came into the house; Dad had suffered a stroke. Ian flew me off to Vancouver and drove down for the weekend with Ben. Dad wanted an electric shaver, so Ian went out to buy one. It was one of those very quick visits, just to let my dad know I was there for him. At that point, he was able to recover enough to walk. His brain wasn't affected. Ian and I drove back to Calgary after our visit.

Through all the hard work for the last six months, Ian was loosing weight, a lot of weight, and rapidly; the opening of the store, Christmas, expectations, and so on were the stress factors. Ian was also complaining of stomach pains. Considering men don't like to go to doctors, I suggested that Ian should go. So, he went for tests, an x-ray in Southcentre. As a matter of fact, nothing showed up, so the doctor told him to buy Pepto-Bismol for his upset stomach. Ian loved his beer and scotch. Possibly, that could be it. Ian still had pains, so I suggested that he go back to the doctor. This time, they put him through a CT scan. And, this time, something did show up—cancer cancer in his pancreas. I didn't know what pancreas was. But, I certainly know now. We were both sent to Ian's specialist. It was carefully explained that, depending on the growth of the cancer, it could be taken out, except I'd have to learn to give Ian insulin shots. I said I could learn. That was the only solution: operate. We were also told of the probability of it spreading. That meant *death*. I remember sitting in the doctor's office, just simply not believing that Ian would die. He won't die; he would make it. We went home, only to wait for the doctor's call for booking. Ian called his doctor brother in Germany, Ralph, and told him what was happening. (Later, Ralph would tell me that he knew the end result.) He gave Ian and I hope. Ian went to the Rockyview General Hospital in early April of 1991. Ralph came over from Germany to comfort me, not Clifford. Ian had a lovely view of the mountains, a private room on the top floor. I would go and visit him twice a day. Ian went through his surgery. I met with Dr. Ralph Hayes and Ian's physician who Ralph went to medical school with. We were called into a room.

Ian was not going to make it. I was frozen. I had no tears, just frozen. The doctor was going to give Ian the news once he was out of recovery. Ian's cancer spread into his liver like wild horses. They called it a galloping cancer. Ian was loaded, one walking cancer cell. I sat in Ian's empty room with Ralph, frozen. They finally wheeled Ian in. He didn't know we were there at that point. Ralph and I went for coffee because Ian was still sleeping. As time went on, he had woken up and was informed of his condition. He was hooked up to everything—morphine and stuff. When Ralph and I returned, I asked Ian, "So, how are things?"

Ian said to me, "You know."

In my mind, I answered, *Yes, I knew*. Then, I just quietly said to him, "Yes, I know." Ian didn't want to talk anymore; he wanted to be alone. Ralph and I left. I told him, "I'll be back the next day." Back at home, the house was relatively quiet. We all knew Ian was dying. Now was the time to inform my family. My dad's wife was shocked. We didn't tell my father for some time, as he was ill; we didn't want this to disturb him anymore than we have to. He had a stroke in January and was still going through therapy. Shelly and I now worked the candle store; it gave Shelly more hours. She was happy to run the place. One day, I went to Zaros and saw that John was there. I told him that Ian was dying and should be dead in a week. This was the first time he had heard it. He bought me a beer. I thought that was nice of him. Ian taught me how to do payroll and showed me his way of recording invoices. Clifford, at this time, was still doing the books for the candle store. Ian was in great pain and wanted to get out of the hospital. He was told he could no longer drive his car, so I went to pick him up. He was so glad to be home. His routine changed. I let him drink all, or what, he wanted, smoke all he wanted, eat all he wanted, and call whoever he wanted. His doctor prescribed a large bottle of morphine for him, which I put in a special cupboard I prepared for Ian's medical things. Our master bedroom became a hospital room. Ian's doctor also prescribed me Valium. I could take it when needed. I was working the best I could under the circumstances. But, I was probably in denial and was really walking around like a zombie. Our home began to look like a flower shop. Flowers from Finland, Germany, Florida, and Ontario were arriving daily. The phone was constantly ringing. Ian had his will and personal effects in an envelope with a title "In the Case of My Death." I was to open it later. I ran the store daily. Soon, it became known to everyone in the mall that Ian was dying. I had a great support group everywhere. It was touching. Ian told Ralph that he was left out of their dad's will. Ralph was mad and was going to contest the will. Ralph left shortly after seeing the household was okay. I was so thankful for Ralph's help. I really needed the support of family. Ian was slowly losing more weight, and Ralph told me that when he lost his appetite, it was getting closer. I made special dinners for Ian in the hope of getting some food into him. It was just so painful to see him pick one little bit, swish it around his plate, and leave it. I would just remove his plate without saying a word. Ian and I spent the evenings together, watching TV. He was in his spot, and I was in mine. I bought him a heating pad and got him all the necessary things for his comfort. Rockyview General Hospital gave me a special document for Palliative Care section of the hospital. When Ian gets bedridden, I could just zip him in the hospital without having to go through the paperwork. It was already done. This was a horrible waiting time—watching this man deteriorate to skin and bones. One day, my girlfriend from Toronto called me at the candle store. She had called the house and spoke with Ian. She thought she'd call me and ask if I knew Ian was going to a funeral home tomorrow to pick out a box. I had no idea of this. When I got home, I carefully questioned Ian. At first, he wouldn't say anything, but, apparently, he had made arrangements to get a funeral home to pick him up in their limousine to arrange his funeral arrangements. This was going to happen tomorrow morning, while I was at work. Very carefully, I got it out of him. I telephoned the funeral home and said all was fine, except I was coming along as well. (The last thing I needed was Ian to sign any documents). Shelly was willing to work that morning, especially after I explained what Ian was doing. By this time, Ian was walking with his cane. Anyway, we ventured off to the funeral home, way up in northeast Calgary, way out of our way. Anyway, I let Ian walk around and look at each box. My god, this was awful—to watch this man turn around and say to me: "I want this" or "I want that." I said okay to everything. It wasn't that common that a sick man would pick out his own stuff. I was so glad to get out of there. Can you imagine what would happen if Ian signed a $10,000.00 contract?

Ian liked wearing pajamas to bed. I bought him some lovely Christian Dior pajamas, he looked good in them. Ian wanted to die at home, but I really didn't want him to die at home, especially not in our bed. One morning, I woke up and Ian was soaking wet, a warm wet; he peed the bed. I got him in the tub and all, cleaned him up, and got him downstairs, then I continued to clean up the bed. I decided to put plastic on the mattress. When Ian came to bed that evening, he got mad at me because he thought it to be infantile. Ian started to stink. There was a very strong, unexplainable smell that goes with death. After the operation, Ian wasn't healing. One of his stitches opened. I saw some goop draining out of it. I told him to lie down on the floor. I got some Q-Tips, went into this hole, and pulled out some black goop with the texture of snot. The smell was unbearable. I held back my own desire to puke. I kept saying, "Ian, I've got it. It's coming out. Hang on, I'll get some more out." I kept rolling this goop around the Q-tip until I finally said, "I got it all out." Ian smiled at me, and I smiled back at him. It was as if we both believed that I got the cancer out and he would be okay; we were both in denial.

I could feel that Ian was getting closer. He was loosing his speech and was unable to walk to the bathroom. He peed the bed again. It was time to put him back in Rockyview. He didn't want to go. I said, "Ian, you'll get better care there." I called Richard DeVries about the transfer of the candle store, and he had sent legal documents to me by courier for Ian to sign. Richard directed me and Ian over the phone as to where to sign. Ian's handwriting was not the same, but it was signed. A home nurse arrived and helped me dress Ian into something comfortable before the ambulance came. I drove my car behind the ambulance. Ian was checked into a private room. I stayed with him for about an hour, doing crossword puzzles. I bought a parking pass at the hospital so I could just drive in and out. The parking lot attendant thought I was a new mother and was returning every day to feed the baby. I guess my times were regular. "No," I said. "My husband is dying." She appeared shocked. I don't know why; you'd think people are dying all the time in the Rockyview every day, and visitors and family just might share that. At first, Clifford and I would go to see Ian at least twice a day. As Ian was going down, I only came once a day, usually around dinnertime. Clifford was happy to stay home. One day, I went over to the hospital to find that Ian was bubbling all over the place. He was strapped into a chair while the attendants were changing his bed. He was so skinny and old looking. One nurse thought I was his daughter. I said, "No, I am his wife." Other days, Ian couldn't do a thing. I would do my bit like trim his mustache. He was just sort of lying there, all wired up. His speech was going. One day, I said, "Give my hand a squeeze." He did, but it was ever so lightly. There was no strength. Every evening, I would say, "I love you, and I'll see you tomorrow." One evening, I felt that I would not see Ian the next day. My gut feeling was right. A few hours later, at 2:00 A.M., April 22, 1991, Ian's doctor phoned me to let me know Ian had died and that he was sorry. I got up, woke Clifford, and we both went downstairs. I made the necessary telephone calls to the key people, and they called the next group in line. Shelly opened the store for the next week. She hired extra help. She had insisted that I called as soon as I heard. I opened a beer and started to dismantle my stovetop. I decided to clean my stove. Odd, but that's what I did. By the time I finished with the stove, it really was spic-and-span. I couldn't sleep. Clifford was silent in the family room, watching TV. There was something terribly wrong with Ben. I went to bed at around 6:00 A.M. in the morning and tried to get some sleep, but the phone kept ringing. Ben knew his beloved master had died; he had a poo by the back door and wrecked the horizontal blinds on the door. I didn't get mad at Ben; Ben was distraught. In fact, I took Ben to the vet, and the vet didn't know why Ben was upset. It wasn't until the end of the visit that I told the vet that my husband just died. Well, that was it. It took Ben several months to recover. Ian and I hadn't lived in Calgary long enough to have a full house for his funeral. I went to McInnis & Holloway on Elbow Drive. It was on the southside, for those of us who lived in the south can come. I picked out a box similar to the one I picked out for my mother—royal blue with white satin. Ian wanted to be buried in his wedding suit. My god, it was too big for him. There were a few flowers in the funeral home, and Richard DeVries showed up, along with Paul, Ian's friend, Ralph from Germany and our coworkers from Southcentre Mall. It was a very small and sad affair. I started to clean out Ian's closet and gave his clothes away. I gave Paul, his good friend, Ian's very expensive fishing gear and sold to his son Ian's brand new bicycle, which I bought for him but Ian never rode. The only things I left in Ian's closet were his .22 rifle and its bullets and his baseball cap, one that said "Time for a Beer" with a clock that actually worked on the front. It was an ugly yellow hat, but I kept it. I also kept his cane. The Collie Club did something special—a memorial trophy that said, "Ian Hayes Memorial Trophy for the Best Smooth Collie at a Show." I was very overcome by this. It was a beautiful silver bowl mounted on an oak base. I was to later find out that the president of the club said I had requested this trophy. I never did such a thing. The president came and asked me if I would accept this offer. I donated $100.00 to the club in Ian's name. I cleaned my name with that story.

CHAPTER SIXTEEN

Rockyview Hospital offered grief sessions for those who lost loved ones. Clifford and I decided to go to the chapel at the hospital. You could go, as often as you liked. I entered a room of mostly women. I was the youngest one there; there must have been around forty of us. The preacher asked every one of us to get up, say how our mates died, and whatever one wished to say. I got up and said, "My husband and I were married twenty-two months ago. He died of cancer in this hospital at the age of forty-four." Then, I sat down. Clifford got up and said his thing about being Ian's father. It was a full afternoon. We could go back, but I didn't want to. That was enough for me, and Clifford didn't think I needed therapy like the women who have been married to their mates for fifty years.

Now, for the paperwork: I went to our commercial lawyer, Mr. Ron Peterson, to handle Ian's estate. I was to receive $100,000.00 life insurance. Ian's car was life insured, so the $25,000.00 owed was paid. I was also to receive a widow's pension. Upon going down to Canada Pension Plan, I was ashamed; I was the youngest in the line up, the only white woman, and probably the only Canadian citizen. I received $85.77 a month. As I aged, the amount went up. At that time, I though it was a joke—$85.77. But, I took it anyway; I was entitled to it. Being a widow was different, when I went to work at the mall, people, for a while, would point at me. "That's the wife of the guy who died." Also, those who read the obituaries, there were the scam artists. For some time, I'd answer the door bell only to find no one there. No one on the other end of the phone either. It was scary. One thing I did was hire a security guard for the day of the funeral. These people would know if there was an empty house that day. It is very cruel how people think, but this is reality.

The Hayes family got together and decided what to do with Clifford. Ralph and Eileen hated Clifford and didn't want any responsibilities for him whatsoever. I didn't mind the chap; we were best of friends. Clifford chose to stay with me, it was best that he stayed with me. He had everything he needed: Ben, me, a room, TV, his own bathroom and, most importantly, company.

Clifford was in his eighties; he can stay put. Well, here I was, in this huge, beautiful house. I asked Clifford what I should do, and he just said, "Carry on." Ian and I didn't even get the chance to decorate this place; he didn't even make it to our second wedding anniversary. For some time, people came over with casseroles, casseroles, and more meals. I was so grateful; at that time, no one really wanted to cook. Things started to drop off in about two months. Everyone was getting back to their lives. I was back at the candle store with Shelly, and I was waiting for my $100,000.00 to come in. It did, in June of 1991. Boy, that was nice. I decided to go to Hawaii, first class, so I booked a trip for two weeks. I continued to wear my wedding rings. Nothing changed that way. I had someone look after Clifford and Ben while I was away. Clifford thought it was nice to go on a holiday. I prepaid my room and requested a room with a view. When I got to Hawaii, at midnight, I was tired. I booked into my room at the Outrigger West. In the morning, I found that I was overlooking a garbage dumpster for the hotel. I went to the main desk and said, "I want a room with a view; that's what I paid for." So, they put me up on the tenth floor, where I had a view as long as I stood on a chair. Anyway, I was content with this. I'd go up to the roof, by the pool, and have a few beers, relaxing my hours away. It was nothing out of the ordinary, just a vacation under the sun. I wasn't as motivated as I was in my first Hawaii trip; I just wanted to be alone and go to the pool and the Rose and Crown Pub. This was in July, and it was one of Hawaii's hottest summers ever on record. I got tired of the heat. I wasn't really enjoying the shopping and restaurants. I went to a different restaurant daily. One day, I was walking down the main street and saw this wristwatch in the window just shining at me. I thought, *No way, it's too expensive*. Nonetheless, I went in and bought it. A Christian Dior watch for only $1,000.00. What a deal.

One day, I went to my room. My suitcase had been opened, and there was pee in my toilet. I went down to the front desk and demanded another room. They gave me another room on the twelfth floor, overlooking the water. I hated this hotel, the Outrigger West. I just wanted to leave Hawaii. On top of it all, I missed my flight going back. There was my stepmother, waiting for me at the airport, and I didn't show up. I called her and made plans to get the flight out the next day. In fact, I went to the airport very early and sat in the first class lounge, just to make sure I wouldn't miss my flight. I flew to Vancouver and spent a few days in Vancouver with my father. Then off to Calgary. I had money, a paid-off house, a paid-off car, a small business, and was financially set for life, if managed properly. Back in Calgary, I continued my volunteer work with the Woodbine *Grapevine*, the Collie Club, and, of course, the store. I was occupied. One thing I did, considering I was so very successful in real estate flipping, was to buy a rental property in Abbeydale, a small, lower-middle-class section of Calgary. I paid $95,500.00 for this house. I rented it out for $800.00 a month. I had a $15,000.00 mortgage on it. In no time, I would pay this house off—a good investment property. I secured my money. I took Clifford to a new restaurant twice a week. We had our schedule weekly. Life was good, content, considering I had no lan. I had to carry on. When I returned to Calgary, I started the usual paperwork, accounting, and so on. Then, I noticed a piece of paper by Clifford's papers. It read, "Paul Dalziel owes Clifford $5,000.00 payable in three monthly payments six months from now." I was shocked. I asked Clifford what it was about. Our neighbour, Paul, while I was away in Hawaii, went over to ask Clifford for $5,000.00 and said that I had said it was all right for Clifford to lend it to him. Paul used my name to get $5,000.00 out of Clifford. I was fuming. I let it go for now—just for now. I told Clifford not to do this again. Well, time was going on. I decided to have a party to let everyone know that I am still around and alive, that I am not grieving forever. Cliff thought that would be nice. I had Zaros make up a catering plate, and I bought invitations and selected a small, select group of people. John Aikens was one of my guests, as well as Shelly and her husband, Rolly, a friend, and Arnie. Everyone was invited to bring a guest, wife, girlfriend, or whoever. This was October 1991. John came over by himself; all dressed up in a suit and tie with two bottles of wine: one red, one white. I had lots of booze and food. Everything was all right, except the mall closed Zaros down the night before, so I had to rush to Safeway the next day to get a catering platter. (I'll find out what is going on with Zaros later).

I put on music and games. John was paying a lot of attention to Clifford. I was being a great hostess. Rolly was very drunk, and I suggested that he shouldn't drive; he left anyway. It was late, but everyone had fun. John stayed in the spare bedroom, Shelly went home, and I and Clifford went to bed. Needless to say, John stayed. I've always had a feeling for him. He was very kind and gentle. The next week, we played cards and drank. I was wondering that John should want to have clean clothes by now, especially underwear. John slept in the spare bedroom. We were getting closer. One evening, he came into my bedroom with just his underwear on. He slept with me that night and from that night on. I really enjoyed this man. He was like a big teddy bear: soft, gentle, smart, a C.A., everything. My weakness is falling for smart men. Plus, he turned me on sexually. Clifford liked him because he was treating me nicely. John decided to show me his house—the house that his wife, Elsa, and him shared. It was just five minutes away from my place, a nice house, but not as nice as mine. John picked up his computer, desk, clothes, and all his things; his wife had removed all of hers. Arnie, a friend of both of us, helped John move into my house. This was also in October 1991. I didn't know John was now officially divorced from Elsa and that a foreclosure was planned; John had to get his stuff out before the sheriff shut the place down. Three days later, his house was shut down. I did not know what exactly happened. I was just happy that he was safe and okay with me. How could his wife do this to him? Poor John. He basically moved in with his computer, clothes, and a ten-year old Grey Buick Skylark; he had nothing else. Before John moved in, I had a ticket to Vancouver in November of 1991. My elementary school, David Lloyd George, was having a 1967 reunion. John wanted to come with me, so I bought him a ticket. This would be the first time my father and stepmother would meet him. So, off we went to Vancouver. I was happy to see everyone again. I was bragging about my new man—that he was a C.A.—my house, store, dogs, and how well I was doing. The party was great. I couldn't believe how fat we all were now. Many of us were with kids, married, or divorced. The girls who organized the party had the old music playing, and John and I danced and socialized. It was fun. Then, we were back to Calgary, back to work. Because John was so academically smart, I let him take over the books. I knew the store had a $25,000.00 line of credit with the Canadian Imperial Bank of Commerce (CIBC), which Ian had signed when we opened. Our banking was across the way. This line of credit was up to its limit. The store wasn't doing all that well. Some time that year, the manager left and a new hotshot woman took over. She pulled my line of credit; $25,000.00 was now added to my $15,000.00 mortgage on my rental property. Candle & Flame had no operating line of credit anymore. I just assumed that that woman wanted to make a name for herself; I wasn't the only small business she hit. I was hoping Christmas would do it for me. I wasn't going to put my personal money into the store. I carried on working the store, and John would hang around a lot. My friends really didn't approve of John, but he was nice to me, and I was happy with him. That's the main thing. For Christmas, I bought John a stainless steel and gold Gucci watch, designer shirts, slippers, cigarettes, a designer housecoat, and little things. He started to cry when he opened the watch box. I draped Clifford with new slippers, a sweater, and things an eighty-year old man can use. We had a lovely Christmas. I cooked a fine meal and set out the silver and crystal. I always made a big deal for Christmas, as I'd never know if this was Cliffords last one or not. I always found John striking, a tall (six feet, two inches), large-boned man with a very loud laugh. His legs were long and thin, along with a fifty-year-old beer belly. His hair was always stylish, and, sometimes, he had been told he looked like Donald Trump. The only faults I overlooked were his gorilla way of eating, the huge gap between his front teeth, his huge flat feet, and his face's reaction to some soaps that made it red.

As spring was coming along into 1992, I realized that the candle store isn't really going to provide a proper income. I wasn't sure at this point, but I started thinking about another business. In the meantime, my cousin from Finland, Leena, had married Vesa, and they were both transferred to Los Angeles to do research in a children's hospital for cancer. They both have their doctorate degrees; both very smart people. Leena had a new baby that was born in Finland, and they were coming over here with practically nothing. I wanted to visit them. I haven't been in California for some time; time to go. I had someone look after Clifford, and John and I went to visit my cousin in February 1992. We went to Las Vegas first and played the slot machines. I provided John with spending money, beer money, and cigarettes. We both made money. In fact, I was $400.00 up. We rented a New Yorker and drove to Los Angeles, Glendale to be exact. It was so pleasant to see Leena and Vesa. Their baby was very tiny. We went to all the Hollywood hotspots, the beaches, malls, and thoroughly enjoyed ourselves. John and I had fun. In fact, Leena had nothing, not even a crib for their baby, so I gave them money to buy suitable things for the baby. She later sent me pictures of the articles they bought. Then, back to Calgary; holiday time's over.

Clifford always had both papers delivered—the *Calgary Herald* and the *Calgary Sun*. I also had cable for him. Anyway, I'd ponder through the businesses for the sale section, and I came across a neighbour pub for sale. I said to John, "Pub for sale, what do you think of that?" He thought we should look into it. John looked after the business that way. We met with this agent, and he told us to go up to the Waterworks Pub on Strathcona Road, SW.

"Be discrete. The staff may not know if it is for sale or not," he reminded us. We went up during the day, on a Wednesday, sat around, and had a beer. We kind of thought it was cosy, so we decided to go back up there on a Friday night. And we did. John knew the Chinese cook there by the name of Winny. I guess John frequently went to a restaurant downtown where this guy once worked. He always took John as a big shot Revenue Canada Taxation heavy.

Anyway, John and I discussed this. "Beer is recession proof, isn't it?" "Should we put an offer?" "Yes." "Okay." We met with the landlords of this building, David Halphern and Murray Zimmerman, and the sales agent at the realtor's office. David Halphern actually owned the mall while Murray was his son-in-law who did his scapegoat jobs. They were a team, a very strong Jewish team. Apparently, David once owned a very famous hotel in Calgary, which he sold, enabling him to buy various malls and apartments in Calgary. Anyway, Richard DeVries, my lawyer, was to set this sales transaction. John put in $30,000.00 of the money that he received from his ex-wife. I put up $70,000.00, of which a lien was put on my personal home. The Bank of Montreal provided the loan. I should have this paid off in no time. What could possibly go wrong? I remember that David wanted me to sign a personal guarantee. I said, "No, I happen to like my house."

However, the night before the transaction was officially signed, the staff at the pub had a party and totally wrecked the place. Winny had let the fire extinguisher off, and there were broken glasses, tables, and chairs. Richard DeVries came to the pub to see the devastation. This transaction was on hold for a day or two. The owner lived in Victoria, BC and wasn't always easy to get ahold of. I wondered if I should buy this place, but I thought, *A bar is a bar*. The transaction was settled, a liquor license was issued, and we were in business in June 1992. There was a restaurant on one side, which was always empty, and the bar on the other side. John took to the place and gradually introduced ourselves to the customers and suppliers. The Finnish cook showed us her ways, and Winny, the Chinese cook, showed us his ways. The bartender, Kevin, was a great guy and took on the day job. We got rid of the manager, Charlotte. She gave me a hard time, so I immediately got rid of her. As the months went on, John would sit in the office and do the accounting. I would be there back and forth from home to the bar. I also worked the candle store. Shelly was fully running the store and doing a good job. I looked after Clifford during the day. As time went on, I also began to trust some but not others. All our staff, except Kevin, wasn't trustworthy. Our customers were middle to upper class with attitude problems. Strathcona, the area the pub was in, wasn't my kind of atmosphere. John seemed to have taken control over the place; it was like he didn't want me around there. It was his bar. He never seemed supportive with me at all. I thought, maybe it was the ten-year difference. The Alberta Liquor Control Board passed a law that we could have the wall removed between the restaurant and pub. This would enable us to increase seating capacity for the bar. Considering we did no business from the restaurant side, this was the way to go. Quite a few bars in Calgary were now becoming just neighbourhood pubs. One of my candle suppliers' husband was in commercial renovating. We had him come up and give us an estimate on extending the oak bar all around like a horseshoe shape and a few other odds and ends. We also needed to buy more bar stools. Where the restaurant was, we also had stand-up bars with stools. I went to the bank to borrow $15,000.00; it went against my rental property. So, what I paid $96,500.00 for now had $40,000.00 against it. But that's okay; the expansion would generate more business.

John was always saying, "I'll do it. I'll do it, I know what and where to go as far as the government is concerned." That was his job. He had worked in many government positions and knew the ins and outs. He was in charge of the legalities as far as the construction, liquor license, and other regulations such as fire and liability. I looked after the daily bank deposits and the socializings. All was going smoothly. We rented a pool table, bought a shuffleboard, and we set up dart boards, lots of things customers can do. Before, there was just darts and lounging. We really did a good job in expanding the interest, and sales were increasing. We always paid our bank loan, rent, and suppliers. As time went on, we hired someone responsible for the evenings so that John and I can both have the odd evening off. Then, I noticed John spending more time there and would come home drunk. He seemed to isolate himself from me, and there was one bag at the pub by the name of Elaine Brown who wouldn't leave him alone, although she just got married. I took this all with a grain of salt; that's a pub. The hours were long, from 10:00 A.M. to 3:00 or 4:00 A.M., all around the clock. Sometimes, John and I would sleep there. It was Stampede again on July of 1992. The landlord advertised a band by the mall, and free hot dogs for the kids. Murray ran these affairs. This was to help all five of us merchants running a day care, beauty salon, dry cleaner, the pub, and a convenience store. The program didn't work, except for those who got the free stuff.

One nice afternoon, John and I were sitting on the patio of my house. We had a few beers, just enjoying the weather and each other. John got down on his knees and proposed. I accepted. I told Clifford, and Clifford had my blessing; he liked John. Besides, rather than be common law, one should be legally married. The day he proposed was July 14, 1992, I married Ian July 14, 1989. He knew because it was on the coasters. John had no money for a ring; we'd get one later. It was Stampede time. John and I decided to go, all dressed up in our duds. We drew a salary from the pub so we weren't broke. We walked around and I played the games. I won a huge, huge pig and various other stuffed toys. Anyway, it was time to leave. It was around 5:00 P.M. John was driving down Macleod Trail at Southland when the cops pulled him over. I wondered what he did. Nothing out of the ordinary; apparently, John was driving with an expired car sticker. On top of that, they made him blow, and he blew over. Well, they towed the car away and took him to District Six.

They asked, "Why were you driving impaired?" John said that his future wife was more impaired.

That is what the cop told me. I said, "Really?" Anyway, they let me go to District Six with them. I waited in the cop shop for them to finish all the things they needed to do. Then, we called a cab and went home. I said to John, "Why wouldn't you get a sticker for your car? That's a dumb way of getting an impaired charge." Well, John's car was now out of commission. He had to go to traffic court. I went with him, and I said I didn't know where it was, John knew. He pleaded guilty and handed in his driver's license for one year. I didn't think John was impaired, but I guess he was. He didn't blow that much over. Because of this, I drove him up to the pub every day, did the deposits, and looked after the banking, Clifford, the candle store, and so on daily. I left him to run things up there. Then I would spend the evenings with him and drive him up at night and drive home at 3:00 or 4:00 in the morning. This was beginning to take a toll on both of us. We needed good night management so John and I can have a life as well. We were able to find a good guy. The rules were all followed and things worked smoothly. John seemed distant with me, not very loving. One day, I told him I changed my mind, and I don't want to marry him anymore. He said I had to, or he'd sue for breaking the ritual clause. I didn't know, until months later, that that law was dropped years ago, and that John had no recourse over me for breaking an engagement. John had a usual routine in the mornings: he'd open the pub and get his cigarettes. He always had a cigarette in his mouth; he could talk, walk, and run with a cigarette in his mouth. The only time he didn't have a cigarette in his mouth was when he was sleeping and showering. One of my customers pointed this out to me; before, I didn't notice. In this business, staff come and go. We hired a new cook by the name of John. We called him little John. My John, big John, would do most of the hiring. In fact, he was looking after everything. In the bar business, it was centred around a lot of low-lifes looking for work. This Winny guy was always stoned on something and would be hospitalized. My Finnish cook was mouthy and always boozed up, like I mentioned, the odd cook that would show up for a week and leave without notice. John and I talked about wedding plans. He wanted the reception at the pub. I didn't; I wanted it at home. "My marriage was at home. Let's have our friends there." John adopted this pub; it was his pub. The reception would be held at the pub. I didn't trust this little John guy, as things started to disappear. He'd always suck hole to John; most of the staff did. They knew they couldn't get away with anything with me, so they really, really sucked to John, making him feel like a worshipped king. John was glowing in his newfound fame. This little John would ask big John to order certain steaks, qualities, and so on, and my John would. Apparently, these steaks never saw the people's plates. While we had a new cook, we thought we'd change the menu. John and I had a meeting with the cooks as to what we can do to enhance the food. Kevin was also putting in his good words. We sold a lot of French fries. We blanched them, which was far better than frozen fries. Our fries were fresh from the potato. We did try the frozen fries and noticed people left them, so back to blanching them. As time went on, I noticed Elaine Brown frequented the place late at night, every night, with or without her husband. No big deal, I just always found her arrogant and constantly drooling all over my John. But he loved every minute of it. Was there something going on? As John and I were preparing the menu, he hired Elaine to do the printing; her husband had a printing company, and she worked as a secretary there before she married him. I didn't know that John and Elaine had spent several days together, putting this together. She came up one day with a proof. I was somewhat interested in her comments to John—she never addressed me, only John—with what I would call somewhat flattering comments for a business transaction. She was beginning to piss me off. I began to really hate her. One evening, I wasn't there, and, apparently, Elaine and her husband had a great big fight in the pub and walked home. My John followed her for a bit. In the morning, Elaine's mother phoned me to let me know that Elaine is a nice girl and that her husband moved into her house. The house was hers and so on. I said, "I really don't know what happened last night; I wasn't here." After the conversation, I wondered why her mother would call me. There had to be things going on at this pub that John doesn't share with me. With this, I said to John, "Elaine and her husband's company are not going to do the menus; I'm taking charge and will find someone else." With this, I called Elaine to basically shove her menu up her ass. With that, she said she wasn't coming to the pub anymore. Good! A few weeks later, she popped in during the day. John was not in and left an invoice. I didn't pay it with our company cheques; I went and got a Postal Money order 30 days later. John insisted we pay it. She's out of my way. Along with the Waterworks Pub came a baseball team, a very good team consisting of the neighbours. They wanted new shirts and baseball stuff. We did get new shirts and stuff for them. Red and white were the pub colours. Kevin helped in the design. Apparently, the Waterworks Pub baseball team won the league. John and I were happy about this. They brought in business during the summer. Anyway, I hired a new printing company and got new menus in the pub colours. I got criticised when I chose red on white. It was apparently hard to read in a dark pub. The customers were right.

With little John, things went missing. In fact we experienced our first break-in. Our security system went off at around 4:00 A.M. Someone had broken the front glass door and tried to break into the office. Apparently, this was a nonsuccessful event, but it cost money to get a new window in the door, plus to call our insurance agent, Royal Insurance Canada. Our representative was a customer of our pub. He lived in Strathcona. We had bad, bad, staff; only one good one, Kevin.

This Chinese guy, Winny, was getting on my nerves. John never noticed conflict toward himself, only conflict with me and others. I could read too much through these low-lifers. I guess John would drink all day and night. I did too, but only carefully because I drove. I usually went elsewhere for a couple of hours. One evening, this Winny guy came into the pub and called me every single filthy word he could think of. I went into the office where John was. Winny came after me, screaming filthy words at me, then he pushed

John against the wall, and he started to bleed on his hand. John called the police to come and get this guy out of here. John didn't seem to care about the verbal abuse I took, but rather his good image. He seemed caring enough. This Winny guy left for good and found some crap job downtown. Then, on several occasions, he'd show up at the Waterwork's and phone 911 on us for no reason. The cops knew this game by now. This Winny was bad news, so was his friend, Judy, who lost her job at Alberta Utilities for being stoned all day long. These are the type of things you are surrounded by in this business. I was beginning to hate the people, the hours, the area, and the pub. We had another break-in, but it was centred on the hatred toward me, as I was told, not toward John, but me. Once again, the front door was broken, just like the previous break-in. The office door was kicked in but nothing was stolen. We had, at one point, hid money in the office; only an insider would know that. We quit putting money in the office. We had it hidden in a safe place—with ourselves. We could see footsteps in the snow. Small feet. Because of these break-ins, John and I both started to work every night till closing. Sometimes, we would be sleeping there, only to go home in the morning to freshen up and return. Another chap who would express his hatred toward the landlord was this Lebanese guy next door who owned the beauty salon. The landlord being Jewish and he being Lebanese caused a stir sometimes. They were arguing over the lease, I think, or arguing about something. Whatever, it wasn't healthy. He threatened to burn the place down for many months. No one believed him; he was always talking stupidly.

We had the other business, the candle store, but it wasn't making money. Possibly, I should close it down. John told me to close it down, so I sent him off to the big executives at Southcentre to tell them of my plans. They didn't buy our shut down idea, and said they'll probably sue us for $10,000.00. On October of 1992, I closed the shop. It was like a midnight move, but the rent was paid. The store security wouldn't let me out, so I called Richard DeVries. Richard knew of my plans and, in fact, informed me exactly how to do this. He came down to the mall, and I got my stuff out. Arnie helped. We loaded everything in the van—all the glass shelving and products. That was it. When Shelly came in the morning, I was gone. Shelly was really mad at me; she didn't know. Years later, I told her that John told me to shut it down. She ended up working at the mall in a much better job anyway. She wasn't mad at me anymore. She hated John. Ian had wanted me to keep the store going. I promised him I would, but that store was what we created together; my heart wasn't into it. And no one was interested in buying it, although John and I did go to Edmonton in August for a quick buying trip for my Christmas products. At that time, I didn't have plans to shut the store down. This was when John met my first husband, Bill Hayes.

CHAPTER SEVENTEEN

The economy was dead. This was September of 1992. John and I were getting married on November 8, 1992. I had arranged the priest, photographer, and limousine. John arranged the reception with the cooks and staff. The staff was sweet; they would decorate the place for the wedding. We would close the pub for one evening for this private party. John and I picked our rings from Wong Ken's Jewellery in Southcentre Mall. They were very pretty, white and yellow gold bands with six small diamonds. We had them engraved—an old Asian tradition. I moved my previous wedding rings to another finger. The new wedding rings wouldn't clash with my existing diamonds. I also had Ian's sapphire and diamond wedding ring made into a necklace for myself. I paid for the rings. John and I went to the wedding store and purchased our custom-made invitations. Then, we went to city hall for the marriage license; he paid for that. Little John cooked for us, Elsa (my Finnish cook) set up the shuffleboard as a buffet, and Kevin stocked up the bar with booze. Things went very smoothly. John and I were very much in love. He would be my third husband, my last husband. John's high school friend, who was a dentist, and his lawyer wife were our witnesses, along with my longtime girlfriend from Edmonton, Marion. Clifford also witnessed and signed the marriage register. John bought me a black and white suit with gold-coloured buttons. It was the in style, just suitable enough for having gone through this before. John had his only suit dry-cleaned, and I bought him new, shiny shoes. I paid for everything. The priest arrived with his wife, and then the photographer. I put Ben in the car. Ben was a good watchdog. If someone was walking down the road while we were doing our lines in the living room he would start barking. One of our guests video-recorded the affair from start to finish. The affair seemed long, and then I became John's wife. The photographer took pictures and left; I never saw him or the photos ever again. My other guests had taken pictures. We had a lot. John hurried to open the champagne and signed the documents. I went out to get Ben from the car. It had started to rain where we were, and it snowed up by the pub. Everything was timed. We had a moment to socialize at the house and before the limo came. We all went up to the pub. Our guests were already there, being served by our staff. The staff really decorated the place nicely. There was a pile of gifts on a separate table, along with a guest book. We both went around and did our socializing. Elsa and little John did an excellent job with the food. (Kevin was in charge of the bar and also in charge of the pub while we went to Reno for only a week). We hired a band for the evening, and the party was on. Because of the severe weather that just pounded the roads, those who had to go far left early. John and I left around midnight with Clifford while the party stayed on. We had an early flight to catch. We were both hungover, but we made our flight. John had a little trouble crossing the border, I didn't know why. Once aboard, the stewardess announced that the party setting in seats thirteen are on their honeymoon. The flight from Calgary to Reno wasn't a long one. We were going to the Hilton Hotel. We booked a car. The Hilton was not in the downtown area. We had a beautiful suite on the top floor, overlooking Reno. The management had champagne for us. I was in seventh heaven. We went down for dinner and gambled some. That evening was lovely lovemaking. In the morning, we got ready to see downtown Reno. I drove downtown and parked the car; we walked all over the place. We were trying this place and that place. It was in November, and Reno wasn't that warm. The next day, we drove around Lake Tahoe and visited Caesars Palace there. We also stopped in Crystal Bay, a small town on the edge of Nevada and California. I won some money in keno there, around $600.00. I was very impressed with this drive, so beautiful, and the mansions around this lake were big. Anyway, we proceeded around the lake, stopping here and there, enjoying our day. We went back to our hotel to relax. The next day, we'd venture elsewhere. John telephoned Kevin to see how things were working back at home. Everything seemed fine at the pub.

We lost money in Reno. I didn't like that much. The only money we had won throughout the whole trip was the keno win. Our trip was coming to a close. I really wanted to be out of Reno. We waited for our flight beside two older women. They were on the same flight to Calgary. They had won $200,000.00 on 6/49 and split it between each other. Wow! I was impressed. I would video-recorded our trip. This was when I noticed that John would always say, "That's enough," wave his hand, and say again, "That's enough." He never really showed much enthuasium for a newly-married man. But then, I didn't want to compare him with Ian. They were two very different people. Back at the pub, there was another break-in. Kevin didn't want to tell us while we were in Reno. Someone stole food and was trying for money. Approximately $800.00 was taken. Kevin wasn't very good in depositing money. He never made one deposit all week. Kevin was getting tired of whoever was doing this. I suspected it was little John, so did Kevin, but my John just worshipped this guy. John was dumb this way. One day, Kevin decided to set up traps, like put extra cash in his till. His till was very close to the cook's entrance. One day, $100.00 was taken. That was when we got Kevin a lock for the cash register, and, if it should open, a bell would ring. These break-ins were now twice a week. John told me he was going to sit in the pub one evening with a cop from District Two. I never heard from John nor did he answer the phone at the pub. I guess he was doing some investigating up there. John and I started sleeping at the pub. In fact, someone bought us two very nice air mattresses. But, someone knew our car. There were no break-ins when my car was there. Then, one day, we got a call from security that there was another break-in. This time, the cigarette machine was sitting outside on the sidewalk. We were both getting very sick of this. Our insurance company now enforced that we put bars on our windows, or they will not insure the pub anymore—another expensive cost coming out of our own pocket. It just felt like we were losing control of this business. I suggested to John that we sell the pub. It was really taking a toll on our early married life, being wakened up many nights all week, the long hours, and the abuse. But John wouldn't have anything to do with that idea. He loved this pub; I hated it. There were lots of rumours going around, one being that I sold my share, or it's for sale; to whom, who knows? Every now and then, someone would ask me something, I thought it odd. The landlord's fat son-in-law was always cruising around. In December of '92, it was thought that John and I should go to Toronto for a week. I would center this around my birthday and the Credit Valley dog show. John also wanted to show me his boyhood home, Grimsby, Ontario. He grew up there and, apparently, was an alderman for many years there. He was in charge of the town's money, the treasurer. I was impressed. We made new rules and plans for the pub and was assured by Kevin that no goofs will happen. So, off we went. We stayed with my girlfriend, Janice, at Pape and Danforth Avenue in Toronto. I rented a car and showed John Beaverton, Ontario. We visited Marja, but she was out Christmas shopping. Her son was there. He showed me the most beautiful female puppy; I wanted her. When Marja came back, I asked her for the puppy. John encouraged me to go back to breeding. It was my love. I spoke with Marja, and she said I could take the pup back to Calgary with me. We made arrangements to meet at the dog show at the end of the week. In the meantime, John and I stopped at Irene and Stan's place. I showed off my new husband. John also saw where Ian and I lived. I was not sure they liked John, but no one said anything. We had a full night of partying. The other neighbours came over; it was their twenty-fifth wedding anniversary. We all had fun. John and I returned to Janice's. She was very hospitable, always cooking up something lovely. One evening, John and I had gone for a subway ride. Walking back, John stole some fruit from the fruit stand and peed his pants. I made him take the fruit back. I don't know if he did or not, but he was gone for a few minutes.

John left me in my room and played board games with Janice. She gave him shit when he grabbed her breast. She said, "Go into the bedroom with your wife. Don't you ever touch me." I didn't know that this incident took place until much later. Since I married him, John didn't seem to be with me; he was in his own world, like he felt that he was now secure, had a place to live, a bar job, my money, a wife when needed, and all those wonderful customers he worshipped. He changed. The next day, Janice was fuming over his behaviour but kept her cool. That day, John and I drove to Grimsby, Ontario. Here I met his stepmother who wouldn't have anything to do with him. She slammed the door in our faces. There was no way she was going to let us in.

John said, "This woman has hardening of the arteries. Let's go." He showed me his first house that had a pool, and his childhood home. We also went to the city hall and met with his old friend who was now chief of the place. They pulled out all the old photos of my John as an alderman. I was very impressed. Apparently, John had shared his first home with an older woman but never married her; it didn't work out. Evidently, he was an alcoholic and smashed her brand new Camero. It was published in the local papers that Alderman John Aikens was charged with impaired. He got off his charge. While we were in the Niagara area, we went to the falls. It was freezing cold around 7:00 in the evening, and the two of us nuts, the only people there, were taking pictures of the falls. It was terribly cold. From there, we went over to the United States' side for a beer, drove back to Hamilton, and got a motel for one night. John wanted to show me Hamilton. He was a C.A. there for Revenue Canada in his early years. He had places to show me. We bummed around Hamilton and proceeded back to Toronto. All was well back at Janice's. John and I were going to go to Meaford the next day. Morning came—we weren't going anywhere—we were snowed in. A tree broke in half across the street because of the weight of the snow. It was stay-inside day. We never did get out to Meaford.

The day before our last day in Toronto, I took John to the Credit Valley dog show. That was where I would meet Marja to pick up my new pup, which I named Grace, simply because she was. We spent the day there and returned back to Janice's. She was really mad at me for bringing a dog into her apartment even though her apartment allowed pets. I said, "For God's sake, Janice, she'll just stay in her crate for one night and John and I will be gone tomorrow. What's the big deal?" I really have no use with people who don't understand the ownership of animals. Anyway, John, Grace, and I were back to Calgary the next day. Ben loved his new playmate, a female. Clifford liked the new arrival as well. Anyway, Christmas of 1992 was arriving, so we put up the tree as usual. This would be mine and John's first Christmas married. We continued our pub business as usual, but I began to really wonder if there was more going on there than I know about. The three of us had a lovely Christmas. New Year's was arriving.

On New Year's Eve, John got all dressed up to go to the pub. I asked, "Will you be back?"

He said, "No, I'll be spending New Year's there."

I said, "We spend every day there. Aren't we going out somewhere else together?"

He replied, "No, I'm going to the Waterworks." I knew I had no plans on spending my New Year's there. Clifford and I spent the evening at home. I went to bed at 10:00 P.M., missing New Year. I woke up at around 12:45 A.M. John never returned home, nor did he call. I fell asleep again. I woke up at around 3:30 A.M. I called the pub. The place was rocking and rolling. I said, "John, close the place down. I'm worried about our liquor license. Come home." I phoned again, but he wouldn't talk to me. He was very drunk. Our cook, Elsa, did the lying for him. She said he had gone to the back to sleep. In the morning, there was no John. I drove up to the pub at around noon; no one there. I couldn't get in as my keys weren't on my key chain. Some husband, some New Year's Day. Around 5:00 P.M., on the first, John came home, all hung over and stinky. He had my set of pub keys. I was really, really mad at him. I was also very hurt. I remember he and I argued. Then, he went out to shovel the snow. I went in, got Ian's .22 rifle, and just stood in the hallway by the garage, holding it in a vertical position, watching John shovel the snow while the garage door was open. I was just fuming. John came in and put the rifle back in the closet upstairs, so I was told. But, I thought that I had put the rifle up in the closet because I thought this was stupid. John was just indifferent to me. His bedroom manner began to change. Although he was never a very touchy person, he soon slept with his big back to me. If I opened my eyes, all I would see was a big back. John was never intimate to me after our marriage. He would go to bed, slump his big, buffalo body on the bed, and go to sleep or pass out. He would never touch me, say good night, or kiss me. No "I love you," nothing. I began to think I made a mistake in marrying him. I was thinking of getting an annulment, but we owned that stupid pub together. Well, for better or worse, carry on. I was carrying on into 1993. Calgary was having a cold winter. John and I usually had a cozy fireplace going. He occupied one couch while Clifford and I had the other in the family room. Needless to say, I wasn't the happiest wife. For the pub, we did our buying. Fridays and Saturdays were our money making days. We stocked our freezer full of food and the bar full of booze for the weekend. On January 8, 1993, at around 4:00 A.M., our phone rang; our security system went off at the pub. John and I were getting used to this and had our track outfits usually ready in the corner of our closet. As we were driving up Sarcee Trail, stopping at Bow Trail to wait for the left turn signal, I could see huge flames coming from the mall. "John, our pub is on fire." He started to cry; I didn't know why. As we drove up and around, we approached a major mess. Fire trucks were all over the place, smoke bellowing out of our pub. Flames were high in the air next door in the beauty salon. All the businesses were smoked, watered, and fire damaged. All of us merchants, except the Lebanese owner of the hair salon, showed up to watch the fire. John and I were on the news in front of our pub. The police and fire department told us to go home and return at around 1:00 P.M. There was nothing we could do right now. So, after standing for one hour in the freezing cold, we went home for some sleep. Back at home, we had to bang on the front door and scream up to Clifford's bedroom because he was still sleeping and couldn't hear us. Although the dogs were barking their heads off, it seemed we were at the front door forever. Once John and I got freshened up, we returned to the pub. While there, we saw the landlord with his fat son-in-law, Murray. I brought up my video camera. We learned that it wasn't an ordinary fire; someone bombed the place. It blew a hole right through our pub wall and the hair salon next door. The roof was gone. The carpet was soaking wet, and the kitchen was full of soot. Apparently, the landlord had professional people come in and rescue the goods. All open booze was thrown out. Someone had unhooked the freezer, so all the food was spoiled. There were professional cleaners for the black-smoked kitchen, engineers, insurance people, arson squad, police, and the fire-relief people who were removing all remaining stuff like the pool table, bar chairs, and cash register to their place of business. These people would spend weeks cleaning this stuff. They had degrees in fire safety and preserving things. They would clean our stuff. The cash register would even come back cleaner than it ever was. They can take the thing apart and clean the chips. I was impressed with their business. Murray and John were always whispering together, and when I'd come along, they'd break off their conversation and do something else. Something was sour about this pub, the landlord, Murray, and John. There was something going on that I don't know about, and it wasn't in my favour. It wasn't until some time later did I clue in. I took a video of the dry-cleaning place, the convenience store, and the pub. The day care was toast. The owners of the day care lost their shirt. They never returned. Our pub would reopen, as well as the convenience store and the dry cleaners, but there was other stuff going on that we would only find out months later. After spending a couple of hours at the pub, John and I went home. Actually, I hung out at Caesar's South Lounge, a very elegant, high-class lounge. John could normally find me there. Well, there wasn't anything much to do except let the professionals put our place of business together. John and I spent lovely days at home playing cards, watching TV, and solving any telephone calls we got concerning the pub. Apparently, this time off lasted longer than we wanted it to. The landlord was stalling and playing games with the contractors. He insisted for about three estimates. Some contractors knew the Halphern people and wouldn't quote him at all. They were known for not paying or for slow paying or for just being really annoying. I registered the actions in my mind of the Halphern people's business ways, and, mostly importantly, how they treated people. John and I continued to play cards and go out the odd day. Our day was routine. John would get up without acknowledging me, put a cigarette in his mouth, sit on the toilet, shower, put his housecoat on, floss his teeth, go downstairs, put on coffee, read the paper, then go to the den and play on his computer. If we weren't going out, he'd be in his housecoat all day. If we planned on going out, he'd put on dress pants, sometimes jeans and a dress shirt. I usually wore my track outfit around the house. Clifford, John, and I played more cards. Of course, my dogs enjoyed me being home. I cooked elaborate dinners, and I thoroughly enjoyed this time with John. A new pub called Gator's Pub opened in our neighbourhood. It was the only pub in Woodbine, and I could walk to it. John and I were the pub's first regular customers. I got to know the owners, Nick and Corrina, well. They were very nice people. While John and I sat around at home, we had to push the Royal Insurance to pay us living expenses. Our staff was toast, and push we did. We barely got much. I had American Express, Aerogold Card, VisaGold, and regular CIBC credit cards. All my cards had very high limits on them. John and I started to live off my cards. No big deal, I was expecting at least a $70,000.00 pay off from Royal Insurance. Right now, we had to get the pub up and running. The arson squad spend an hour at our home. We all new the Lebanese guy next door bombed the place. Apparently, he had moved his best furniture out of the place one evening and opened shop on 17th Avenue. He even went to Lebanon and returned; the arson squad had a copy of his ticket. To make a long story short, he never got charged because it couldn't be proved, although, two weeks later, a fire was set in the office of the landlord; we suspected it was him. This was definitely a racial war between Halphern (a Jew) and the tenant (a Lebanese). The police at District Two called our mall Gaza Strip. While we were bumming around, Gator's was putting a baseball team together. I thought it would be nice to join, so John and I joined; it cost $50.00 each. We practised once a week at a ballpark nearby. On our first practise, we had a regular practise, no big deal. After a couple of practises, I didn't feel wanted on the team. The younger chaps really wanted to have a number one, winning team. John and I could hardly play as well as them, them being in their 20s while John and I were in our 50s and 40s, respectively. I expressed to John, "Maybe we should quit."

But he suggested, "Let's try one more practise."

I said, "If I feel uninvited, then I'm not going to bother." John was never, never ever supportive or comforting toward me in private or public. Anyway, we would spend time at Gator's and Ruffino's, a new Italian restaurant up the road with very good food. I still went to Caesar's South and the Point & Feather to play the video lottery machines. We were now heading into March and not much was going on at the pub. It was like David was holding up transactions galore. A temporary wall was put up where the existing wall originally was. This would enable us to at least open the pub while contractors were being bullshitted around by David Halphern. A new carpet went in. Our bar was okay. There was new paint, new everything about the ceiling, and the kitchen was repaired. It was like owning a brand-new place. We were just waiting for the day we could open. The staff from the local radio station frequented our place. They were waiting for our place to open, too. They had only one choice in their area now—Schooners, a fish and chip place. We got a call from one of the contractors: he needed us up at the pub to acknowledge where the wall should go. I wanted the wall to go back to its existing place, but the landlord wanted the wall to take over the hair salon as well. I didn't want anymore space because the landlord wanted $1,000.00 more in rent. We were paying $6,000.00 a month for rent; that was enough. It almost seemed like we were working for the landlord. He would price us out of business. We don't need more space; we don't need to pay more rent. David said he'd give us a deal for a couple of months, and I simply said, "No." So John and I signed the document for the contractor to put the wall back where it was originally. While John and I were up in that area, we decided to go to Schooners. All our customers were drinking there. So, we sat down. Elaine Brown came over to us in a hurry and quickly said hello to me and John. Then, they were glued-eyed together, speaking sweet things. Her hands were all over his shoulder. I stood there like an asshole, patiently waiting for them to close their intimate gossip. When she did, she went and sat at the bar. I don't know why, but I sat down and ordered two beers: one for me and John. The whole time we sat there, my conversation with John was nothing; he was facing Elaine Brown and couldn't keep his eyes off her. It was like I didn't exist. It was personally humiliating, and I hate humilation, public or private. I said to John, "Let's go." As we left, he kept turning back to look at her. So, I gave him a push and said, "Let's go." I argued with him on the drive back home. This is where I noticed he could very well keep a cigarette in his mouth and verbally humilate me with his cigarette going up and down in a vertical position without any trouble. He was 100 percent on that woman's defense. I also noticed that he had a really ugly smirk that I would be seeing daily. I was trying to be the loving wife; John was not being the loving husband. I became unhappy, or too confused as to what kind of marriage I have. Anyway, back at home, I continued my elaborate dinners and looked after Clifford, John, and my two collies, Ben and Gracie.

Back at the mall, the other merchants were having their, own bickers with Halphern as to the cleaning up and to getting their businesses up and running. Halphern had the power to manipulate people. He enjoyed manipulating and pushing people who were trying to make a living. It gave him great satisfaction. I would get my turn. The best was yet to come. It was getting closer to the pub's reopening. The convenience store was ready; we all were. I put on a black Suede suit, and John put on his suit. We opened on April 2, 1993. We did some word and mouth, and the landlord put an advertisement in the *Calgary Sun*: WATERWORK'S PUB, NOW OPEN!

Day one, some of our customers came in because of the word and mouth while others just saw we were open. John walked around, shaking hands and greeting everyone with his loud voice. He always was shaking hands; it was as though his hand was always extended outward. It was actually abnormal. Still, there was a cold feeling toward me from the people, and I really couldn't understand why. I didn't spend much time there, and when I was there, I was there to pick up John. There were times when he would take a Mayfair cab home. John carried on with his routine; I carried on with mine. I said to John, "Let's sell this place," but no, he wouldn't have it. From April 3, David Halphern would call us once a week, every Monday morning, and demand rent. He wanted his $6,000.00 rent for April. I said, "How could we possibly pay rent when we just opened?" He said, "No." He wanted his rent. I figured Halphern would, at least, give us three months free rent so we can rebuild our clientele and catch up financially. The Bank of Montreal was patiently working with us. But David wouldn't hear of it. John wasn't with me much. He was always drunk. In fact, our neighbours in Woodbine labelled him as the "drunk-I-married," even the people in the 7/eleven and the people who walked their dogs labelled him as such. John Aikens was the neighbourhood drunk who lived at 134 Woodbrook Road SW. I was really beginning to hate this program. Halphern called constantly for rent, threatening to close us down and takeover. He sent his fat son-in-law down to our home, and he sent down his daughter down to our home for cheques; money that we didn't have. The insurance wasn't paying anymore. John signed a very mickey-mouse insurance policy, which put us in a loss. I would not receive $70,000.00. That was it. John said he knew everything. I was worried that if David took over the pub, I'd lose my house, or at least have a $70,000.00 mortgage on it that I don't need. I really wanted out. The daily harassment from Murray and David and John's daily drinking and verbal abuse toward me, and his ignorance, was taking a toll on my happiness. John's daily bed routine, nonintimacy, and his buffalo-sized body thumping around my house like he owned the place bugged me. We had sex, but not loving, especially when he was in his housecoat, which he lived in, with that cigarette in his mouth, and, at meal times, slopping down my food. He'd eat three helpings to Clifford's and my one. John was up at the pub a lot, and I was getting mad at him.

One day, he had gone out with some customers elsewhere, or maybe with Elaine, who knows. It was around suppertime, when I should be at the pub. I could see John wiping the bar, him standing behind it, wearing Ian's "Time for a Beer" baseball cap. I was roaring mad. I went in and told him to immediately come home. That smirk and his verbal abuse just set me off. I picked up the ashtray and threw it at him. He darted off like I was attacking him. He went and joined some customers in the corner. They bought him a shooter, but not me. I was sitting at the bar. I voiced my opinion, "Why didn't I get a shooter?" People bought John drinks, never me. Someone in the corner bought me a shooter. When it arrived, I slowly pushed it along the counter and onto the cement floor behind the bar. I left in such humilation. John came home drunk at around midnight.

CHAPTER EIGHTEEN

In the morning, John did his usual flossing, and that started to make me sick. I drove him up to the pub; I wasn't going in. He did his usual routine, went and got cigarettes, and, on the way back, with a cigarette in his mouth, he said, "Everyone hates you," while giving me that smirk. I went to Caesar's South's lounge. I started going there every day. I got welcomed and treated much, much better. I also went to Gator's every day. Another baseball practise was coming up on April 26, a Monday. This would be our last practise—then the real game starts. John and I got ready to play. It was a cold day, so John put on long underwear, his Harry Rosen track pants that I bought him, his runners, and a couple of sweaters. I was in my jeans and a T-shirt. Before I went to play, I took off my jewellery and put them in my jewellery box. Then, off we went to the park. On the way there, I voiced my opinion again that I didn't feel welcome, and that if it remained the same this time, I'll go back to Gator's and get my money returned. While John and I were getting ready on the bench, John just left me sitting there. It was obvious that he ignored me and went to play catch with someone else. I sat there for a few moments and just watched his behaviour. I was hurt and angry more than anything. I left the field and went to Gator's. When I got to Gator's, I voiced my opinion to Nick. I said that I didn't feel welcome, and I want my money back. I was fuming inside. I stayed at the pub. Several hours later, John showed up with the team. I expressed my opinion to John; he didn't care at all about my feelings, not one bit. We started to argue, and I went to reach for Ian's baseball cap that said "Time for a Beer." Because John is so tall, I couldn't reach the cap. He did his humilation stunt once again—that "I-was-attacking-him show" and started walking back home. I was furious. I got into my car and drove up to him walking home. Again, he voiced out that he was being attacked by the five-feet, one-inch petite woman. To get his attention, I drove up on the curb; he made it like I was running him down. He got into the car. We started arguing. He punched me in the face, and my glasses slightly cut me vertically between my eyes, just above my nose. I began to cry. All this time, he had a cigarette in his mouth.

I just drove home. I opened the automatic garage door and in I drove. John got out. I was determining if I should go in the house or not. I drove back out of the garage but stopped. I thought, *No, go into the house.* As I went in, I put my purse on the kitchen island, said hello to Clifford, and let my dogs out. I was just standing in the kitchen, staring at John who was helping himself to whatever. I started to argue with him. He had that ultimate smirk that no one can top. That smirk can just set anyone off.

As I was standing in the kitchen, I was fuming; John had a way of ignoring me. To get his attention, I threw the Windex bottle at him. He came racing around the island in the kitchen, pushed me down, and started kicking me on the shin with his left leg. He was just kicking, kicking, kicking, kicking, and kicking with his foot with full force. While I was crouched down on the floor, my mind decided to say to me, *"No one* ever *does this to me."* When he stopped, I went upstairs and got Ian's .22 rifle. I came downstairs and stood at the northeast side of the island. John was at the northwest of the island. I was holding the rifle in a vertical position. John returned to clean the floor. I positioned and fired the gun off, and the bullet lodged right in the crack of the dining room door, about six inches from the floor. I was sure I could never do this shot again. All this action was within a few seconds. There was silence, and then John got up from the floor and said, "Darling, you *shot* me." As he placed his foot on the floor, he started hopping around the island like a rabbit, screaming. I had no intentions, whatsoever, to hit him. I went into shock. John said, "Phone 911." So, I did.

I said, "We were in the backyard, and it went off." Not true about the backyard. The woman on the phone tried to keep me on the phone, asking questions. I hung up and put the gun in the hallway by the laundry room. I didn't notice, but John had gone upstairs and retrieved fresh underwear and socks. He knew he was going to the hospital. The two of us were in the kitchen. Clifford was in the family room, watching TV. I had no idea where the dogs were. I guess they went to hide. Then John looked at me with that smirk. I knew from then on that he was going to toast me. He had a really ugly look on his face. (Mind you, I don't blame him)

The ambulance guys came first, put John on a stretcher, and told him to get the cigarette out of his mouth. John said to one of the ambulance guys, "She shot me fellas. How do you charge your wife?" The police were right behind the ambulance guys. I just stood in the kitchen, beside the island, as the police searched the place. They left my front door open. The police asked me why I shot my husband. I couldn't think straight. Never at that moment did I mention John was beating me up. The police asked trick questions. Meaning, regardless of whether you answered yes or no, it wouldn't sound to your favour. They took John to the Foothills Hospital as per his request. (He also knew Jackie, his friend who was studying to become a nurse, worked there). It was close to the Waterwork's Pub. Plus, the Foothills Hospital had the equipment for shooting cases. The cops said I could call a lawyer. I first called Richard DeVries; he was shocked to hear from me. He gave me a list of criminal lawyers. Richard is only a corporate lawyer. The first on his list was Don MacLeod. I called him; he was in. He gave me instructions as to what to say and what *not*. I mentioned my dogs. Possibly, they are outside. I needed to get them before the police took me downtown. Don told me not to make a big fuss over my dogs, that it wouldn't look good. The police told me to take some money downtown with me. I don't know why, but I just took my wallet with my credit cards in it. They walked me out of the house with one cop ahead of me and one behind me holding a gun. I was put into the back of the police car. The cop kept asking me why I shot John, but I wouldn't answer these guys. The cop said there were charges, and I said John would drop the charges. The cop said that they have charged me with owning and firing a weapon in the danger of public peace and assault. These guys took me to District Six and put me in a cubicle. Of course, I was in there so long, and I had to pee. I was banging on the door for them to let me out. They finally let me out for a pee. They escorted me to the locked washroom. I was to bang on the door when I was ready to come out. I have no idea how long I was there, maybe several hours. I shot John at 8:00 P.M. From there, I thought I'd be able to go home, but I was informed that they were taking me to the downtown jail. The drive was around twenty minutes. As we approached the back alley of the jailhouse, the young cops said they had to handcuff me. I started to laugh in their face. Although, I didn't say this, what was going through my mind was, *I'd rather fuck you in the laneway than run down the street and jump on the C.T. train*. I think I would have gotten in deep trouble with a comment like that. These men were young enough to be my sons. They handcuffed me, scratched my watch in doing so, and took me up an elevator to some floor. As I entered, I could hear screaming; police were making fun of other inmates. One old bum was picked up with some marijuana, and the cops were really making fun of him. The old bum was laughing. I guess he was stoned. As soon as they saw me, all became quiet. It was like I didn't belong there.

While there, I could hear the older cop ask another cop "Why did she shoot her husband?" It was a Monday night, and it certainly wasn't a full house. While I was sitting there, handcuffed, they removed my belt, hairpins, watch, shoes, and anything sharp. They even checked for false teeth. I was fingerprinted and pictured with my own number. I found all these interesting rather than annoying. I was put into my own cell on the ladies' side. I found that interesting also. I had my own open toilet, steel bed with open cut squares in it, a cement chair, and table; no toilet paper. I asked the cop if he would bring me some paper. He did. So, I used the toilet. I sat on this bed and stared at the bright lightbulbs that would, apparently, stay on all night. I was beginning to get curious as to how the engraving got scratched into the wall. The cops removed everything sharp from me. For some time, I just sat and listened to the other women screaming at each other. Then, some time later, two more women joined me. One was picked up for making a disturbance in a pub on Electric Avenue, Calgary's young drinking section of town, while the other was charged for assaulting her boyfriend. But, apparently, she had a large cut on her cheek and was sent to the hospital first. When she was sewn up, the cops brought her to the downtown jail. The two asked me what I did. I said I shot my husband.

The tough girl said, "You'd better get a good lawyer." For a while, I tried to sleep on the steel bed and used the toilet paper as a pillow. But, no one can sleep on this. They removed the two girls and put them somewhere else; I had no idea where. While I was there, the girls down the hall were masturbating, and they shared this with me. I just sat there wide-awake, waiting for morning. Several hours later, I saw a new cop. I just assumed it was shift change, and that it will be morning soon. It was a long, long night. I was removed from my cell to a holding cell, one wherein you'd await the judge to set a court date or something. I remember this girl who set the date for Monday next week. I can't remember what all that went on, but I was released from jail on $600.00 bail. I had to come up with $600.00. I telephoned a lawyer that was on the list in the cops' telephone booth in the jailhouse. He came over, and I showed him my leg, which was swollen and getting blacker. Who knows what he said, but I wanted to be out of there. The police accepted my Gold Visa Card. I bailed myself out of jail with my Gold Visa Card. Can you imagine, if I was up to my credit limit, I'd still be sitting there. It was around 10:30, and I felt tired and stinky. I went walking to find a phone booth to call Clifford and to call a cab. I called Clifford to inform him that I was on my way home. I waited for a Mayfair cab outside of Calgary City Hall. Once home, my dogs were there to greet me. Thank God. They could have been all over the neighbourhood, lost. However, Clifford forgot to put them out. Dog shit was all over the living room and dining room. I let them out, but what good was that?

Clifford told me the cops asked him if I shot John. Clifford said, "No, Anita wouldn't shoot John." Clifford said the cops went through my purse and around the house. Poor old Cliff thought I had been out to an all-night party. I went upstairs to bathe; I was going to the Foothills Hospital to see John. I got all prettied up in my black silk blouse and so on. I went to Safeway and bought flowers with an "I love you" card. Safeway was next to Gator's, so I popped in for a quick beer. I did that on purpose, so everyone would see me. That evening, the cops had gone to Gators to ask questions. They knew I spent the night in jail, but no one said a thing to me. I left for the Foothills Hospital. I had never been in this hospital before. It was a huge hospital. I walked through hallways and hallways, took an elevator to the seventh floor, and located John's room. He was by the window, in a room with another man. As I walked in, he looked very surprised, not welcoming at all. Immediately, hospital security came and hauled me out of his room. They asked John permission, if it was okay for me to go into his room. The hospital personnel were worried that I might come back to finish the job, and that I'd shoot other patients.

I said to the hospital security, "Do I look like someone who is going to shoot someone?" The security guard, who was young enough to be my son, said, "No." This was the projection John gave to everyone—that I was a very dangerous woman. John said I could come in. I placed the flowers and card by his bed. I said, "John, you've got to say this was an accident." Then I saw that smirk. I knew John was going to toast me; I just knew he had his own selfish plans. It appeared he didn't want me around, so I left. I was to pick him up the next day. I asked him if there was anything he wanted, and he asked me to bring up Ian's cane. The next day I went up to get him; I noticed that my flowers and card were moved to the corner of the room, away from him. Beside his bed were two books. As I was patiently awaiting his official release, I thumbed through these books. One book had a lady's handwritten message on the front page. As I read the message, it reminded me of the way Elaine Brown speaks and writes. As I went through this book, I noticed that it was about touching, feeling, love, love-with-your-partner kind of book. The other book was of pictures of countrysides. We were ready to leave, but John wanted to take the books home, although he said he got them from the hospital library. I said, "Will that be okay? Are you willing to return them?" I didn't know the Foothills Hospital had a library. (Maybe they didn't). John wanted me to meet his roommate and tried to humilate me; I could feel it. As I was walking down the hall, the nurses were just staring at me with tacks coming out of their eyes. John didn't want to take the card or flowers home. We stopped at Gator's pub and went home. John relaxed, and I worshiped him in every way. He slept with me, and our marriage carried on. I had an appointment with my new criminal lawyer on April 30, 1993. I put on my Suede black suit and went downtown to explain what had happened. I showed Don MacLeod my bruisings. I actually took off my nylons in his office to show him my leg. He requested that I take pictures and make an appointment with my physician. John took the pictures, and I saw Dr. Narang. I told her that my husband kicked me many times to get my leg looking like this, and I had shot him. The bruising now reached four and a half inches long, four and a half inches wide, and there was two and a half inches sticking out of my shin bone. It hurt and was hard. I asked Dr. Narang, "Couldn't I just stick a pin in it so that it will release any goop and pressure?"

She said, "No, it will stay hard and sore and go down on its own." She prescribed some medication. I remember meeting John. We were walking through Southcentre, and people were staring at my leg. Once again, I saw that smirk on John's face. John had a permanent bullet hole in his leg. Apparently, it was just a flesh wound, but John made such a big stink about this. In fact, there was no damage to his muscle or bone, and his leg cleared up faster than mine did. As time went on, nothing out of the ordinary happened. John and I continued as husband and wife. Sex was the same, his bedroom manners were the same, and so on. My lawyer and I had weekly meetings. He said my case was very serious. I asked, "Is it?" I have no idea what was going on behind the scenes, but the Crown added two more charges: intent to wound and aggravated assault. So now, I had four charges. Throughout my appointments with my lawyer and while he was doing whatever research lawyers do, I wanted to get rid of John and divorce him. Don MacLeod said I couldn't until after the trial; it's too sticky against me. The Crown wanted to charge me with attempted murder. My mouth fell when I heard that part. Something was going on that I didn't know about. It became apparent that John and I could no longer run the pub. There were still bickering about the construction and the wall. John and I hired Nick, our friend from Zaros, to manage our pub with the option to buy. Nick lived in that area. He was all too welcome to manager the pub for us; all I wanted was a buyer. With that, we got rid of all the staff and Nick brought in his own. There was great animosity toward me from the staff. I guess John told everyone that the idea was mine. We were getting calls from the labour board, so I changed our home phone number. Bringing Nick in was a good idea. With Nick's specialty cooking, John and I went to an auction to buy a pizza oven, pizza-dough maker, and meat-slicing machine. We asked Clifford for $5,000.00 to pay for this. This would generate sales, and we'd have the best pizza delivered to customers' homes. Nick would have his right-hand man deliver the cash to my Woodbine home daily. John and I stayed home. I was now in hiding. As time went on, Nick decided that David Halphern wanted way too much rent, so Nick would not buy this pub from us. Damn. It was agreed that Nick would stay on as manager until a purchaser was found. Nick was spending money, our invoices were rising, and less cash was being brought to us. In hope of keeping the landlord from taking the pub from us, John, Murray, and I met in Richard's office. I didn't like the agreement much, but I felt we better take it. Murray would take any extra profits and catch up on the owed two month's rent, pay the bank loan, and pay Revenue Canada. John and I could not collect a wage. At this point, we had the books. John had noticed Murray had helped himself to the till and left notes as to how much he took. Apparently, he would go up to the pub Friday and Saturday nights and take anywhere from $600.00 to $1,000.00. This hurt us in paying suppliers. There was no control anymore, so I wanted a buyer. With the pub's mess and my shooting troubles, I became very depressed, and it would get worse. Murray signed an agreement that he'd follow the above conditions, and he voiced that John could go to the bar, but I couldn't. I said, "If John goes to that bar, I'll divorce him." That was the end of the meeting. As time went on, John was beginning to constantly push me against the wall or repeatedly kick me. We fought about everything, but mostly about the books. John was also drunk every day. He got the booze and money from me. I gave him anything he wanted: sex, money, booze, food, cigarettes, anything. John lived very, very high. Some time around the summer of 1993, an offer came in for the pub. I was really happy. There would be $80,000.00 in trust after realtors' fees. But, there was a problem with the liquor license. Because of the construction delays and David Halphern, there were delays with the negotiation with the city. The purchaser agreed to run the pub and pay Halphern the rent until that problem was solved. It was an unusual transaction, but it was suitable for now. In the meeting with Richard, Murray, John, and I, were informed of this person's purchase interest and his interest in running the pub. Richard would handle it all for us. However, I was also informed that Murray and David had not paid the bank loan, and the Bank of Montreal pulled the loan. I asked how much, and Richard said it was $150,000.00. I immediately burst into tears in his office. How could my loan of $70,000.00 now become $150,000.00? A mortgage of $150,000.00 would be placed through Richard and Granville Mortgage for the next couple of months. Richard, Murray, David, and the new purchaser would try to solve the liquor license problem.

In the meantime, I was going through a daily mental cruelty and, soon, weekly beatings from John. I was constantly bringing up Elaine's name, the books, and telling him, "You never support me. You never support me." John would explode. Throwing me against the wall and/or kicking me was his style. One day, he pushed me backward onto the spiral staircase. I rolled myself around and went upstairs very hurt. I guess John went to watch TV. I was beginning to really hate him. One day, I was in the Jacuzzi. I was under the tap, rinsing my hair, when I got stuck there; I couldn't get up. I called John for help because I couldn't get out of the bathtub. He helped me out of the tub, and I tried to stand. My back was in *pain*. I stood ever so slightly to dry my hair. I told John that there was something very wrong. I went to lie down. In the morning, I was in great pain still. John phoned this chiropractor and made an appointment. John had to help me out of bed, but I was unable to put pressure on my tailbone. He had to carry me to the toilet and carry me off. He had to help me get dressed. I slowly made my way to the car using Ian's cane. I wanted to drive, so I carefully and very slowly put myself in the driver's seat. The doctor's office was way up in the northwest side of the city. Once there, I checked in and sat down. I made my way into the patients' office.

The doctor checked my back. We were making small talk, and he said, "Your husband is supportive."

I said nothing, but just looked into his eyes. *Yeah, right*. Apparently, my back was so swollen around the tailbone. The doctor sent me home to lie down with a cold pack for a couple of days, then come back so he could fix it. So, off we went. John made the cold pack every few hours, helped me out of bed every twenty minutes for a fifteen-minute walk, and back to bed. John made supper and brought me up my favourite tomato soup with cheddar cheese in it. One day, I didn't want to eat my soup and toast, and John just *lost it*. I thought he was going to hit me. This went on for four days. This was when I started reading Stephen King books. This was also the beginning of spending most of my time in bed, upstairs, reading. I went back to the chiropractor, and he was able to do his thing; the swelling had gone down. I looked up the first date of my visit—June 3, 1993. However, I was still walking with a cane as the pain was still there; I would for another month. I continued going to the chiropractor for the next two years. All the while, I was awaiting my trial. I was some scared puppy. John would constantly say that I'm going to jail and giving me that smirk. He really made my house his home; it was like I was just a cook or a maid. In fact, I had a maid, Louise. She would come once every two weeks. John would do his regular routines, and we'd go out for a beer or supper. Finances were getting low, so I sold my truck for $5,000.00. That money went out quickly. For the first time in my life, I had a cheque bounce. While John and I went out, his boozing would put a toll on his manipulation and humilation toward me. He was now constantly humiliating me in public. With his horrid words, he would embarrass me, and people around would feel sorry for me. John was not getting very liked. The fights and his ignorance were pulling me down, down, down. That was his ultimate plan. I am a tough cookie and very strong minded, but John was able to break me. There isn't a man out there like him, as I told my lawyer. He has a PhD in mental and physical cruelty. John was slowly destroying my self-esteem and spirit. People around us could see it; I couldn't. One day, I slipped out of the house with my cane and went to Gator's bar. Everyone knew John had beaten me up, but nothing was said. I just said I hurt my back. John was nice to me during this back thing. I used to slip out of the house and go to Gator's much more often, in fact, daily. This was the start of John constantly looking for me, almost stalking. John would drive up very slowly and see my car parked outside of Gator's. He'd park and come in. John was not very well liked, but people tolerated him because he was my husband. One nice sunny afternoon, fat Murray joined John and me on our back deck. I was still walking with the cane. We were getting close, possibly, in solving the Waterwork's Pub's sale. I'd be so happy to get out of this deal, put the money back onto my house, and carry on. As money was getting tight, John started applying for accounting jobs. However, everywhere he went, he got rejection letters and two interviews. Because he doesn't have a driver's license I drove him to his interviews and waited outside. When he came out of this one interview, he was excited. He thought for sure that he'd have the job. Maybe things would work itself out. I was in love with John. I supported him, and I was good to him. If we got rid of the bar and he gets a job, possibly, we could repair the damage in our marriage. After all, it was for better or worse. I was hoping the pub would not affect my mortgage, so John and I went to look for another house. I wanted to do my kennel business, so I looked at a house south of Calgary. It was five acres, with indoor pool, boarding kennel license, and had a nice floor plan with 2,000 square feet. I liked the house, but it needed TLC. I told John about it, and, one day, we drove by it. He liked the look of it on the outside. This would give me a job at home, and I could drive John to work and pick him up in the city. In fact, John even had an interview in Okotoks, which prompted us to look down there. We stopped at the bar in Okotoks, and I loved the video lottery terminals. I always did very well playing these machines. John was in his suit because he had this interview in Okotoks. We had a couple of beers. There were some people visiting from England sitting next to us. I was friendly, laughing, joking, and really enjoying myself.

As John was drinking more and more, he started verbally cutting me down in front of these people. It was very rude and humiliating. When John went to the bathroom, one guy said, "What are you doing with him? He treats you like shit. He's not for you." I knew what he was saying. I had a lot of credits on my machine, and, when I went to the bathroom, John cashed in my credits. I was furious with him. He handed the money over and kept some for beer and cigarettes. Anyway, it was time to go back to Calgary.

We stopped at Gator's and I said to Corrina, "That's what I married, John being so good looking in his suit, but you know what I got." Corrina and Mike were getting married, and John and I were invited. It was in September 1993. All summer long, I would support her with her up-and-coming marriage. We became friends. Back at home, we continued looking after Clifford and looking for work and a kennel property. John and I even looked at mobile homes.

Today, they are very attractive. There was thought of buying an acreage way south of Calgary and setting up kennels there. That was the purpose of looking at mobile homes. John had another interview in the far northwest of Calgary; it was an evening appointment in the portable of the community there. I drove him up there, went to the bar for about forty-five minutes, and came back to pick him up. We went back to this bar as I was playing the lottery machine there and was winning. John had drank two jugs of beer in the forty-five minutes we chose to stay there. I cashed out, and we went home. July '93 was the year everyone came to visit me. Marja and her husband, Bill, stayed with us. I had bought my beloved Grace and Ben from her. She and her husband were doing a cross-country drive and stopped to see the Calgary Stampede. So, we all went. John did his "I-could-attack-him-anytime" thing. There was an odd air in the house. Something was wrong. However, all my visitors would never have guessed that I shot John a couple of months earlier. When my guests saw everything they wanted to see, they thanked me and left. Another guest was my stepmother, Marg. She didn't know exactly what was wrong, but she knew John was drunk every day. Also, my stepsister visited me. What a year for visitors. Once in a while, I would go to the den with John and play cards on my computer. John had these books carefully stacked on his desk. I never said anything, but those books bugged me. We did the same things every day. I went to Gator's, Ruffino's, and Caesar South daily. John knew where to find me. He would usually find me, park his car, and join me. Don't forget that he has no driver's license, so he would not venture too far out of the neighbourhood. One evening, I was at the Point and Feather pub. I had 3,000 credits on my machine. It was a lot and I was starting to get an audience. I stayed there until the machine was dead. I came home and showed John, who was relaxing in his housecoat, all my money. I placed it on the kitchen island, counted it—$2,000.00 to be exact—and put it into my purse. One evening, I was at Gator's with the owners. I spent one really late evening there. It was actually closing time; the door was locked.

Then, all of sudden, Corrina said, "Here comes John." He was in his housecoat and slippers. They wouldn't let John in, so I told him I'd be home soon. John walked back to his car and went home. I laughed so hard, we all did. But it wasn't funny. I couldn't see it, but everyone else could; there is something terribly wrong with John's brain. The next day, there were rumours everywhere about John in his housecoat. One day, John was in the den. I ripped out a page of his book, the one with the note, and *he lost it*. He went ramping, raving, and screaming all over the house. He put this note back in the book. He continued ramping and raving, and I left the house. This was the beginning of me leaving the house.

One day, we were out for a drive, and I felt my period starting, I said to John, "Run to Safeway for me and get some Super Tampax." I gave him the money. When he came out, he took the box out of the bag to show me if he bought the right thing. At that point, I grabbed the box out of his hand, threw it onto the floor, and said, "I don't read French." Well, after that, he started beating the daylights out of me. People started to stop and look into the car.

As soon as people started to stop at the car, John said, "Get going. Get going." Upon arriving at home, I decided to have a warm Jacuzzi, go to bed, and read a Stephen King novel. It was a warm day in July. Clifford was fine, and the dogs were fine. I would just slowly try to relax my brain by reading. I got into bed naked, with my legs up, holding the book.

About one and a half hours later, John came upstairs. I smiled at him and said, "Hi." I thought, maybe he wanted some loving. But, instead, he came up ramping and raving with this note from the book and just plowed the right side of my face with his hand. I dropped the book and put my hands up to my face for the next blow. I crawled on my hands and knees along the bed, saying, "Don't hurt my back. Don't hurt my back." He was screaming at the top of his voice. As I crawled along the bed, I tried standing up into the left corner of the bedroom. He came around the bed, screamed and whacked the top of my head, screamed and whacked the top of my head, and screamed and whacked the top of my head. This went on thirty times. I was trying to protect my face, teeth, nose, and breasts. When he finally stopped, I looked up at this big, bare back. Had I had the rifle that moment, I would have killed him. At that moment, I went to the phone for 911. He grabbed the phone out of my hand and said that if I phone 911, he would kill me. I was crying; he wasn't kidding. I put the receiver down. He left the room. I called Corrina. She came and got me. My face was turning black; it was like I have black eye shadow on one side of my face. My right hand and shoulder were getting black, too. I stayed at Gator's for a while then went home later. Corrina drove me back and waited to make sure everything was okay I went to my room, to bed. John slept on by himself in the spare bedroom for four nights. In the morning, he came into the bedroom to see the damage he had done. By this time, the bruisings were really black. It was much worse than the beating I took when I shot him. I called my lawyer, and he told me to get pictures. I went to see my physician; the top of my head was really, really sore. My eyes were black. She gave me a prescription for the pain and for reducing the fluid on the top of my head. It was painful for many days. In fact, it hurt even to wash my hair. The doctor asked why I didn't go to a woman's shelter. Why? That's what John wanted me to do. It was my house, my collies, and my father-in-law that I look after. I wasn't leaving my house. John wanted me to leave the house. From that point on, I hated John. Up until then, I hoped and tried to repair our marriage. But, from that point on, he knocked the desire right out of me. I was stuck with this guy until after the trial. From then on, daily, I would leave the house and not return until late at night. John was losing his meal ticket. He would start to look for me at different places. Whenever I see his car in front of Gator's, I'd hide in their back kitchen. He'd come in and look for me. Although he could see my car there, I could also be in Safeway. One day, I was with Bill and Kathy. John came into Gator's and joined me for a while. He was getting very obnoxious. Bill and Kathy said I should stay overnight at their place, so we left. About an hour later, John showed up, in his housecoat, at their place. Bill said that I was staying overnight, so he left. The next day, I returned home. John was nice. I guess, through his incredible mental cruelty and beatings, to him, I was not the same little girl anymore. I was severely depressed and worried about going to jail for four years. Depending on the outcome, maximum was four years. I'd loose my dogs, my house—and what would I do about Clifford? This was always on my mind. So, my routine was to go out the door every day. One day, I was at the Point and Feather. I was speaking with a friend when John came in. He wanted me to come home.

With the attitude John projected, my friend said, "Stay with me tonight. He looks like he is going to lose it and hit you again." So, I did. I told John, and he went home. When I would come home in the mornings, John would always greet me at the door. It was getting closer to my pretrial. My lawyer requested $15,000.00 upfront or no dice. Where am I going to get $15,000.00? My houses were mortgaged to the hilt. I took Clifford to have an intimate dinner with him at Caesar's South Steak house. I explained everything to him and asked him if it would be possible to get my share of my estate now, so I could pay the lawyer and keep up with the bills. Clifford agreed. Some time, out in the hall, I saw John looking for me. They would not let him inside the diningroom, so John waited in the lounge. When Cliff and I finished, we went into the lounge. Clifford would have one beer, and that's it. Anyway, the three of us went home. The next day, I booked an appointment with our commercial lawyer. It was all signed legally. Within a month, I got $80,000.00—my share. I gave my criminal lawyer a certified cheque for $15,000.00; that was just the first payment. I paid just in time for the pretrial. I was getting sicker and sicker about the trial. I had no idea what to expect. John knew because he had been in court many times. John got crueller and crueller. I decided I was going to commit suicide. I had a bottle of Activan pills. I took this bottle and put it in my closet, under my T-shirts. On the eve of August 9, I downed the bottle. In the morning of August 10, I woke up, much to my displeasure. However, I was very stoned. I got up and puked and puked. I was dizzy and walked funny. Apparently, I did my usual morning things. I had a Jacuzzi bath and put on my black silk shirt and jeans. I was wearing my Indian slippers, which I usually used in the house. John knew I wasn't all there, so he asked me to go to the bank and get him some money. He took me to my car, put me inside, turned it on, and sent me my merry way. I wasn't feeling all that right, and my car was weaving around. Anyway, I would just easily go to the bank and return. As I was going along, I approached a red light. I went for the brake. Because my car seat was set up for higher-heeled footwear, I hit the car ahead of me ever so lightly. I put my car in park and this Chinese guy got out of his tiny car. I got out of mine, and no damage was done.

He said, "Let's go over to the far right side and exchange addresses and phone number." So I did. But, once again, I hit his car ever so lightly. I was mad, swearing under my breath. After all was done, I carried on down the road. I decided that going to the bank was too risky, so I turned to go back home. I also puked all over the steering wheel and dashboard. Apparently, I hit the curb, totally wrecked the undercarriage of the car, and had a flat tire. I slowly carried on along the shoulder with my emergency lights on.

Then, along Anderson Road, two cop cars stopped me. I wondered what was going on. It was the same cop, Constable James, who was at my shooting incident; they knew me by my first name. The cop asked, "Anita, what are you doing?" I said I was going home. He said, "No, you are not. You're coming with us." Apparently, the Chinese guy I so lightly hit was an off duty Royal Canadian Mounted Police officer. He phoned District Six and said I did a hit-and-run. I said that was a lie and I had his name and telephone number right here. The cops asked if I was drinking. I hadn't been drinking. Then, they said I seemed stoned. I told them I took PMS pills the night before. I wasn't going to tell them I committed unsuccessful suicide with Activan. The cops took me down to District Six, towed my car to Tower Chrysler, and called John. Because the cops knew us, they knew John could not drive down in his car; he had no license. So, John came down in a Mayfair cab. The cops charged me with impaired with a drug and dangerous driving.

John came to pick me up. On the way home, he said, "I knew you were going to get in trouble." Ian's brother came to visit. No problem, but I didn't see much of Ralph. John kept me in my bedroom to sleep and told Ralph I was sick. John didn't want Ralph to see that I was stoned. I slept there for hours. John never came up, not even once, to see if I was okay or to bring me food. It was like he knew I was trying to commit suicide, and he was hoping I would die. I stayed home for the next few days.

CHAPTER NINETEEN

The pretrial was in the next few days. John and I went down to the courthouse. My lawyer and the crown prosecutor were there. I just froze in this place. It seemed like a long time sitting there with all the crap going on back and forth. To make a long story short, for this moment, the judge decided that there would be a further trial and told me not to think of getting off. John and I left the courtroom together. We went to the Bay. I bought new underwear, went to the washroom, and put my new underwear on, as my period started during the trial. I breezed through that one without embarrassment. John and I wondered around downtown and went to the Elephant & Castle lounge. When at downtown, that was my hang out. I didn't know what was going on in the trial. I never mentioned anything to John, nor did he say anything to me. I just knew I was in deep trouble. John was walking around like a king. Only God knew what he was thinking. After our downtown trip, we went to Gator's. No one there knew we were at my pretrial. Anyway, I was physically uncomfortable and wanted to go home, so home we went. I went upstairs to bed to read more Stephen King. Nothing was going on with the pub; Richard just said that the money was coming. It wasn't a big issue at this moment. I trusted Richard's professionalism in looking after the Waterwork's mess. When I felt better, I went on my usual routine. When a man would show attention to me, I fell for it. Anyone who would say I am pretty or something like that got my interest. I needed love and was looking for it elsewhere. It was Labour Day weekend, and most bars were closed. John and I wanted to go out for a beer; we were having a good time. We found a place that was open, the Olive Grove. It was a Sunday. We were actually enjoying each other. We sat in the lounge, and, from time to time, I would play the video machines. Just as John and I were content, right out of the blue, a true fluke, in walked Elaine Brown and her husband. They sat at the table next to us, even though there were ten other vacant tables. Immediately, John and Elaine glued their eyes on each other. I just sat there, stewing. Elaine borrowed money from her husband and began playing the machine behind me. In other words, she had a full view of John, and my back was to her. I watched John's facial expressions, and I could tell when they were glued to each other in between the sounds of the machine. I lost it; I turned to her husband and asked, "Did you know your wife is having an affair with my husband?" And on I went. The owner actually had to take me out of the restaurant; I had put on quite a show. They were going to phone the cops. I left the lounge, walked to a McDonald's to use the washroom and to phone a cab.

As I was walking, John was in his car, driving down the street. He saw me, and screamed out of his window, "I am not going to support you on this one," and drove off. The cab came and took me to a bar that was open—the Point and Feather on 90th Avenue. I knew one guy there. I had company, and we talked for many hours. Internally, I was fuming. It was around closing time, and he asked me if I would like a ride home. I said, "Okay." Rather than turning right, he turned left and took me to the park across the street. This park has a lake. In fact, it is the lake that supplies Calgary's drinking water. I said, "You're going the wrong way."

He said, "Let's go for a walk, okay?" He took me down to the lake, forcefully took off my jeans, and had sex. When this was all over, I left my underpants there because they were wet. This guy drove me home but only dropped me off at the top of my street. I got in at 3:00 A.M. I quickly put on my nightgown and went to bed. In the morning, I told John what had happened. He wasn't mad at me, he was furious with the guy. John looked up his name and address in the phone book and called the guy several times. I said I had left my underwear at the lake because they were wet. John spent his time in the den calling and calling this guy. I didn't know what he was saying. I was in the Jacuzzi, getting refreshed and getting ready for my day. I went down to the den and asked John, "When are we going today? Are we going out?" He said we are going out.

So, off we went. We drove to the park. John insisted that we look for my underwear. We walked and walked up and down the beach for my underwear. I got tired and went back to the car; John stayed looking for my underwear. We must have been down there for two hours. Then, finally, he came over to the car. I don't know if he found them or not. We drove on, and he stopped by this house. He asked, "Is that the guy's car?" I said, "Yes." Then, all of a sudden, John got out of the car, opened the trunk, and took out a huge axe. He came over to show this to me. I got scared, jumped into the driver's side, and drove off with the trunk door still up. I drove around the corner, stopped, and put the trunk down. I went home. Hours went by, and then John came home. Apparently, John had been pacing up and down the street, swinging the axe and screaming, "You fucked my wife," and on and on at this guy who was with his wife and kids inside of their house.. John threatened to smash the guy's car windows in. Evidently, the guy phoned the cops. By the time they arrived, John was walking down the street, in his suit and tie, swinging the axe.

The same cops that were at the shooting stopped John and asked him, "What are you doing with the axe?" John said he was going to cut down a tree. They took him down to District Six. He got charged. To this day, I don't exactly know what John had done. I am only quoting what John told me. His court case was coming up in February of '94. John would go out of his way to humilate anyone. I believe he wanted to show my underwear to that guy's wife. I was starting to believe that I married a real nut. Because of this, John decided to add more mental cruelty to the list; he decided not to have sex with me. This went on for some time.

Then, one evening, I said to John, "If you don't have sex with me, I'll go looking for it." He started to have sex with me again. Sodomy joined the ritual. People didn't understand why I let him stay; I was following my lawyer's instructions. I could not get rid of John until after the trial. Why didn't you phone 911? I did. How come you let the credits on your cards get so high?

During the eight months of waiting for my trial, I let John have whatever he wanted, so he wouldn't toast me in the trial; John lived like a king. Sometimes, I would lock John out of the bedroom. So, one day, he decided to change locks with the spare room; John would never be locked out of the master bedroom. It was time for Corrina's wedding. John and I got all dressed up, had our best behaviour, and went to the wedding and reception in September of 1993. Corrina looked lovely. It was a lovely wedding, and I was so happy for her. I had duplicates made of the pictures I took and gave them to her. As time went on, I was very unhappy, scared, and depressed. I continued my usual routine. John continued to look for me whenever I disappeared. One afternoon, John drove up to Gator's. Rather than coming in, he drove his car backward and forwards for about twenty minutes in front of their large glass windows. The customers, owners, and I were getting a little worried; it just showed how mental John was. Then he drove off. One day, I couldn't find my rings. For a week, I was without my rings. It was rumoured that John pawned them off. I called the cops and put in a claim for my missing rings. A week later, John gave me my rings back. To this day, I have no idea, what happened to my rings. One day, I joined a friend at Austin's pub. John came in and I said, "Honey, come on and sit down." I bought John a pint of beer, but, before I knew it, he threw the whole pint in my face. Just like that. I threw my beer at him, but missed. He got up and left, then turned around, came back, and handed me my Bay card. Everyone couldn't believe John's behaviour. Those who had not seen his actions were now convinced that John is truly an asshole. Then, the next day, I was at Austin's with the same friends. John came in, stared at me, and walked out. John's behaviour since the shooting was the talk of the town—big time. Although John was going around saying he's the victim; in reality, I was. Just so John wouldn't find me so easily, I started going to the Stetson Village Inn on MacLeod. It took him a long time before he'd find me. I found comfort there. In the meantime, should John find me, he was obnoxious. I was normally asked to stay at someone's house. But, not every day was rotten; I tried to get along. One day, we were driving home. I parked the car, got out, and decided to kick the empty paint cans in the corner of the garage before going into the house. I said hello to Cliff who was standing around the island. John came in like a raving idiot and asked why I kicked the paint cans. I told him I was frustrated and I just kicked the cans. Well, at that point, he picked me up and started pushing me toward the garage. I was screaming, "Cliff, help! Help!"

Poor old Cliff was standing at the garage door, screaming, "Stop it! Stop it!"

John pushed me against the garage door. I was screaming, "Don't hurt my back! Don't hurt my back!" He finally stopped, and I went up stairs, got into the Jacuzzi, went to bed, and cried. Each day was a day of mental pain. I'd go off anywhere. I was at the Stetson Pub one day, and John came in, raving. The bouncer was watching John's behaviour. He thought John was going to hit me. I left just to get John out of there. I started going out without my wedding ring, and John would come looking for me to put my ring back on.

So, I'd take my ring with me but not wear it. If I saw him coming, I'd put it on. At this point, it didn't matter. However, in John's eyes, he didn't want to lose his meal ticket. That's all I was to him. One evening, on October 30, 1993, I was at the Point and Feather with some friends. It was a Friday night, and the pub was full. While I was there, John walked in wearing only his housecoat and slippers. We both turned around in amazement.

He said, "Come home."

I said, "I'm not walking out of this bar with you looking like that." He left. I stayed overnight with my friend. Everyone was just blown away by his behaviour. Plus, he pulled his coat open to show me he was wearing only underwear. It was embarrassing to me, but that was what John was trying to do. That went all over town and was the talk for many months to come. I was at home one day, and John went out. I didn't know where he was, but I didn't care. Then, I got a call to come and pay his bar bill. He was charged $100.00 in fine meals and booze. John did this to me about three times. One day, he came home really drunk and went to bed with me. He was really hungover, but he mentioned to me that he was missing his wallet. He told me he was at the Point and Feather, so I called the Point. The manager said that he was barred from the Point, and so was I. But why me? I said I was going to divorce John soon. What a lousy judgement call. But it didn't matter; they didn't want me in there because he'd come looking for me. That housecoat scene was just awful. I went upstairs and said, "John we are both barred out of the Point and Feather. What did you do in there?" The next day, I went to Gator's, and Nick mentioned that John had been threatening to smash the windows of his pub with a crowbar. The owner asked me not to come in for a while. I wasn't barred; I was welcome as soon as I got rid of John. In fact, I could be there, but I got their hint; they were getting scared of John.

One day, John was losing it. I called 911. The woman on the other end of the phone asked, "Is this a problem house?" I said, "Yes." "Has he hit you?" I said no. John was screaming at the top of his voice, right in my ear, then I put him on the phone. The girl listened to him, and he said hello in a soft, sweet voice. Then I was on the phone, and he'd scream at his loudest again. I'd put him on the phone, and he'd answer with a soft sweet voice again. They sent over the cops. Only one problem, one cop would take my side, one his. John always had his charisma on queue for the cops; he was able to turn everything around and told them that I was attacking him. Then the cops would leave. I called my lawyer once, during one of these 911 calls, but he just hung up. One day, Clifford and I were sitting on the couch, watching TV. John came over, took my beer, and threw it in my face. Clifford said in the best way he could, "Don't do that." John went and sat on the other couch.

He turned around and said to me, "You are such a cunt. Living with you is such a high price to pay."

With that comment, I froze. A few seconds later, I said, "I don't know why you wear your wedding ring." I just hated John. As we were getting closer to the trial, my lawyer wanted another $10,000.00 certified, so I got it for him.

Also, I was spending more time with my lawyer, approximately twice a week. I wanted to get this over with. Either I am going to jail, or I can get rid of John. I had no support while waiting for this. I had no brothers or sisters; my support group was my two lawyers, Richard and Don, and John knew this. I had it all planned. Should I go to jail for four years, Richard would get John out of the house and rent it out for me. Cliff would go to Ralph, my dogs to Marja. I had everything in order: one envelope here, one there. Should I do weekends, I could handle my affairs under those terms. While waiting for my trial, Don MacLeod was sending me to a psychiatrist. I went for several sessions. My lawyer was going to prove, if needed, that I am not a dangerous person.

The psychiatrist said to me, "It is your misfortune that John has come into your life. Otherwise, this would not have happened to you." How true. What a big mistake marrying John. While all this was going on, I still looked after the Collie Club memberships. John and I were invited by some collie-owner friends with regards to purchasing one of their show males. Buster was his name. He was a beautiful male. John and I bought him. We spent several weekends at their place, about one hour north of Calgary. I also continued my dog shows and stayed with friends in Edmonton and Medicine Hat. I was showing Gracie off. John and I weren't getting along; he was trying to humiliate me with my doggy-club friends. No one knew that there was an upcoming trial. Not anyone in the dog business knew I shot John. So, Buster and Grace are both in our names with the Canadian Kennel Club. But, Ben did not welcome Buster; he beat Buster up. There was a big dogfight in the family room. That meant Ben and Buster had to be separated all the time, when eating, peeing, and just plain socializing. The dog purchase and shows were in July. One evening, I was staying overnight with Bill and Kathy. John came looking for me in his housecoat and slippers with Ben, Buster, and Grace in his car. It was a deterrent, should he pass by a cop. Anyway, Kathy said I was staying overnight, so he quietly went home.

The next day, I said, "John, you can't put Ben and Buster together." John would lose it and I left the house. Since my August accident, I didn't get my car back until November. That's why John was out in his car. Or we were out together. He was taking a chance in driving. I would usually walk to Gator's. One evening, John was loosing it, and I left the house and ran. I ran and ran. I cut through the park on the way to Gator's. It was dark out. I could see John driving slowly along the road, looking for me, so I kept running. I went to Gator's, but John found me there. He behaved, got me, and took me home. I didn't want him in there. Actually, we could still go there; they just didn't want trouble. This was around November of '93. I continued doing my thing. The one thing I wanted to do was go to Vegas. I bought myself a ticket for a one-week stay in Vegas. I booked myself into the Flamingo Hilton on the strip. My lawyer had called me and asked me to come into his office. I said I couldn't because I was going to Vegas. John was standing beside me when he heard this. John looked at me funny. I told him I was going by myself; that he's not coming. It did bug him. Upon arriving at Vegas, I did the usual things. I love the one-armed bandits and away I went. During my week there, I went to just about every hotel on the strip and downtown. I played almost every game. I was on a mission trip; if I should do four years, I'll spend my money so John can't have it. Also, the criminal record thing would alter my entry to the United States. That would bother me more than anything else. So, Vegas was my mission trip. Like always, the weather was warm. My suite in the Hilton was pleasant. I was going to go all out. I went to a different restaurant every day. John called me every morning in my room. It was one of those "I-love-you calls" or how late I was or if there was anyone with me. He asked if I have won any money. However, a week in Vegas is too long. Near the end, I wanted to go home. I had a lovely meal in the Hilton—lasagna. The sauce tasted funny. But, I just figured that the sauce down there was this way. Just as I reached the last game near the lobby, a spinning wheel game, I decided to play. I was winning, then, all of a sudden, I felt funny. I puked the lasagna in the garbage can next to the game. I assumed I was food poisoned. A female security guard walked me to my room. The next day, I came down and the same guy was at the wheel. I promised him I wouldn't puke today. The days grew closer to the end of my stay. My flight was leaving at midnight. But I had to have my suitcase out of my room by noon. The hotel would put it in a secured spot. So, I was out of my room by noon and I've got all that boring time to wait. I went to a few free shows, played the machines some more, and drank the free booze. By 11:00 P.M., I was drunk. Oh, my God, I am going to be late for my flight. I rushed for my luggage and took a cab to the airport. I was running through the airport and fell. I got up and somehow got to my gate. I got my boarding pass and sat down. A big, black security guard came over and said that I lost it, and that he may not let me on the plane. I thought, *What a bunch of bullshit*. Anyway, they let me on the plane, but they wouldn't serve me any booze. I was mad. I went up to the stewardess and asked why. She gave some lousy comment. I said I will not fly Canadian Air again and I gave her my Canadian Points card. She said she wouldn't take it. Finally, she took it, but it was sent back to me. I have never flown Canadian again. Years later, the company folded.

CHAPTER TWENTY

Back at home, I was spending a lot of time with my lawyer and going out, staying away from John as much as possible. One day, he found me at Austin's. He came in and joined me at the table. He was mouthing off, "You had it coming. You had it coming. You've been a spoiled brat all your life, and I'm glad I'm the one who has ruined your life." God, I hated this man. As we were getting closer to the trial, the beating and the sodomy stopped. But the mental cruelty was there, and sex was there. I asked John one morning if he loved me. He turned around and, with his deep, loud voice, said, "No." John was smart; he didn't want any charges against him. He wanted this trial to proceed. That's why he quit beating me. He also didn't want a divorce, and he didn't want me to use sodomy as a way out. If he should get countercharged, my case would be thrown out. John couldn't possibly risk that. My lawyer informed me that it was jury-picking time. I didn't want a jury, but he suggested that I should have one. The judge was a tough female; better get a jury. This was new to me. I wore the dress suit I wore to my marriage to John and my fox and lynx fur coat. It was wintertime. I entered this room in Queen's Bench. A whole bunch of people were sitting in there. I was nervous. My lawyer saw me and motioned me to sit up front. Before I went on the bench, three guys were ahead of me. Apparently, they killed someone while being in jail. They were brought into the courtroom from the jailhouse. All three of them were in the accused box. I didn't like the smell of this. Their lawyers were going through a lot of people. The courtroom was getting empty with people. It was my turn to go in the accused box. The judge read the charges to the courtroom, all four charges. People were looking at me, really looking at me. I felt so stupid. I was also scared. Two prospective jurors called and said they couldn't sit on the panel because of whatever reason. One said that the case was too emotional for her. The audience turned out to be six men and women. My lawyer addressed me to go outside for a minute. He stayed in the courtroom. Then I had to come back in. I didn't know what was going on. Then, I went back out. He said that one of the jurors picked could not sit on the panel. I had to go back in. Finally, it was all squared away. I could leave. I met my lawyer several days later, and he told me to dress down; I shouldn't look to prosperous. I was not to wear my fur and only wear my wedding ring in the courtroom, not my other diamonds. Anyway, that was done. One early Sunday morning, the police were at the door; they asked for John. He showed up in his housecoat. The cops presented legal documents for John as the victim. John was smiling at his papers. He came back into the kitchen and said to me, "You're going to jail." He was giving me that smirk. With that, I just heaved a mighty spit at him. John looked at me funny and just carried on cleaning.

Clifford heard that and said, "She shouldn't be going to jail; you should be." That was the first time Clifford let out his real feelings about John.

Clifford hated John. My dogs hated John. Everyone hated John. My forty-first birthday was on December 7, and I wasn't jumping for joy, not when my trial was on December 13 (Monday). I had all these thoughts. Maybe I'll be spending my forty-first birthday in jail and so on. It was freezing cold outside, my December wasn't fun. On the morning of December 13, I got all ready for my first day in Queen's Bench. I dressed down like my lawyer said. I always wore short-sleeved outfits to show the jury how skinny and tiny I am. I never gave John any money for a haircut as I wanted him to look messy. John would alternate his clothing also. He really wanted to look good. As we proceeded into the room, I was to sit in the accused box. There was no comfort there. A bench seat was what it was. The jury had plush, comfortable seats. John, the victim, sat in the visitor's section, right behind me. There was a security guard beside me. This was an extra expense. John was feeding the prosecutor that I was very dangerous, so they hired a security guard. Although I was "highly dangerous," John was still living with me—nobody thought about that. The beginning was basically the police and ambulance people stating what they remember of this incident. It was an all-day thing with a lunch break and coffee break. John and I could leave the building at lunch, but, for coffee, we went to the court lunchroom downstairs. All kinds of other trials were going on as well. The media went from courtroom to courtroom to get their stories. John and I went to the Elephant & Castle in Eaton Centre for lunch. I had tea while John had a couple of beers. My lawyer told me not to drink booze, so I didn't. John did. This trial was only supposed to go on for three days, but it went on for five days. After day one, John and I went home. In the morning, I was in the papers. John cut the article out, brought it upstairs, and showed it to me in bed. I was just devastated. The next day, it was my turn on the stand. The judge looked at me straight in the eye. She scared me. Although, throughout this trial, I could tell she was brilliant. The prosecutor, the Greek bitch, was horrid. I hated her. The first thing the judge asked me was to tell the jury how my second husband died. Just as she said that, one female in the jury burst out laughing very loudly. It almost set the room in giggles. I said he died of cancer. The Crown started asking me questions. She referred to John as my friend throughout the whole trial.

She asked me, "Did you ask John, while in the hospital, to please say this was an accident?" I said, "Yes." At this point, I wondered how the Crown would know this. That's when I realized that John had been feeding the Crown with all sorts of information, true and untrue. John had been feeding the Crown for eight months behind my back. The usual questions went on back and forth. At one point, the Crown screamed at me at the top of her voice and said I deserved to be hit. How professional was this broad? "Did you hit John."

"Yes, I hit John, but he wouldn't feel anything." This Crown was pushing and pushing me. I finally said, with my hands tightly squeezed together, my head up in the air, that I am going through severe mental cruelty. John, sitting in the seats, made a voiced jesture, "Yeah sure." I also went through the motion of the bruising I had. It basically went back and forth with my lawyer and the Crown, with the usual breaks. My lawyer would ask, "Are you and John having sex?" "Yes." "Are you and John sleeping in the same bed?" "Yes." "You are coming here together?" "Yes." If there was anything I felt was important to say, I would be cut off, or simply couldn't say it. When I think back it, I shouldn't have been so truthful; I should have lied a bit here and there. The judge brought out the .22 rifle. I was to show the jury what I did. The judge handed me the rifle. As she handed this to me, I put on a funny smile, an embarrassed one. I found the gun heavy, but it certainly wasn't heavy that night. I was motioned to stand in the middle of the courtroom so that the jury could see me. I showed them how I held this thing and what was going through my mind. I said that while I was down there with this thing, I shot at the door and placed it back upstairs. That's it. My time on the stand was over. It was John's turn and my lawyer told me that he was going to make a fool of John. While John was on the stand, it was proven that he was a liar and had been all his life. It was proved to the jury that John has never been a chartered accountant, although he projected himself as one. He was black-balled for this in the courts. His first wife divorced him for mental cruelty; it wasn't John who divorced her. He said he was with his wife ten years, which was a lie. He also has an impaired charge. But, while on the stand, John went out of his way to bad mouth me: that I drink more than he does; that I start in the morning, drink all day, order beer in at night, but that he doesn't start to drink until noon; and that I start all the fights first and always hit him first. John admitted to beating me up, he admitted to taking the pictures of the bruising. John was worried about getting countercharged, he was on that stand defending himself. He couldn't back off now; he had pushed it too far. My lawyer said he was going to make a fool of John, that he did, but not enough to convince the jury that I was an okay kid and that John is cruel and wicked. John was very, very charismatic and intelligent while on the stand. He played the poor victim; that he was the one who got shot. The trial was pretty well a redundancy of the pretrial, with one surprise for the Crown. My Doctor, Dr. Narang, appeared as a witness. She told the jury that Anita Aikens visited her office with severe bruisings on her shin and arms. She could not tell the jury as to how many blows to the leg I took, but it was intense. In other words, John Aikens was really, really beating his wife. This was when there came a possible countercharge against John. When the court was discussing this, I saw John hurrying out of the courtroom and to the washroom across the hall. He was scared that he'd get countercharged. This would certainly blow his plans. No big house, no fancy car, no pub, no rental property, no cash in the bank, and, worst of all, no imprisoned wife. I asked my lawyer what was going on, he said that it was too late to countercharge John, I thought that was odd. But, I left that up to my lawyer. After all, I was told I had the best lawyer in town. Five days of this had put a heavy strain on my mental condition. John was glowing in his own pride—whatever that was. On Friday, December 17, 1993, the jury originally convicted me for intent to wound which would give me four years. Somewhere in all this the judge reread the act on that charge, in other words, convict "Beyond a reasonable doubt." The jury gave me a not-guilty verdict on that count. They also gave me a not-guilty verdict on aggravated assault. But, they gave me a guilty verdict on the weapon and assault charge. The weapon charge ruined my life. Well, John wasn't successful in sending me to jail for four years, but he was happy with the conviction, he had wrecked my life. John was very proud of this. And, worst of all, he walked into the horizon cleared. When I heard the verdict, I started to cry. My lawyer immediately came over and told me to stop crying, I shouldn't let the jury see me crying. I thought to myself, *How could I stop?* The judge did say that this was a very difficult and unusual case. The judge told the jury that they can sit in the courtroom to hear the sentencing. Only the women jurors showed up, the men left. The women were giggling and smirking and looking at me with great jealously. They were so proud to wreck my life as well. I sat in the accused box with a look of great hatred. The women went to the Crown and said, "Did we do it right, did we do it right?" "No," the Crown said, "no, we were supposed to convict her on all four counts." While all this shuffling was going around, the humilation within me was escalating. Then, all of a sudden, my lawyer was going to file an appeal. The sentencing was postponed until December 23, 1993. Those poor women didn't hear the sentencing; they had to read about it. The courtroom cleared, John left on his own somewhere. Actually, he went to the Inn on The Lake Bonavista. It was a very posh bar, where you'd find yourself very rich, single old women. For some reason, I believe John knew now that our marriage was toast and he'd better look for someone else to take care of him. I ended up sitting in the courthouse, awaiting my conviction papers, which I have kept to this day, laminated and stuck on the wall. After all, not too many women have convictions papers about shooting their husband to brag about. Once that was done I took a cab to my corporate lawyer's office. Richard DeVries gave me the comfort I needed. I was distraught and suicidal. I was in the news, *CBC Alberta*, TV and newspapers. This affected my charity work. No one knew about my problem until it became public. My phone kept ringing. It was so humiliating. December 23, 1993 came, I arrived in the courtroom with a girlfriend; John didn't come. Why should he? He had already done his damage. I was sentenced 75 days (weekends) in jail and one year probation. Also, I was forbidden to own a gun for ten years.

On Friday, December 17, 1993, following a trial before the Honourable Madam Justice A. Fruman, sitting with a jury, the following verdicts were reached:

Count 1: Mrs. Aikens was not found guilty of discharging a firearm with intent to wound contrary to section 244(a) of the Criminal Code, but was found guilty of the lesser and included offence of assault causing bodily harm contrary to section 267(1)(b) of the Criminal Code.

Count 2: Mrs. Aikens was found guilty of possession of a weapon for a purpose dangerous to the public peace contrary to section 87 of the Criminal Code.

Count 3: Mrs. Aikens was found not guilty of aggravated assault (unlawfully wounding, maiming, disfiguring, or endangering the life of the complainant) contrary to section 268 of the Criminal Code, but was found guilty of the lesser and included offence of assault causing bodily harm.

Count 4: Mrs. Aikens was found guilty of assault with a weapon contrary to section 267(1)(a) of the Criminal Code.

Convictions of assault causing bodily harm and of possession of a weapon dangerous to the public peace were entered and the remaining verdicts were conditionally stayed.

CHAPTER TWENTY-ONE

BACKGROUND AND CIRCUMSTANCES OF THE ACCUSED:

Anita Elizabeth Aikens is forty years of age. She completed high school in Vancouver, British Columbia in 1972, followed by one year of university education at the University of Alberta. She is a licensed aesthetician. Her employment is secretarial positions throughout most of the 1980s.

In July of 1989, Mrs. Aikens married Ian Hayes. The couple moved to Calgary where they operated a retail business called Candle and Flame Creations Ltd. in the Southcentre Mall. Ian Hayes' father (Clifford Hayes) moved to Calgary to live with the couple.

On Aprill 22, 1991, Ian Hayes passed away from liver cancer. The accused continued operating the retail store following his death.

While Mr. Hayes was still alive, the couple met John Aikens who was himself still married to his former wife. In October of 1991, John Aikens attended a party held by the accused. Shortly thereafter, he moved into Anita Aiken's house, and the couple has cohabited ever since, marrying in November of 1992.

In June of 1992, after John Aikens had seen an advertisement for a neighbourhood pub, the couple invested a total of $110,000.00 in the Waterworks Pub. Anita Aikens contributed some $70,000.00 toward the purchase price.

In January of 1993, due to an explosion in adjacent premises, the Waterworks Pub had to be closed down. When it reopened, following repairs, it had lost a substantial amount of its clientele, encountered financial difficulties, and was sold in November 1993. Mrs. Aikens continued to cohabitate with Mr. Aikens subsequent to the events of April 26, 1993.

Clifford Hayes is now eighty-three years of age. He has cancer. He is hard of hearing. He has resided with Mrs. Aikens for some three years, and she provides him with a home, companionship, and assistance with meals.

Mrs. Aikens herself is presently in the course of reorganizing her financial affairs in the aftermath of the sale of the Waterworks Pub. She hopes to either find employment or become self-employed in the field of dog breeding and care once reorganization of her business affairs is completed.

Mrs. Aikens has no previous record. She has been described as trustworthy and honest. His physician confirms that she (Mrs. Aikens) has provided Clifford Hayes with excellent care. Dr. Parney also observed that their relationship is a good one, based on mutual respect and affection.

THE JURY'S VERDICT:

In cases where the jury has rendered a finding of guilty, the sentencer is bound by the express and implied factual implications of the jury's verdict.

A close review of the verdicts indicates that the jury accepted that Mrs.

Aikens thought the rifle was a BB gun.

The finding under Count 1 is particularly illuminating. It will be recalled that, when the jury was charged, the instructions given them left little room for doubt that Mrs. Aikens had, in fact, been wounded. It would follow that, if the jury thought Mrs. Aikens knowingly discharged a .22 calibre rifle at Mr. Aikens, there would also be little room for doubt that she intended to wound him. Instead, of course, the jury rendered a verdict of assault occasioning bodily harm.

The jury obviously did not think that Mrs. Aikens discharged a firearm capable of causing serious bodily injury or death to a person at Mr. Aikens.

Mr. Aikens himself admits that, prior to the offences, he had kicked Mrs. Aikens at the precise location depicted in the photographs entered as Exhibits 5, 6, and 7 in the trial. Mrs. Aikens testified that she was kicked some twenty times. Some three to four days after the accident, she attended the offices of her physician. Dr. Narang confirmed that the bruising to her left chin was approximately four inches by four inches, with a central area of fluid-filled swelling measuring two and half inches by two and a half inches. Although Dr. Narang was not able to testify as to the number of blows required to cause an injury of this nature, she was able to confirm that the bruising was "deep" and was caused by "intense" force. Dr. Narang also testified that Mrs. Aikens was still limping on April 30, 1993, and that the bruised area was tender to touch. She prescribed painkillers for Mrs. Aikens.

In any event, Mrs. Aikens went to the upstairs bedroom to retrieve a rifle she believed to be a BB gun. She returned downstairs. Mr. Aikens ignored her and returned to cleaning the floor in the kitchen. Mrs. Aikens discharged the "BB gun," causing Mr. Aikens bodily harm.

Following the discharge of the rifle, the evidence of both Mr. Aikens and Mrs. Aikens is to the effect that she could not believe she had shot him. There was no further aggressive or hostile acts toward Mr. Aikens. Mrs. Aikens complied with Mr. Aikens' request to telephone 911. She complied with all requests made of her by both Emergency Medical Services personnel and police officers who later attended the residence.

Mrs. Aikens visited Mr. Aikens at the hospital the following day. Mr. Aikens did not perceive her to be a threat to himself, the hospital staff, or other patients. Upon Mr. Aikens' discharge, he was picked up by Mrs. Aikens and returned to the Aikens' residence with her. As noted, the parties have cohabited since.

Mr. Aikens did not sustain any vascular, neurological, or orthopedic injury. He was hospitalized for approximately thirty-six hours and experienced some discomfort for approximately four days following his discharge. There was no permanent effect resulting from his injury.

SOME GENERAL PRINCIPLES:

It may be useful to consider some general principles before turning to sentencing cases dealing with persons convicted of assault causing bodily harm or possession of a weapon for a dangerous purpose.

DRUNKENNESS:

While drunkenness is not a truly mitigating factor, it, nonetheless, may be relevant in that it is a factor which may assist in determining whether an attack was spontaneous and whether the accused fully appreciated the likely consequences of his or her act.

In an assault context, drunkenness has been considered to be a "highly relevant" factor for sentencing purposes.

Finally, alcohol and drunkenness may be relevant in the court's consideration of the part deterrence play in fixing a sentence. In relation to the deterrence question, the Alberta Court of Appeal has observed that a drunken aggressor gives little or no thought to the consequences of his or her actions or the punishment that might be visited.

PROVOCATION:

Provocation has also been considered to be a "highly relevant" circumstance in fixing a sentence following a conviction for assault occasioning bodily harm.

The Alberta Court of Appeal has also referred to provocation of the offender by the victim as "an obvious mitigating factor."

In a case where the trial court found the accuser's reaction to a kick from the complainant to be excessive, the Alberta Court of Appeal characterized the complainant's action as an "extreme provocation," which should be taken into account in the sentencing of the accused.

HARDSHIP FOR THIRD PARTIES:

An unusual feature presented by this case lies in the fact that Mrs. Aikens has had the elderly and ailing father of her deceased former husband living with her for the past three years. As previously noted, she has been giving good care to him, and the relationship between the two of them is characterized by mutual caring and respect. Obviously, a disposition which significantly impedes that relationship will impose an extreme hardship on Clifford Hayes.

—Case study not important

IT IS RESPECTFULLY SUBMITTED THAT the hardship concern is equally apt in this case because of Clifford Hayes' circumstances and his relationship with the accused.

SENTENCING DISPOSITIONS:

This is a HIGHLY UNUSUAL CASE, given Mrs. Aikens' belief that the weapon she used was a BB gun. Additionally, alcohol, provocation on the part of Mr. Aikens, significant bodily harm to Mrs. Aikens, and the continued relationship between the parties somewhat revealed unusual features.

Further, this is not a firearms offence in the sense that that term is ordinarily understood.

Mrs. Aikens' case presents an unusual sentencing problem because of the unusual circumstances. In order to afford some perspective on the matter, the accused will review some cases involving careless use of a firearm, dangerous use of a firearm, assault occasioning bodily harm with a weapon, and intentional wounding. However, IT IS RESPECTFULLY SUBMITTED THAT, within the continuum between careless use of a firearm and intentional wounding, the circumstances of the case at the bar can be far more closely likened to the cases involving carelessness in terms of blameworthiness.

to 55. Case studies; can be of importance.

CONCLUSION

To repeat, IT IS RESPECTFULLY SUBMITTED THAT, in all of the circumstances of this case, including the alcohol consumption, the provocation offered by Mr. Aikens, the injuries suffered by Mrs. Aikens, Mrs. Aikens' belief that she was using a BB gun, her abandonment of hostilities, her call to 911, her cooperation with the authorities, the nonpermanent nature of Mr. Aikens' injuries, and the continued subsistence of her relationship with Mr. Aikens, the ends of justice in this case can be met by the imposition of noncustodial sentence.

The accused commends the following circumstances to the courts attention:

- Mrs. Aikens has no record
- Mrs. Aikens is of previously good character
- The incident occurred in the course of a drunken, escalating argument
- In the early stages of the argument, the accused herself sustained significant injuries which are documented and required medical treatment
- The accused used a rifle which she believed to be a BB gun
- The accused did not intend to wound Mr. Aikens
- The accused initially could not believe what had happened
- The accused abandoned any further argument or application of force toward Mr. Aikens
- The accused telephoned 911
- The accused was completely cooperative with Emergency Medical Service personnel
- The accused was completely cooperative with the City of Calgary Police Service personnel
- The accused visited Mr. Aikens in the hospital, and he was discharged into her care
- Mr. Aikens' injury had no lasting affects
- The parties continued cohabiting
- The accuser's husband's father lives with her. Mr. Hayes

has cancer and is hard of hearing. A carceral disposition would mean a real hardship for him.

CHAPTER TWENTY-TWO

I was absolutely devastated. Jail? I couldn't believe it. I just couldn't believe that I'll have to find someone to look after Cliff while I spend weekends in jail. I was very open with him. As I was telling him that, John came out of the den in his housecoat and slippers and said, "Darling, I'll look after Clifford while you're in jail." I couldn't believe what I heard.

With great hate and anger, I said to John, "No, you have until the end of the year to get out of my house. I will not give you any money. I will not buy you any booze. I will not buy you any cigarettes, but I will feed you. And you are not sleeping with me." Then, I left the house. Upon my return later in the evening, John approached me and asked if we could have at least a turkey dinner, at least for Clifford's sake. Remember: I had no presents, no tree, no nothing that December. I said, "Okay. For Clifford's sake, we'll have turkey dinner on Christmas day." John went to Safeway and bought the groceries. I did the usual for Christmas. I took out my best crystal and silver and put on a lovely dinner. While at the table, I said to John, "You know our marriage didn't have to get this sour." I've lost my beautiful home, but he didn't know that I bought a smaller home out of Woodbine. I said, "I've got this criminal record, and you expect me to carry on with this marriage?" That's very abnormal. There is something severely wrong with John's brain. John started preparing himself to move out. One morning, we were all standing in the kitchen. I said to Clifford, "John is moving out."

The sweet old man screamed with all the power in his heart, "Good!" That was the very first time I have ever heard Clifford express his anger toward anybody.

John was slowly moving his clothing out. He really didn't have much, basically the same stuff he moved in with, with the exception of the few items I spoiled him with. He packed his car with his clothes. One day, I walked by the den, and I noticed he was crying. I assumed he was crying because I wasn't sentenced to four years. I was thinking that John felt bad because he got shot; that he had gained momentum in the "feel sorry" department. But, in fact, it was quite the opposite. Everyone hated him; they knew John pushed for this trial because of his selfishness. Everyone now hated him, big time. John left my home on December 28, 1993. He went to stay with someone for one week. Then, they asked him to leave. He had called me twice to come back. Then, he went to his ex-wife's place. He was pleading for someone to take him in, but no one wanted his baggage. He lived in his car for several months. In Calgary, it is 50 degrees below zero during winters. Sometime during this period, there had been a warrant for his arrest. I am not actually sure what for, but I know for sure that fraud would play a *big* factor. John ended up running at large, convicted for whatever, and placed in Bowden Institution in Bowden, Alberta for two and a half years. Too bad the jury who convicted me didn't know this.

It was truly my misfortune that this man came into my life. I had never been in trouble before, and had never experienced anything like this before. This really was stuff you see only in the movies. But nothing prepared me for what was yet to come for the next eight years, *nothing*!

Me, Salt Spring Island, B.C., 1970s

John wanted my home in Calgary, Alberta

The heart of my home, where everyone gathers

John and I on our wedding day, November 8, 1992
(Ian's dad sitting on the couch)

Signing with my friend Marion who came down from Edmonton

Dad and me, Calgary Zoo, 1956

Cultus Lake, B.C. 1959

Helen and I, Vancouver, B.C. 1970s

Mom, Vancouver, B.C. 1976

Toronto, Ontario 1980s

Uncle Frans, me, Aunt Anna, Finland, 1985

Ian and Anita, married July 14, 1989, Newmarket, Ontario

Honeymoon in Paris, France

Ian and I are in London, England for a job interview.
Here I am at the Tower of London.